MAKING CONNECTIONS 2:

An Integrated Approach to Learning English

TEACHER'S EXTENDED EDITION

Carolyn Kessler

Linda Lee

Mary Lou McCloskey

Mary Ellen Quinn

Lydia Stack

Contributing Writer

Carolyn Bohlman

Heinle & Heinle Publishers
A Division of Wadsworth, Inc.
Boston, MA 02116, U.S.A.

The publication of Making Connections was directed by the members of the Heinle & Heinle Secondary ESL Publishing Team:

Editorial Director: Roseanne Mendoza
Production Editor: Lisa McLaughlin
Marketing Manager: Elaine Uzan Leary
Development Editor: Nancy Mann

Also participating in the publication of this program were:

Publisher: Stanley J. Galek
Editorial Production Manager: Elizabeth Holthaus
Manufacturing Coordinator: Mary Beth Lynch
Composition: Prepress Company, Inc.
Project Management: Carole Rollins
Interior Design: Carole Rollins/Martucci Studio
Illustration: Jerry Malone/Martucci Studio
Cover Design: Martucci Studio

Manufactured in the United States of America.

ISBN 0-8384-3836-9

10 9 8 7 6 5 4 3 2 1

Printed in the United States of America.
Heinle & Heinle Publishers is a division of Wadsworth, Inc.

Contents

Unit 1 - Choosing Foods

Topics

Unit 2 - Sending Messages

Topics

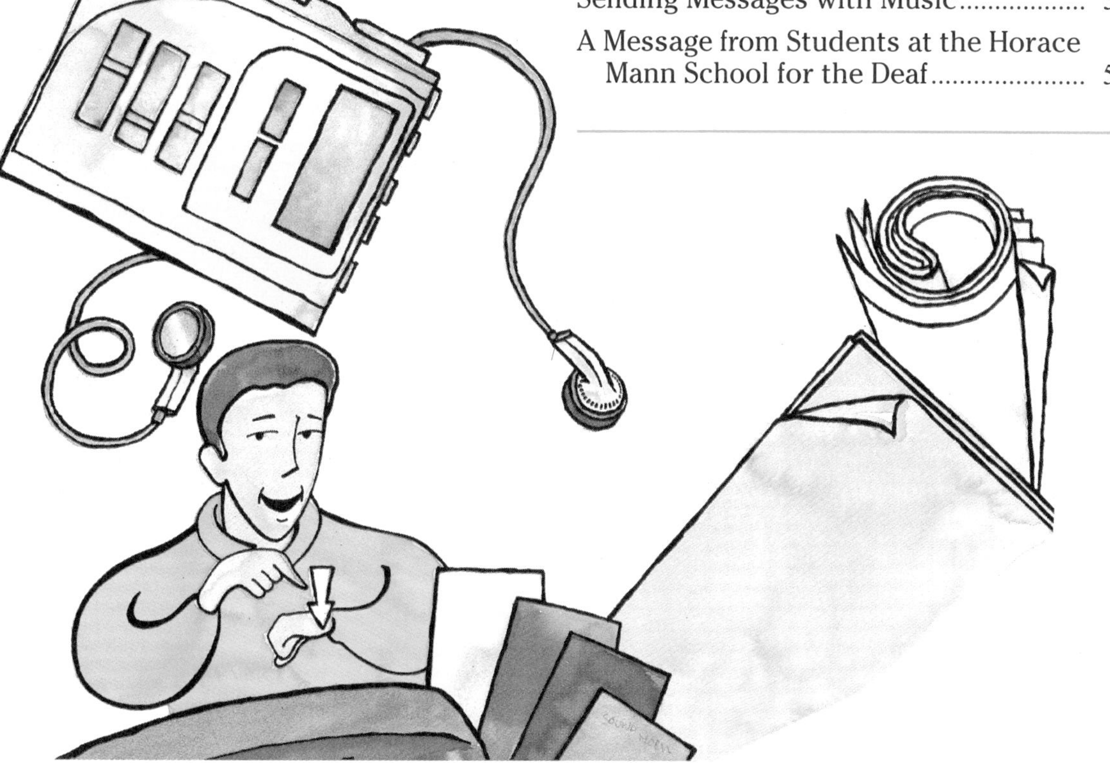

Unit 3 - Setting Goals

Topics

Unit 4 - Making Changes

Topics

Unit 5 - Resolving Conflict

Topics

To the Teacher

Goals, Philosophy

Middle and High School ESOL (English for Speakers of Other Languages) students are faced with a formidable task. In the few short years of school that remain, they must learn both English and the challenging content of their academic curriculum, made more challenging because so much language acquisition is demanded. *Making Connections: An Integrated Approach to Learning English* provides resources to integrate the teaching and learning of language and academic content. Resources in the series help teachers and students develop students' ability to communicate in English as they focus on motivating themes with topics, activities, tools, and procedures that introduce the content areas of science, social studies, and literature.

We are aware of the need for materials that help us to teach to the long-term learning goals we know are most important, and to teach the ways we know students learn best. We know this from our own experiences as teachers, as well as from working and talking with many classroom teachers. *Making Connections: An Integrated Approach to Learning English* is designed to do both: to help secondary students and their teachers reach toward important, essential goals, and to facilitate their learning language and content in the ways they learn best. What are the goals we reach for?

Joy—the joy in life and learning that will make our students happy, successful life-time learners;

Literacy—the ability to use reading and writing to accomplish amazing things;

Community—the knowledge that they live in an accepting community where they have rights, responsibilities, and resources;

Access—access to whatever resources they need to accomplish their own goals—including access to technology;

Power—the power to make their lives into whatever they choose.

What are the ways of teaching and learning that work best, according to our best understanding of language acquisition research? The answer, we believe, is **integrated learning**. In *Making Connections,* we include four different kinds of integration: integration of language areas, of language and academic content, of students with one another, and of school with the larger community.

- **We integrate language areas through active learning.**

We combine reading, writing, listening, and speaking into things that students do. Through interacting with authentic and culturally relevant literature, through activities that involve genuine communication, and through student-owned process writing, students learn the "parts" or "skills" of language in meaningful "whole" contexts.

- **We integrate language with academic content and process.**

Language is best learned when it is used as a tool; when students are meaningfully engaged in something important to them. Learning the language of and participating in processes specific to academic content area subjects are essential for preparing students to move into mainstream content-area classrooms. By teaching language through content, we attempt to do several things at once: we help students to learn to use a variety of learning strategies, we introduce them to science, social studies, and literature content appropriate for their age and grade level, and we help them use accessible language and learn new and essential language in the process.

- **We integrate students with one another.**

We try to help teachers and students develop a real learning community, in which students and teachers use a variety of strategies—including many cooperative learning strategies—to accomplish student-owned educational goals. We acknowledge that students are not all at the same level linguistically or academically, but we recognize that each student has strengths to offer in your classroom, so we provide choices of materials and activities that accomodate a multi-level class.

- **We integrate school with home culture and with the greater community.**

We strive for materials and activities that are relevant for a culturally diverse group and that help students to develop their self-esteem by valuing their unique cultural heritages. We seek to involve students in the community, and the community in students, by providing and encouraging activities and projects that relate to community life and that put students into interaction with community representatives. This active involvement is integral to the development of students' content-area knowledge and language.

In order to reach toward these goals and implement these four kinds of integration, we have used integrated thematic units as the organizational basis for *Making Connections.* Other themes are arrived at in a variety of ways. Some, such as "Checking the Weather," have very concrete connections among the sections of the units. Others, such as "Sending Messages," make more metaphorical connections among sections that treat very different aspects of themes. In all the units, students will make connections across content areas and will revisit themes and use and re-use the language of a theme in different ways. Each unit provides multi-level information and experiences that integrate language and one or more content areas, and includes the following features:

Learning Strategies

In each unit, we highlight strategies to help students with their language and content area learning. We encourage teachers and students to be aware of the applicability of these strategies in new learning situations. Our goal is to create active, capable, self-starting learners. Research has shown that students apply learning strategies while learning a second language. These strategies have been classified, and they include:

Metacognitive Strategies, through which students think about their own learning processes.

Cognitive Strategies, which relate directly to learning tasks and often involve direct manipulation or transformation of learning materials.

Social/Affective Strategies, which involve teacher and peer interaction to accomplish learning goals.

Many of these strategies can be used as **Mediation Strategies,** strategies through which learning is assisted. Transfer of learning strategies from one context to another can be enhanced by combining cognitive and metacognitive strategies. In developing *Making Connections* we have constantly sought ways to assist students in developing their own repertoire of learning strategies. Following are strategies included in the series.

1. Reading Strategies: We encourage you to use a variety of ways to guide students through the reading selections. To accomodate the varied levels of students, you might choose one or a combination of these strategies for reading the selections:

A. *Read Aloud:* You or an advanced student read the selection aloud to the students. Pay attention to your voice. Develop your expressiveness, varying pitch, volume, and speed of reading. Create different voices for different characters when reading literature selections. Don't read too quickly since second language learners need time to process what is read.

B. *Shared Reading:* Teacher and students read together using text on a transparency or a chart or multiple copies of the selection. During shared reading, students at a variety of language levels can all participate in different ways.

C. *Paired Reading:* Two students take turns reading aloud to each other. If they are reading prose, one student can read one paragraph, and the next student can read the following paragraph. If they are reading poetry, students can alternate lines or stanzas.

D. *Silent Reading:* Provide time during class for your students to read. Students need plenty of reading material at different reading levels, selections from text as well as other sources. Set clear expectations for your students during the silent reading time. Everyone must read; they cannot talk or write during this time.

E. *Directed Reading:* Students learning to read in English often need help with their acquisition since content-area schemata may be culturally specific and not part of the second language learner's cultural background. To make difficult material accessible, the teacher divides text into manageable "chunks" and uses strategies such as questions, outlines, or story maps to support student reading. The following activities help students acquire schema:

   1. *Use questions as a "scaffolding" technique.* The use of questions helps to clarify meanings of words, develop concepts, encourage both literal and inferential comprehension, and relate the story to the students' own experiences. For multilevel classes, include questions at a variety of levels, from labeling and recall to analysis. Always include some questions that do not have just one right answer, in order to encourage students to think for themselves.

   2. *Use cueing strategies.* When reading literature selections with various characters, use verbal cueing strategies, such as changes of voice for different characters, pauses to indicate changes in events and dramatic moments, and exaggerated intonation for key words and concepts. Use non-verbal cueing strategies, such as pointing to illustrations or parts of illustrations, and using facial expressions, gestures, and actions to accompany key events in the story. Story maps or content-area charts can also serve as cues. (See graphic organizers)

F. *Independent Reading:* Encourage students to read outside of class. Take students to the school or public library, and encourage them to use this resource often. Help them select reading materials at their interest and reading levels. If possible, develop a classroom library and provide class time for independent silent reading of self-selected materials. Read yourself during this time to serve as a role model.

2. Graphic Organizers: Graphic organizers are visual aids that help students remember the content as they read and then relate that content to their own experience. Graphic organizers can be used in many stages of unit study. As pre-reading activities they prepare students for the text they will read. During a reading, graphic organizers help students understand what they are reading, and after the reading, graphic organizers help students analyze what they have read. Finally, graphic organizers can be used as pre-writing activities, to help students organize material for writing stories, essays, and reports. Many graphic organizers are used in *Making Connections*. Some of these are described below.

A. *Semantic Maps:* Semantic mapping includes a variety of ways to make graphic displays of information within categories related to a central concept. This strategy helps students to demonstrate prior knowledge and add new information. The semantic maps can show relationships among terms and concepts and help students to develop vocabulary, improve understanding, review material learned, and prepare to write.

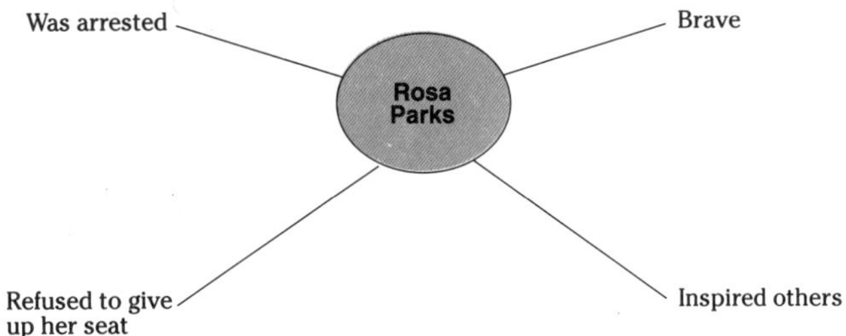

A Semantic Map

B. *Five Point Outline:* This graphic organizer helps students to generate basic information to prepare for writing by asking the basic newswriter questions. The students draw rays coming from a "sun" center and write a question word on each ray: Who, What, When, Where, Why. Then students write a phrase or two about the writing topic that answers each question.

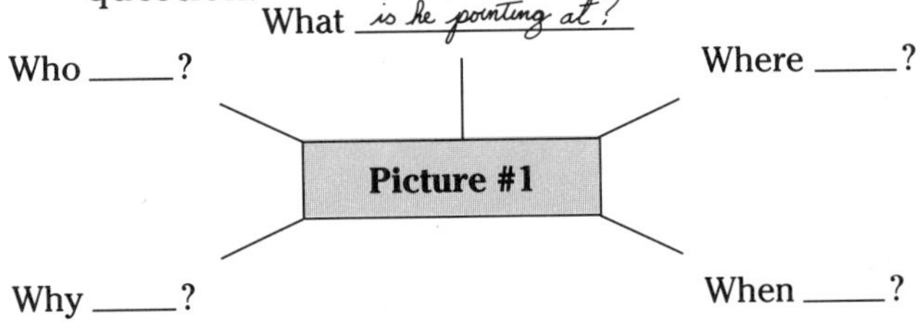

A Five Point Outline

C. *Venn Diagram:* A Venn Diagram uses circles to show similarities and differences between topics or concepts. Two overlapping circles allow students to compare and contrast information. Information that is common to both topics or concepts is written in the overlapping part of the circles. Information that is specific to one or the other of the topics or concepts is written in the circle for that topic or concept.

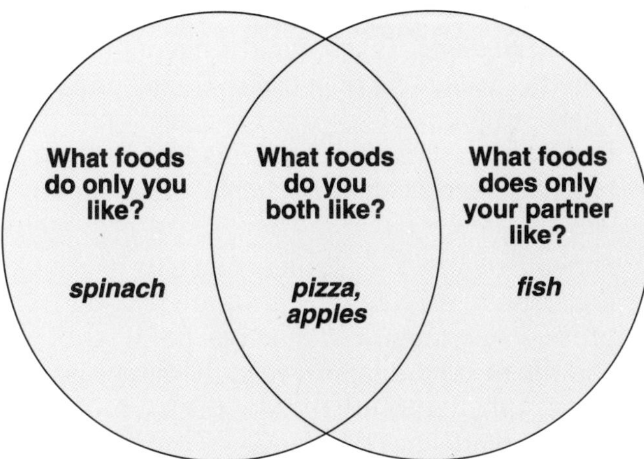

A Venn Diagram

D. *K/W/L Chart:* The Know/Want to Know/Learned (K/W/L) Chart is a preparatory activity that allows students to discover what they know about a given topic and what they want to know. Before beginning to study a topic,

Know	Want to know	Learned
What do you know about the story from the pictures?	What do you want to know?	What did you learn?
Younde lives in a village.	*Where is the village?*	

A K/W/L Chart

students make a chart with two columns. At the top of one column, they write "Know" and at the top of the other column they write "Want to Know." Students meet in small groups and talk about the topic. They also brainstorm questions they want answered about the topic. In the first column students write things they know about the subject, and in the second column they write questions they want answered about the topic. After studying a topic, you may want to add a third column to the chart "Learned," and have students work in groups or with you to write information they have learned while studying this topic.

E. *Graphs:* Graphs are visual displays of data or information that help students' understanding of the information presented. A graph allows students to compare data or information.

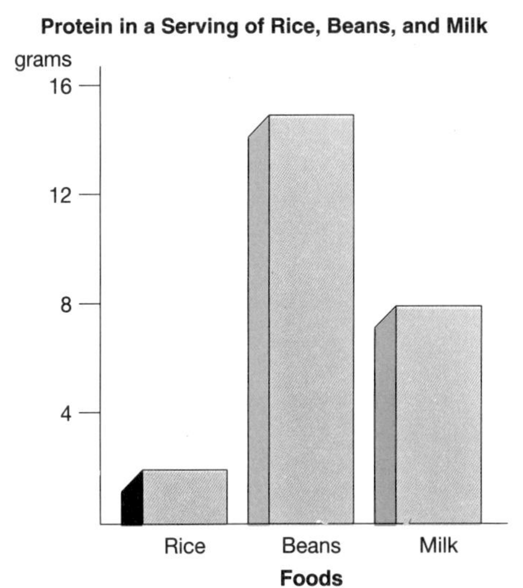

A Graph

F. *Timelines:* Timelines allow students to organize information chronologically, and often to gain an historical perspective. If events happen over time, a timeline can help students match dates to events.

Beginning
went to Port-au-Prince
bought a newspaper
had dinner
sat down with newspaper
End

A Timeline

3. Cooperative Learning: Cooperative learning has been shown to be effective in facilitating both student learning and successful cross-cultural, multi-level student integration. Each unit uses a variety of cooperative groups and activities to achieve these goals. Some of the cooperative learning techniques used in *Making Connections* are:

A. *Jigsaw:* Divide up a task as if it were a jigsaw puz zle. The members of the home group can each become an expert in a small part of the task. Then, when they fit the pieces together, everyone understands the whole. For a reading selection:

1. Divide the reading selection into one part for each group member (4–6 students per group).
2. Each person becomes an expert on one part. To become an expert, students study the reading selection closely.
3. Then each person retells his or her part of the reading selection to the group and the home group can ask questions of the expert.
4. Either groups or individuals then answer questions on the entire reading.

B. *Think–Pair–Share:*

1. Students think about an experience they have had that is related to the topic they are studying.
2. In pairs, students tell their experience to each other. Students take notes as they listen to their partners to prepare to retell their partners' experiences.
3. Two pairs of students get together and each student tells his/her partner's experience to the group.

C. *Choral Reading:* Two or more students read a poem, a story, or a play out loud in unison.

Divide the selection and students into high voice parts, medium voice parts, and low voice parts. Students practice reading in their groups until they can read their parts in unison; then the three groups come together to read their parts of the selection in the correct order.

Language Focus

Language is learned best in meaningful, useful contexts. From meaningful contexts, many opportunities arise to teach language concepts as they are needed. In *Making Connections,* we have provided suggestions both in the student texts and in the teacher editions for teaching language features as opportunities arise in the text materials or in the language students are using.

Although learners of English are not yet proficient in using English, they are proficient users of another language or languages, have had many academic and non-academic experiences, and are capable of high-level thinking. Language educators are challenged to provide appropriate materials for these students, materials that challenge them intellectually without frustrating them linguistically. The carefully-chosen reading selections in *Making Connections* provide students models of high-quality language, with the sophistication and complexity appropriate to the students' age levels. Readings offer new vocabulary in context and serve as a source for learning about the mechanics of language in authentic contexts. Reading selections provide a common text that students can use to negotiate meaning and to participate in lively discussions about the topics.

Each unit of *Making Connections* includes a number of Language Focus boxes that use content and context as opportunities to suggest practice in using particular language forms and functions. We encourage you to use these Language Focus boxes to inspire contextualized practice—drills, conversations, dialogues, and chants, for example—to build your students' language abilities.

Content-area experiences in science, social studies, and literature

We have chosen three content areas for focus in *Making Connections* because of their importance to student success and because of the importance of language to success in these areas. In science, we introduce the language of science (and frequently mathematics language as well) through offering authentic scientific experiences with materials that are accessible to an ESOL teacher. In social studies, we take advantage of the multicultural nature of ESOL classes to introduce the processes of the social sciences—the study of history, geography, culture, and economics. In the content area of literature, we have provided a variety of genres to enhance content-area learning as students begin to learn the language they need to talk about literary works and move on to create their own.

Writing

Making Connections applies a process approach to writing: it offers students opportunities to select topics and experiment with writing activities using themes and forms inspired by the science, social science, and literature content. We have included activities at all stages of the writing process including Prewriting, Drafting, Responding to One Another's Writing, Revising, Editing, and Publishing. We want students to see the writing process as something they can do and we want them to see authors as real people.

Choices for Teachers and Students

Every ESOL class is a multi-level, multicultural class. In order to meet the needs of these diverse groups, and in order to empower both teachers and students, *Making Connections* offers many choices. Teachers can choose among the many activities in the units to provide experiences most appropriate to their classes and can sequence these activities as needed. They can also individualize by choosing different activities for different students in the class. Each unit includes an Activity Menu of experiences and projects that will help students to integrate and apply the material from the unit. Both teacher and students can make choices among these culminating events to suit them to student interest, level of ability, and needs.

Components of the Making Connections Program

Student Text

Making Connections: An Integrated Approach to Learning English integrates the teaching and learning of language and academic content. The student text provides students opportunities to develop their ability to communicate in English as they focus on motivating themes with topics, activities, tools, and procedures that introduce the content areas of science, social studies, and literature.

The Activity Menu at the end of each unit provides opportunities to help students relate their learnings around the unit theme to one another and to review and explore further concepts developed in the unit. Following each unit is a collection of supplemental readings related to the unit topics. We have included these readings in response to requests from pilot teachers for more literary selections related to unit topics.

Teacher's Extended Edition

This Teacher's Extended Edition provides:

- an introduction to the thematic, integrated teaching approach
- a description of several approaches to presenting literature selections
- a guide to the study strategies that appear in the student book
- detailed teaching suggestions for each activity
- suggestions for extension activities
- listening scripts

Workbooks

Workbooks provide additional practice in using the vocabulary, language functions, language structures, and study strategies introduced in each of the thematic units. Workbook activities can be used in class or assigned as homework.

Video

Video provides powerful and memorable language input and can stimulate much student response and interaction. The video provides reinforcement and expansion of the themes and language introduced in each of the thematic units. It brings real-life community contexts into the classroom with highly authentic situations and language. Included with the video are complete descriptions of extension activities.

Assessment Program

The Assessment program consists of several components and accommodates a range of assessment philosophies and formats. Included are:

- a portfolio assessment kit, complete with a teacher's guide to using portfolios and forms for student and teacher evaluation
- two "progress checks" per unit
- one comprehensive test per unit

Color Transparencies

Color transparencies provide enlargements of visuals from the student texts. Many teachers find it helpful to view visuals with the students as they point out details. They may also write on pages using blank overlay transparencies.

Activity Masters

Reproducible activity masters support activities from the student book by providing write-on forms and graphic organizers for students' use. Activities for use with these masters consistently promote active student roles in engaging experiences.

Tape Program

Audio tapes provide opportunities for group and individual extended practice with the series materials. The tapes contain all the listening activities included in the student texts. Scripts of the recorded material are included in the Teacher's Extended Edition.

About the Authors

Carolyn Kessler

Carolyn Kessler is Professor of English as a Second Language/Applied Linguistics at the University of Texas at San Antonio where she teaches graduate courses for the master's degree in ESL. She serves extensively as a consultant to school districts for ESL programs and has published widely on bilingualism, second language learning, and literacy. She has taught ESL both in the United States and abroad and is a former secondary language and science teacher.

Linda Lee

Linda Lee is an ESL/EFL teacher and writer. She has taught in the United States, Italy, China, and Iran.

Mary Lou McCloskey

Mary Lou McCloskey coordinates the Atlanta Satellite of the University of Oklahoma Bilingual Education Center. She has developed integrated curriculum and consulted with school districts across the United States. She is past second vice president of International TESOL.

Mary Ellen Quinn

Mary Ellen Quinn is Visiting Professor of Mathematics at Our Lady of the Lake University. As a consultant in science and ESL to school districts throughout the country, she has presented many papers on bilingualism and science education both nationally and internationally and has published in those areas. She has been curriculum director for elementary and secondary schools as well as a secondary school teacher of ESL, science, and mathematics.

Lydia Stack

Lydia Stack is resource teacher for the Mentor Teacher and New Teacher programs for San Francisco Unified School District. She was formerly the ESL Department Head at Newcomer High School in San Francisco, and has consulted widely with school districts across the United States in the areas of curriculum development and teacher training. She is past president of International TESOL.

MAKING CONNECTIONS 2:

An Integrated Approach to Learning English

Carolyn Kessler

Linda Lee

Mary Lou McCloskey

Mary Ellen Quinn

Lydia Stack

Heinle & Heinle Publishers
A Division of Wadsworth, Inc.
Boston, MA 02116, U.S.A.

MAKING CONNECTIONS *Book 2*

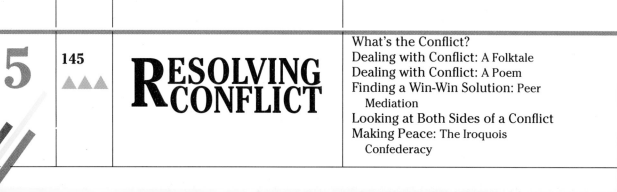

LANGUAGE FOCUS	STUDY STRATEGIES	LITERATURE
Expressing Likes and Dislikes Asking and Answering Questions about Likes and Dislikes Comparing Likes Making Polite Requests Making and Responding to Suggestions Asking and Answering Questions Giving Measurements Comparing Two Things Comparing Three or More Things	Making a Venn Diagram Selective Listening Classifying Taking Notes in a Chart Making Bar Graphs	How to Eat a Hot Fudge Sundae by Jonathan Holden How to Eat a Poem by Eve Merriam Watermelons by Charles Simic A Round by Eve Merriam
Asking What Something Means Asking for Information Reporting What Someone Said Describing Cause and Effect Asking for and Giving Information Making Guesses Stating an Opinion Giving Reasons	Brainstorming Using Pictures Making a Know/Want to Know Chart Classifying Quickwriting Taking Notes in a Chart	Younde Goes to Town (A Folktale from Ghana) That's Nice by Stephanie Todorovich Can We Talk? Deaf Donald by Shel Silverstein
Stating Goals Asking For and Giving Information Agreeing and Disagreeing Giving Advice Describing Future Plans Suggesting Possibilities Describing Past Events Describing a Sequence of Events	Using Pictures Making a K-W-L Chart Using Context Making a Story Map Making a Timeline Summarizing Quickwriting	Bouki's Glasses (A Haitian Folktale) David Klein by Mel Glenn A Biography of Homero E. Acevedo II
Comparing the Past and the Present Identifying Purpose Making Deductions Asking "Wh" Questions Identifying Cause and Effect Giving Reasons	Taking Notes in a Chart Making a K-W-L Chart Reading a Line Graph Making a Word Map Using Context	An Immigrant in the United States by Ponn Pet The Unexpected Heroine by Glennette Tilley Turney The Microscope by Maxine Kumin Change by Charlotte Zolotow
Making Guesses Relating Cause and Effect Agreeing Reporting Someone's Ideas Asking For and Giving Information About the Past Making Comparisons	Quickwriting Using Pictures Making a Story Map Making a K-W-L Chart Taking Notes Making a Word Map	Stewed, Roasted, or Live? (A Chinese Folktale) Sharing a Culture Law of the Great Peace Adapted by John Bierhorst A Kingdom Lost for a Drop of Honey (A Burmese Folktale)

ACKNOWLEDGMENTS

The authors want to thank colleagues, students, and teachers from whom we have learned much and who have offered strong and encouraging support for this project. We thank Chris Foley, Roseanne Mendoza, Nancy Mann, Elaine Leary, and Lisa McLaughlin for their support in the development and production of this project and for weathering with us the storms and challenges of doing something so new. Our expert office staff—Josie Cressman and Sherrie Tindle—provided intelligent and efficient assistance always accompanied by friendship, and we are appreciative. We also want to thank family members—Erin, Dierdre, and Jim Stack; Kevin and Sean O'Brien, and Joel and Tom Reed—for their love and support during this project.

The publisher and authors wish to thank the following teachers who pilot tested the *Making Connections* program. Their valuable feedback on teaching with these materials greatly improved the final product. We are grateful to all of them for their dedication and commitment to teaching with the program in a prepublication format.

Elias S. Andrade and Gudrun Draper
James Monroe High School
North Hills, CA

Nadine Bagel
Benjamin Franklin Middle School
San Francisco, CA

Kate Bamberg
Newcomer High School
San Francisco, CA

Kate Charles
Sycamore Junior High School
Anaheim, CA

Anne Elmkies, Irene Killian, and Kay Stark
Hartford Public Schools
Hartford, CT

Genoveva Goss
Alhambra High School
Alhambra, CA

Margaret Hartman
Lewisville High School
Lewisville, TX

Carmen N. Jimenez
Intermediate School 184
New York, NY

Rob Lamont and Judith D. Clark
Trimble Technical High School
Fort Worth, TX

Judi Levin
Northridge Middle School
Northridge, CA

Ligita Longo
Spring Woods High School
Houston, TX

Mary Makena
Rancho Alamitas High School
Garden Grove, CA

Alexandra M. McHugh
Granby, CT

Beatrice W. Miranda
Leal Middle School
San Antonio, TX

Doris Partan
Longfellow School
Cambridge, MA

Jane Pierce
Douglas MacArthur High School
San Antonio, TX

Cynthia Prindle
Thomas Jefferson High School
San Antonio, TX

Sydney Rodrigues
Doig Intermediate School
Garden Grove, CA

Cecelia Ryan
Monte Vista High School
Spring Valley, CA

Patsy Thompson
Gwinnett Vocational Center
Lawrenceville, GA

Fran Venezia
North Dallas High School
Dallas, TX

The publisher and authors would also like to thank the following people who reviewed the *Making Connections* program at various stages of development. Their insights and suggestions are much appreciated.

Suzanne Barton
Fort Worth Independent School District
Forth Worth, TX

Keith Buchanan
Fairfax County Public Schools
Fairfax, VA

Carlos Byfield
San Diego City College
San Diego, CA

John Croes
Lowell High School
Lowell, MA

Flo Decker
El Paso, TX

Lynn Dehart
North Dallas High School
Dallas, TX

Cecilia Esquer
El Monte High School
El Monte, CA

Marge Gianelli
Canutillo Independent School District
El Paso, TX

Nora Harris
Harlandale Independent School District
San Antonio, TX

Richard Hurst
Holbrook High School
Holbrook, AZ

Betty J. Mace-Matluck
Southwest Educational Development Laboratory
Austin, TX

Jacqueline Moase-Burke
Oakland Independent School District
Oakland, MI

Jeanne Perrin
Boston Public Schools
Boston, MA

Ron Reese
Long Beach Unified School District
Long Beach, CA

Linda Sasser
Alhambra School District
Alhambra, CA

Donna Sievers
Garden Grove Unified School District
Garden Grove, CA

Stephen F. Sloan
James Monroe High School
North Hills, CA

Dorothy Taylor
Adult Learning Center
Buffalo Public Schools
Buffalo, NY

Beth Winningham
James Monroe High School
North Hills, CA

Making Connections 2:

An Integrated Approach to Learning English

TEACHER'S EXTENDED EDITION

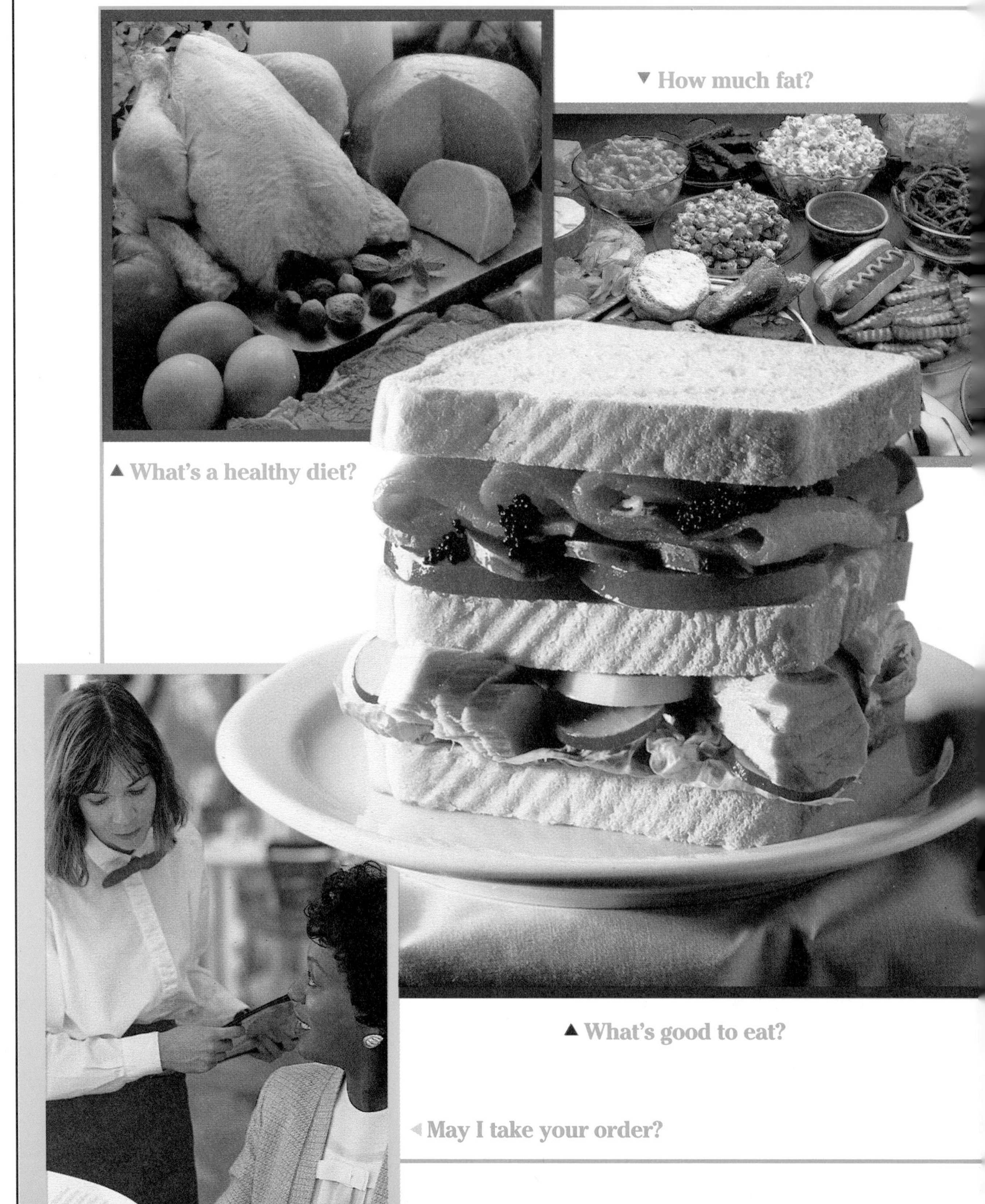

▼ How much fat?

▲ What's a healthy diet?

▲ What's good to eat?

◄ May I take your order?

How did the potato
get to North America?

CHOOSING FOODS

How do you eat a
hot fudge sundae?

What's your
favorite food?

Unit 1

Choosing Foods

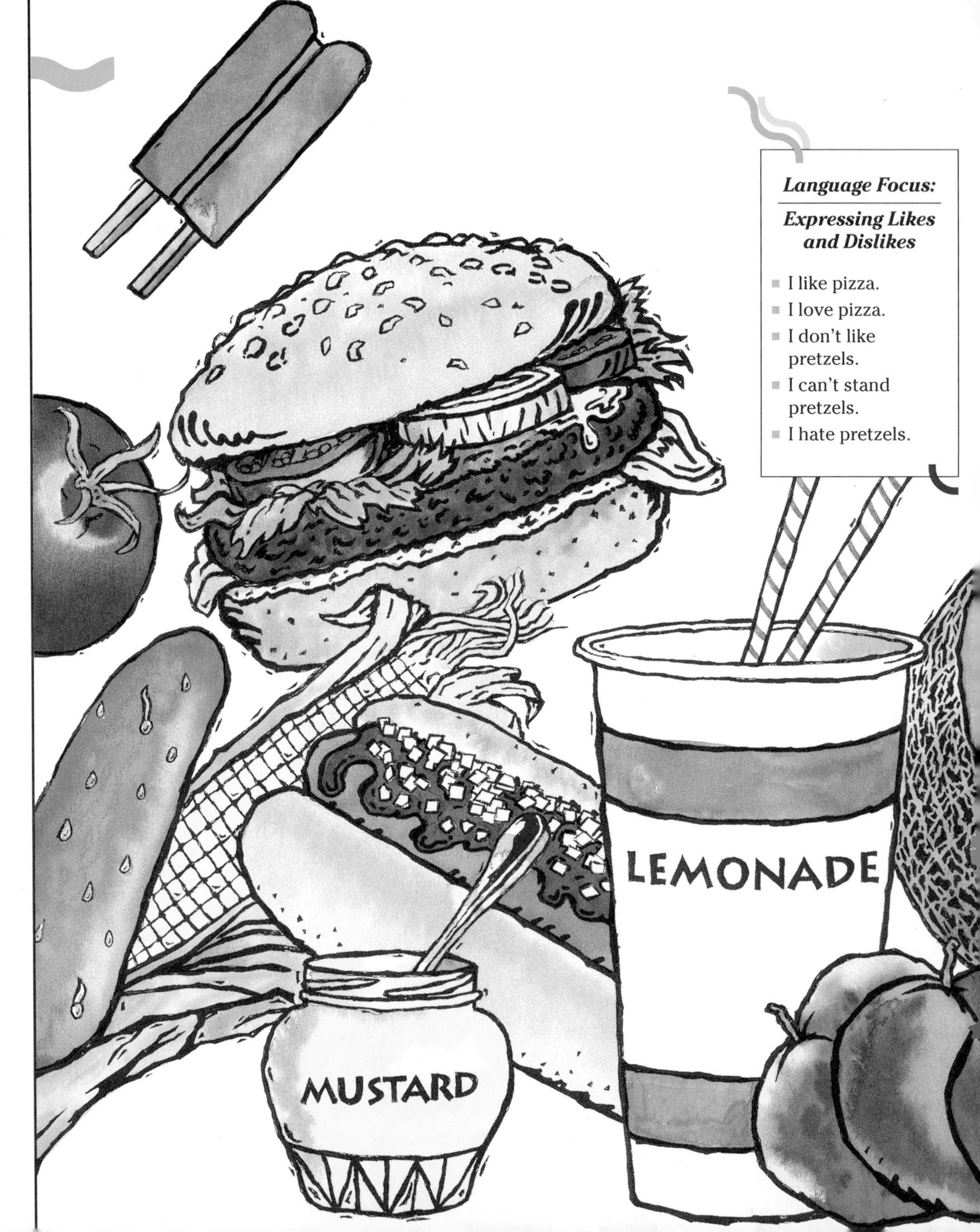

Language Focus:

Expressing Likes and Dislikes

- I like pizza.
- I love pizza.
- I don't like pretzels.
- I can't stand pretzels.
- I hate pretzels.

What's your favorite food?

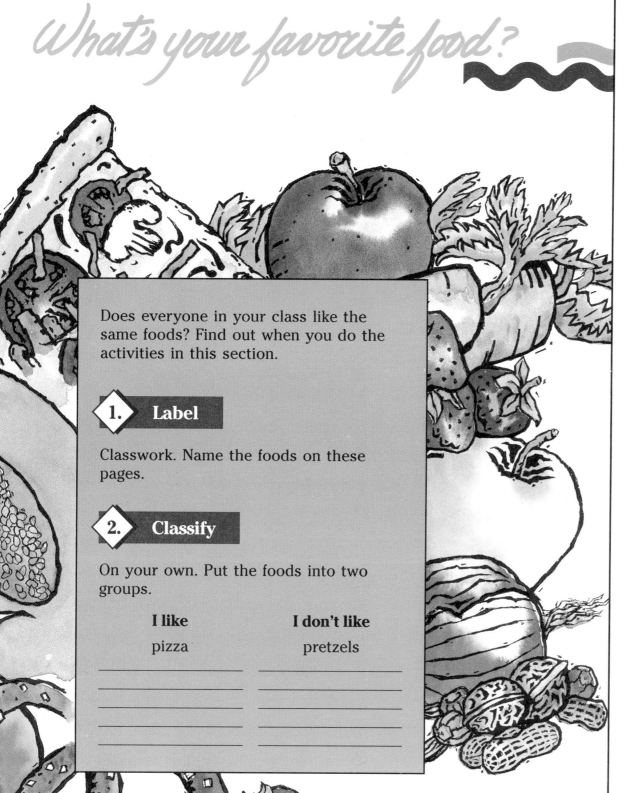

Does everyone in your class like the same foods? Find out when you do the activities in this section.

1. Label

Classwork. Name the foods on these pages.

2. Classify

On your own. Put the foods into two groups.

I like	I don't like
pizza	pretzels

Activity 1: Label

Have students look at the pictures and identify foods they know. Write the names of any new foods on the board. Model the pronunciation of the names and have students repeat after you.

Activity 2: Classify

1. Model the activity by making a chart with *I like* and *I don't like* on the board. Add your food likes and dislikes to the two lists. Use the pictures for ideas and then add other foods. Model the use of the verbs in the Language Focus box, e.g., *I love cantaloupe. I don't like popsicles. I can't stand egg-plant.*

2. Have students make their own charts on another piece of paper. Encourage them to add the names of other foods to the two lists.

3. Have students take turns telling about their food likes and dislikes. Show interest in their ideas by making follow-up comments, e.g., *You do? Really? Me too.*

4. Use the photographs of food on the Unit Preview page to introduce additional food words. Have students add the words to their chart.

Activity 3: Interview

1. Have students look at the Language Focus box while you read the question aloud: *Do you like tacos?* Let different students answer. Prompt them: *Yes, I do. No, I don't.*

2. Model the activity by looking for someone in the class who likes hot dogs. (e.g., *Carlos, do you like hot dogs?*) Continue until someone says they like hot dogs. Write the person's name on a copy of Activity Master 1/1 (AM 1/1). The second item on the list (doesn't like pizza) may cause some difficulty because it's in the negative form. Ask, *Do you like pizza?* and look for someone who answers *No.*

3. Let students practice yes/no questions by asking you about the items on the list. Then pass out copies of AM 1/1 and have students add one or more foods to the list (item h).

4. Have students move around the classroom to find people who like/dislike the foods on the list. Encourage them to talk to different students. Everyone should be talking at the same time, so it might get a bit noisy.

5. Have students report what they learned. Ask, *Who likes hot dogs? Who doesn't like pizza?*

Activity 4: Shared Reading

Use the chant in a variety of ways:

Play the tape and have students listen to the chant while looking at the pictures of food. Have them point to each food as they hear it named.

Have students chant along with you or the tape.

Divide the class into two groups and have them take turns reading a line from the chant. Have the groups use different voices to distinguish the two parts (e.g., a high voice/low voice; soft voice/loud voice).

Language Focus:

Asking and Answering Questions about Likes and Dislikes

A: Do you like tacos?
B: Yes, I do. (No, I don't.)

3. Interview

On your own. Find someone who *likes tacos*. Write the person's name.

Find someone who ________.

a. likes hot dogs ________
b. doesn't like pizza ________
c. hates corn ________
d. loves peanuts ________
e. likes pretzels ________
f. likes carrots for breakfast ________
g. doesn't like strawberries ________
h. ________

4. Shared Reading

Classwork. Listen to the chant. Then chant with the tape.

I'm Hungry!

Pizza, pretzels, popsicles, and peanuts.
I'm hungry. I'm hungry. I'm hungry. I'm hungry.
Apples, peaches, strawberries, and cantaloupe.
I'd like some. I'd like some. I'd like some. I'd like some.
Mustard, ketchup, hamburgers, and hot dogs.
Just a little. Just a little. Just a little. Just a little.
Cabbage, carrots, cucumbers, and onions.
That's enough. That's enough. That's enough. That's enough.
Tacos, tofu, tangerines, and lemonade.
I'm full! I'm full! I'm full!

5. Compare and Contrast

Pairwork. Work with a partner.
Answer the questions in the Venn Diagram.

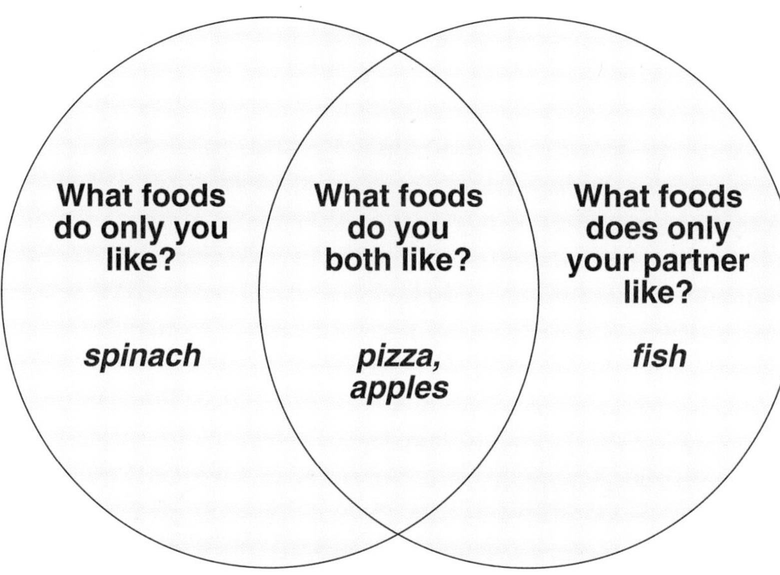
What foods do only you like?
spinach
What foods do you both like?
pizza, apples
What foods does only your partner like?
fish

6. Write

Pairwork. Write a food chant. Use your Venn Diagram for ideas.

7. Shared Reading

Pairwork. Read your chant to the class.

Study Strategy:

Making a Venn Diagram

Use a Venn Diagram to compare and contrast things.

Language Focus:

Comparing Likes

A: I like apples.
B: Me, too.
(So do I.)

A: I really like chicken. Do you?
B: Yes, I do.

Activity 5: Compare and Contrast

1. Copy the Venn Diagram on the board, omitting the names of the foods. Model the activity by comparing your food likes with a student's. Write the foods in the appropriate areas of the diagram. Use the sample dialogue in the Language Focus box as a model. For example, *I like apples. Me too.*

2. Pass out copies of AM 1/2 and have students work in pairs to complete the Venn Diagram.

3. Have students identify a food they both like and report it to the class. For example, *Han and I both like pizza.*

Activity 6: Write

1. If less proficient students need encouragement to begin writing, lead a session in which they give you ideas and you write the chant on the board or on a transparency. Encourage them to practice reading the chant aloud, playing with the rhythm.

2. Have students try different words in a line of the chant to see how the rhythm changes. (Model the revision process by crossing out a word and writing a new word above.)

3. To encourage interaction, have pairs work with just one sheet of paper and one pencil. Have them brainstorm possible subjects for their chant. For example, they might choose to write a chant about foods they like or dislike, using the ideas on their Venn Diagram, or they might choose to write about school food, American foods, or foods they eat at home.

Activity 7: Shared Reading

Encourage students to practice reading the chant aloud to check the rhythm. If feasible, have them record their chants on tape. Later play the tape with all of the chants. If you don't have a tape recorder, have pairs read their chants aloud to the class.

Activity 1: Label

1. Ask about the photograph: *Where do you think the two people are? Which person is the customer? What's the waitress doing?*

2. Discuss the listening strategy. Ask, *What would you listen for if you were taking orders in a restaurant?* Then tell students they will listen to customers ordering in a restaurant. They will write down the customers' orders on a copy of AM 1/3 or another piece of paper. Play the tape or read the script. Repeat the tape or reading as often as needed.

3. Have students compare orders to find differences and then listen again to clear up any discrepancies. (Answers: Dialogue 1, hamburger, order of fries, small cola. Dialogue 2, tuna fish sandwich, apple juice. Dialogue 3, small pizza with onions and green pepper, small salad, large orange soda.)

Activity 2: Roleplay

1. Introduce "Today's Menu." Ask how much the different foods cost. Ask about the foods on the menu: *Do you like French fries?* Then, with a student, roleplay ordering from the menu. Use ideas from the dialogue, e.g., *I'd like . . . For here. . . .*

2. Have students work in pairs to practice ordering from the menu. One student orders food while the other writes down the order on paper or on another copy of AM 1/3. Have them compute the total cost of the meal.

Activity 3: Write

Optional materials: Yellow pages of telephone directory; menus from local restaurants

1. Have students work in small groups. Tell them that they are to imagine that they are going to open a restaurant. First they must choose the kind of restaurant they would like to open. (They can use the yellow pages or newspapers for ideas.) Have them give the restaurant a name.

(Continued on page 7.)

May I take your order?

In this section, you will listen to people ordering food in a restaurant and practice ordering food that you like.

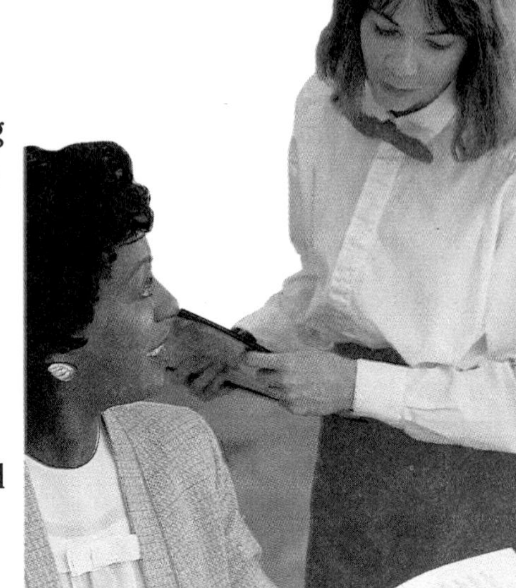

Study Strategy:

Selective Listening

Before listening, ask yourself this question: What information do I need? This helps you listen for the right information.

1. Label

On your own. Listen and write each customer's order.

ZOE'S DELI	
hamburger	1.89
small salad	1.50
large coke	.90
TOTAL	4.29

2. Roleplay

Pairwork. Practice ordering from this menu.

A: I'd like a chicken sandwich and a small salad, please.
B: For here or to go?
A: For here.
B: Anything to drink?
A: A lemonade, please.
B: What size?
A: Small.
B: Anything else?
A: No, that's all.
B: That'll be $5.05.

TODAY'S ME
Chicken sandwich:
Salad: ...small $1.50, large
Lemonade: small .80, large
Hamburger:
Cheeseburger:
Soft drinks: ...small .75, large
French fries
Fish sandwich
.75
2.75
Coffee... small .75, large .90
Milk ... small .75, large .90

Language Focus:

Making Polite Requests

- I'd like a tuna fish sandwich, please.
- Could I have a cola and a hamburger, please?

3. Write

Groupwork. Write a menu for a restaurant.

4. Listen Selectively

On your own. Listen to the dialogues. What are the people going to eat? List the foods.

Dialogue 1

Dialogue 2

> ***Language Focus:***
>
> ***Making and Responding to Suggestions***
>
> A: Let's have cheese sandwiches.
> B: Good idea. (Sounds good.)
>
> A: What about hot dogs?
> B: I don't like hot dogs. What about hamburgers?

5. Plan

Groupwork. Plan a picnic for your classmates.

Activity 3: Write *(continued)*

Then, using the menus collected from local restaurants as a guide, each group can write a menu for its restaurant. The menu should include the prices for each food item.

2. Have groups exchange menus and practice ordering from the new menus.

Activity 4: Listen Selectively

1. Ask about the two pictures: *What are the two people doing? Where are they?*

2. Have students read the instruction line. Review the strategy of listening for specific information. Encourage students to focus on food names when listening to the dialogues.

3. Play the tape or read the script and have students listen for the foods the people are going to eat. Repeat as needed. They can then compare lists and listen to the tape again.

(Answers: Dialogue 1, peanut butter sandwiches and milk; Dialogue 2, cereal and juice.)

4. Have pairs practice choosing food for breakfast or lunch, using the dialogue in the Language Focus box as a model.

5. Have them roleplay their dialogue while the rest of the class listens and writes down the food they choose.

Activity 5: Plan

1. Use the photograph to generate a discussion of picnics. (Some students may be unfamiliar with this type of meal.) Have them consider how a picnic is different from a meal in a restaurant (e.g., you eat outdoors, you cook the food on a grill). Find out if picnics are popular in their native countries.

2. Divide the class into groups and have them plan their picnic. Have each group write its picnic menu. Each group can then present its menu to the class.

Activity 1: Label

> Optional materials: Pictures of food cut from magazines

1. Have students count the number of groups in the Food Guide pyramid (6) and read the name of each group. Have them identify the food pictures in each group and then suggest other foods to fit in each group.

2. Show food pictures cut from magazines (or bring in samples of actual foods) and have students match each food to the appropriate food group on the pyramid.

Activity 2: Classify

1. Working in pairs, students classify the foods in the food chant on page 4. (You may wish to replay the taped chant.) Give each pair one copy of AM 1/4, or have them copy the blank food pyramid at the bottom of page 8. They should list the foods in the appropriate box on the pyramid.

(Answers: Fats, oils, sweets, popsicles; Milk, etc., cheese [on pizza]; Meat, etc., peanuts, hamburgers, hot dogs, tofu; Vegetable, cabbage, carrots, cucumbers, onions, lettuce [from taco]; Fruit, apples, peaches, strawberries, cantaloupe, tangerines, lemonade; Bread, etc., pretzels, crust of pizza, tortilla [from taco]. Note that some of the foods, like pizza and tacos, must be broken into their component parts in order to be classified.)

2. Post the groups' pyramids on the board and have students look for differences.

Activity 3: Identify

1. This food guide pyramid gives the number of servings of food that a person should eat each day. Have students work in pairs and ask each other about the number of servings they need for each group. Model by asking, *How many servings of vegetables do you need every day?* Elicit the answer, 3 to 5. Explain the term *use sparingly* in the sweets group.

(Continued on page 9.)

What's good to eat?

What should you eat to stay healthy? You will find out in this section.

> ***Study Strategy:***
> ***Classifying***
>
> When you classify information, you put it into groups. This helps you understand and remember it.

1. Label

Classwork. Name the foods in each group.

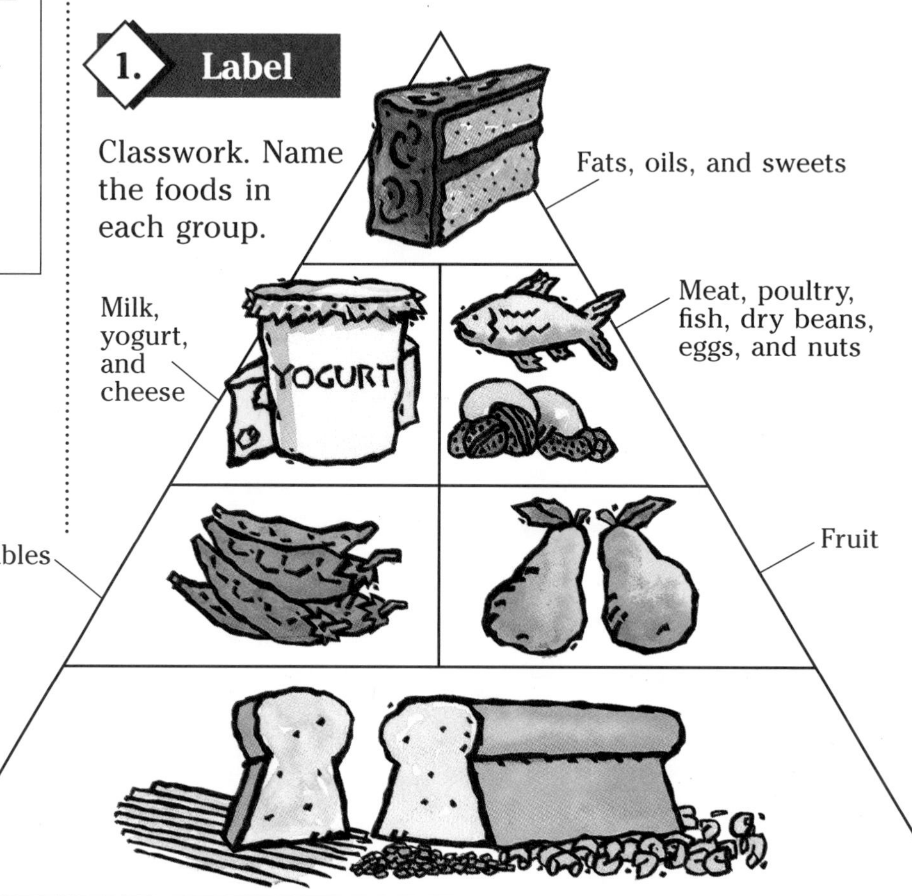

The Food Guide Pyramid classifies foods into six groups. To stay healthy, you need to eat foods from each group.

2. Classify

Pairwork. Reread the food chant on page 2. Group the foods.

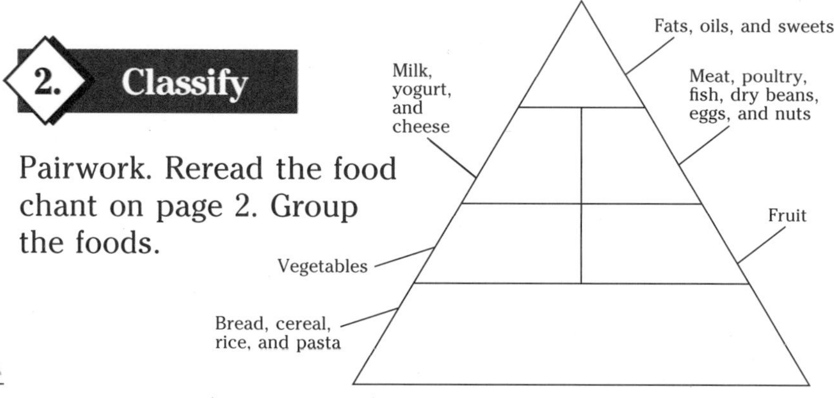

3. Identify

Pairwork. How many servings of food do you need daily from each group?

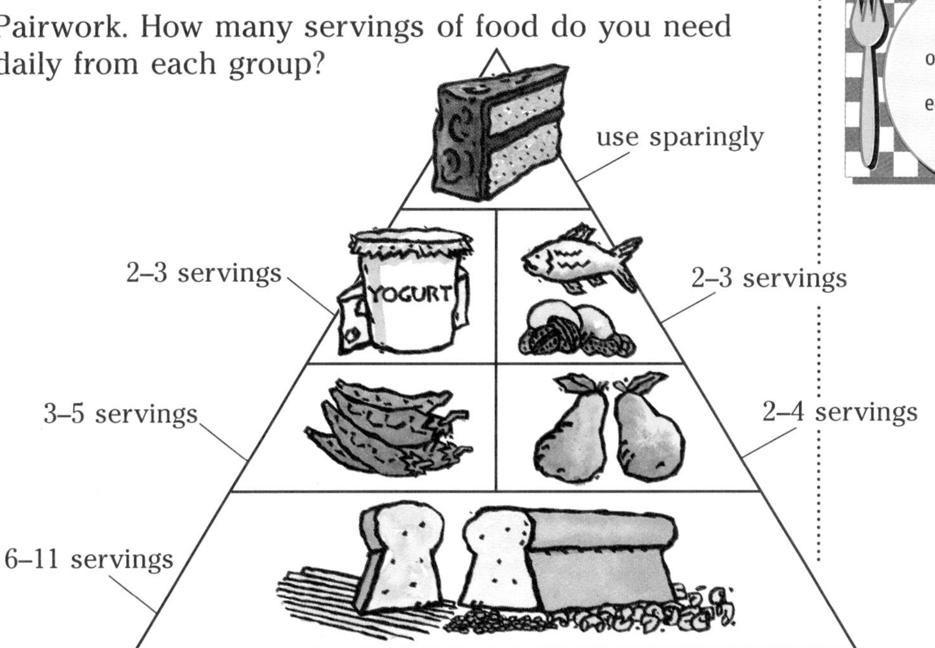

Why do you think the Food Guide Pyramid has the shape of a pyramid?

40 percent of all American households eat dinner with the TV or VCR on.

4. Measure

Classwork. Your teacher will give you information about serving sizes. Then measure one serving of a food.

Materials: measuring cup, tablespoon, sample foods from each group

one slice of bread

one cup of raw leafy greens

one cup of milk

one egg

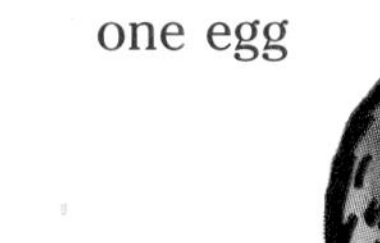

one orange

These pictures show one serving of different foods.

Activity 3: Identify *(continued)*

2. Ask the pairs, *Why do you think the Food Guide Pyramid has the shape of a pyramid?* (Because you need many servings from the groups at the bottom of the pyramid but just a few servings from the groups at the top.)

Activity 4: Measure

Materials:

measuring cup, tablespoon, sample foods from each food group. [Easy ones might be cooked rice, fruit juice, spinach, diced carrots, yogurt, peanut butter, cooked beans.]

1. A serving of food according to the Food Guide pyramid is usually smaller than one helping of food. For example, a plate of spaghetti might be three or four servings. Before students can evaluate their diet, they must understand the size of a serving of different foods. List these serving sizes on the board:

Bread, cereal, rice, and pasta group:

1 serving = 1 slice of bread; half a bun or bagel; a half cup of cooked rice or pasta.

Milk, yogurt & cheese group:

1 serving = 1 cup milk; 1 cup of yogurt; 2 ounces of cheese.

Vegetable group:

1 serving = 1 cup of raw, leafy greens; a half cup of any other vegetables.

Meat, poultry, fish, dry beans, eggs and nuts group:

1 serving = 1 medium egg; 2 tablespoons of peanut butter; a half cup of cooked beans.

Fruit group:

1 serving = 1 medium apple, banana or orange; a half cup of fresh, cooked, or canned fruit; three-fourths cup of fruit juice.

2. Have students get into small groups. Give each group one or more of the foods you brought in. Have them measure out one serving of the food. Have the groups share information with the class.

Activity 5: Measure

> Materials:
>
> Box of breakfast cereal, container of milk, several cereal bowls, measuring cup.

1. This activity gives students a chance to figure out the number of servings in a bowl of cereal. Have the students work in groups. Give each group a bowl and ask, *How much cereal would you eat for breakfast?* (Many students may not eat cereal for breakfast, but they can show how much they might eat.) Have them pour this amount in the bowl.

2. Have the groups follow the instructions in the book and record their answers on a piece of paper. The size of a serving of cereal varies depending on the type of cereal. Have them read the label to find the size of a serving of this cereal.

3. Have each group report the results of their investigation. Use this as an opportunity to familiarize students with American measurement terms of cups and ounces.

4. Ask the groups to look back at the Food Guide Pyramid in Activity 3. Tell them to figure out how many more servings of food from the bread, cereal, rice, and pasta group and the milk group they will need today.

Activity 6: Evaluate

1. Have students look at the pictures showing Jaime's meals yesterday. Together list the foods on the board. Next to each food, estimate the number of servings.

2. Have students get into small groups. Give each group a copy of AM 1/5, or have them make copies of the food pyramid and the evaluation chart on page 11. Warn them not to write in the book. Have students follow the steps in the book. Circulate to answer questions, but give students the chance to work it out. (Students should look back at the food guide pyramid in Activity 3 to evaluate the number of servings.)

(Continued on page 11.)

5. Measure

Groupwork. Measure a bowl of breakfast cereal.

Materials: box of cereal, milk, bowls, measuring cups

1. How much cereal do you eat for breakfast? Pour this amount in a bowl.
2. Measure the cereal.
3. Read the nutrition label on the cereal box. How large is one serving of this cereal? How many servings of cereal are in your bowl?
4. Measure a half-cup of milk. Pour it on the cereal. Is it too much? Not enough? Just right?
5. How many servings of cereal and milk are in your bowl of cereal?

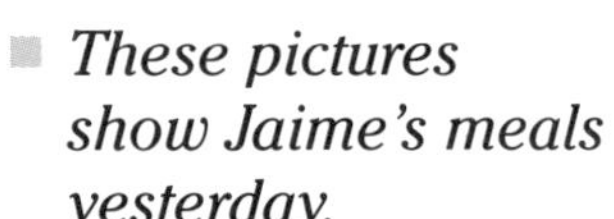

These pictures show Jaime's meals yesterday.

6. Evaluate

Groupwork. Evaluate Jaime's diet yesterday.

1. Classify the foods. Write them on a Food Guide Pyramid.
2. Write the number of servings next to each food.
3. Count the number of servings in each group.
4. Decide if Jaime ate enough, not enough, or too much food from each group. Write your answers in an evaluation chart.

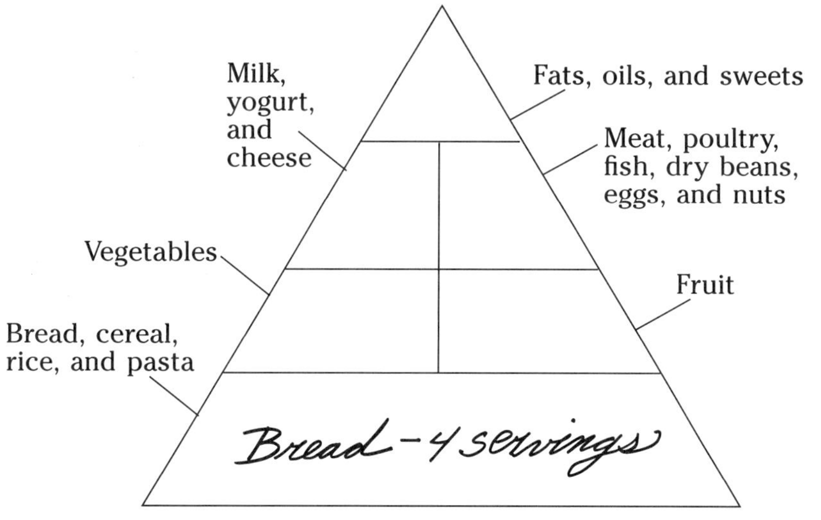

Evaluation Chart				
Food Group	**Number of Servings**	**Enough**	**Not Enough**	**Too Much**
Bread...				
Vegetables				
Fruit				
Milk...				
Meat...				
Fats...				

7. Self-evaluate

On your own. Evaluate your diet.

a. List everything you ate yesterday.
b. Classify the foods. Write them on a blank Food Guide Pyramid.
c. Write the number of servings of each food.
d. Count the number of servings in each group.
e. Decide if you ate enough, not enough, or too much food from each group. Write your answers in an evaluation chart.

My Diet Yesterday
Morning:
large bowl of cereal with milk and small banana
Afternoon:
tunafish sandwich
green salad
glass of juice
bowl of popcorn
Evening:
tofu with vegetables
bowl of rice and apples
bowl of ice cream (small)

Activity 6: Evaluate *(continued)*

3. Have groups compare charts and clear up any discrepancies.

Activity 7: Self-evaluate

1. In this activity students repeat the steps in Activity 6, but this time they evaluate their own diet. If less proficient students need additional modeling before working on their own, show them how you would evaluate your own diet by following the steps listed in the book.

2. Give each student another copy of AM 1/5 and have them follow the steps in the book.

3. Have pairs of students compare charts.

Activity 1: Evaluate

Materials:

five plastic spoons, paper towels, five plastic glasses with the following items:
- a small portion of dry cereal with two dimes, one nickel, and one penny buried in it;
- cut-up carrots, with three nickels and one dime;
- cup of sliced apple or other fruit, with two nickels, one dime, and five pennies;
- a small portion of dried beans, with one penny and one quarter;
- a small amount of vegetable oil and five pennies.

(The coins in the cups represent nutrients. The choice of coins in a cup simply shows that each food contains a variety of nutrients in different amounts. The number and type of coins in each cup do not have a specific meaning.)

1. Write the word *nutrients* on the board. Show the plastic cups to the class, and together identify the foods. Say, *Each of these foods contains nutrients. Nutrients are things that our bodies need to be healthy and grow well.*

2. Invite students to use a plastic spoon to find the coins in each glass of food. Explain, *You found something valuable in each glass of food. Of course, nutrients are not coins, but like coins they are valuable to us. Nutrients are necessary for healthy bodies. Different foods contain different kinds and amounts of nutrients. The different kinds and numbers of coins in the foods you examined represented nutrients.*

3. Have students work in groups to read the introduction to nutrients on page 12. Invite less proficient students to identify the food for each lunch (a. pork chop; b. chicken legs, peanuts, hardboiled eggs, soda; c. cheese sandwich, olives, tomato slices, lettuce, milk, apple). As groups report their answers, more proficient students can explain why lunch c is the healthiest (because it contains different kinds of food).

What's a healthy diet?

To stay healthy, it's important to eat different kinds of food. Find out why in this section.

Classwork. Read and answer the questions.

A healthy diet contains food from different groups in the Food Guide Pyramid. But why do you need to eat different kinds of foods? To answer this question, you need to know about nutrients. You can't see nutrients, but they are the substances in food that keep you healthy. Foods contain different types and amounts of nutrients. No one food has all the nutrients you need. That's why you need to eat different kinds of food.

a. **b.** **c.**

Which lunch shows a healthy diet? Why?

2. Read and Take Notes

On your own. Read for information to complete the chart.

Nutrient Chart		
Nutrient Group	**Function** (What do they do?)	**Good Sources** (What foods?)
Proteins	*help you grow*	*fish, eggs, beans, milk*
Carbohydrates		
Vitamins		
Minerals		
Fats		

Getting the nutrients you need

Nutrients are substances in food that help your body grow and stay healthy. Important nutrients in food are proteins, vitamins, minerals, carbohydrates, and fats. No one food has all the nutrients you need. That's why you need to eat different kinds of food.

Proteins

Your body needs proteins to grow and repair itself. Most foods contain some protein. Meat, fish, nuts, and cheese contain a lot of protein. Cereals and vegetables contain smaller amounts of protein.

Study Strategy:

Taking Notes in a Chart

Taking notes in a chart will help you to organize information. This helps you remember it.

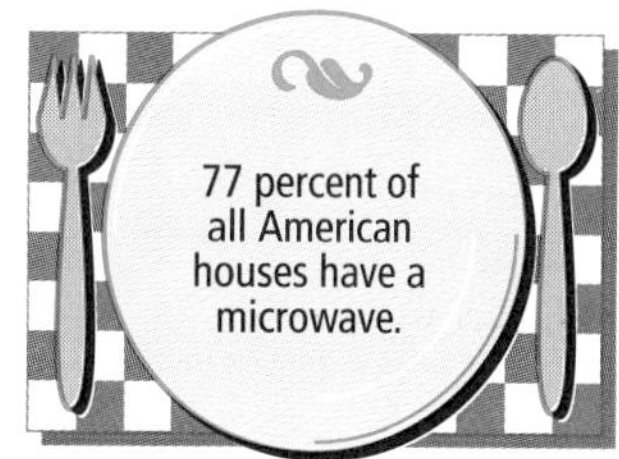

77 percent of
all American
houses have a
microwave.

Activity 2: Read and Take Notes

1. Together study the chart at the top of the page. Read the names of the nutrient groups aloud, and let students repeat after you. Ask questions about proteins, and have students use the chart to answer. *What are proteins? What do proteins do? What foods are a good source* (have a lot) *of protein?*

2. Elicit questions about the other nutrient groups: *What are carbohydrates? What do carbohydrates do? Which foods have a lot of carbohydrates?* Have students predict answers.

3. Have students look over the readings on pages 13 and 14. Together identify the foods in the photographs and read the subtitles. Go back to the chart and ask where they might find answers to their questions about carbohydrates. Have them point to the paragraph on page 14.

4. Read the information in the Study Strategy box on page 13 aloud. Give each student a copy of AM 1/6, or have them copy the Nutrient Chart on page 13. (Warn them not to write in the book.) Students can read on their own and take notes in the chart. They will use these charts in subsequent activities. With less proficient students, you can work together to complete the chart.

(Suggested answers: Proteins—help you grow—fish, eggs, beans, milk; Carbohydrates—give quick energy—bread, rice, corn, fruit, beets, peas; Vitamins—help body work properly—fruits and vegetables; Minerals—help body work properly—fruits and vegetables; Fats—give energy to store—butter, ice cream, sausage, potato chips.)

Vitamins and Minerals

Vitamins and minerals help your body work properly. For example, the mineral calcium helps to build bones and teeth. Vitamin A helps your eyes see at night. Most people get enough vitamins and minerals by eating different kinds of food.

Carbohydrates

Carbohydrates give you quick energy. Your body needs this energy to move, grow, and keep warm. Good sources of carbohydrates are bread, rice, corn, fruit, and some vegetables like beets and peas.

56 percent of
American families
say they eat
dinner together
every day.

Fats

Fats give you energy, too. Your body can store fat and use it later for energy. Everyone needs some fat in his/her diet. However, too much fat is bad for you. Some foods high in fat are butter, ice cream, sausage, and potato chips.

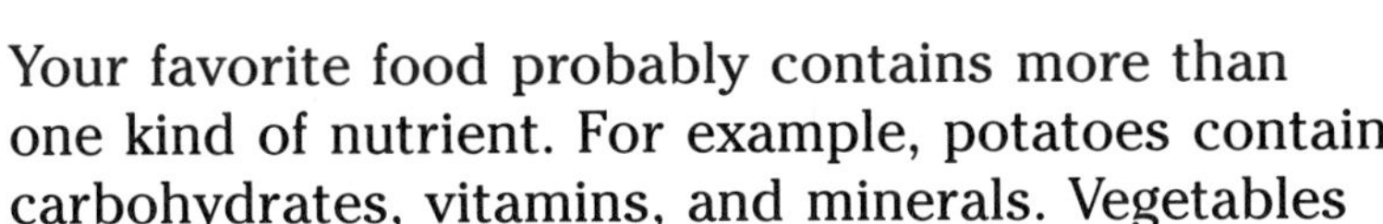

Your favorite food probably contains more than one kind of nutrient. For example, potatoes contain carbohydrates, vitamins, and minerals. Vegetables contain a lot of vitamins and minerals and some protein. An apple contains carbohydrates and vitamins. By eating different kinds of food, you can get the nutrients you need.

3. Read a Chart

Pairwork. Use your chart on page 13. Practice asking and answering questions.

Q: Which nutrient ______?
A: ______.

1. helps your body grow
2. helps your body work properly
3. gives you quick energy
4. gives you energy to store

Q: Which food is a good source of ______?
A: ______.

1. protein	carrots
2. carbohydrate	fish
3. fats	ice cream
4. vitamins and minerals	bread

Language Focus:

Asking and Answering Questions

Q: Which nutrient gives you quick energy?
A: Carbohydrates.

Language Focus:

Asking and Answering Questions

Q: Which food is a good source of protein?
A: Fish.
Beans.

Activity 3: Read a Chart

1. Model the activity by reading the questions in the two Language Focus boxes: *Which nutrient gives you quick energy? Which food is a good source of protein?* Let students read the answers. Have them look at their chart from Activity 2 to confirm the answers.

2. Have pairs of students compare charts by asking and answering the first group of four questions.

(Answers: 1, proteins; 2, vitamins and minerals; 3, carbohydrates; 4, fats.)

Then have the pairs ask and answer the second group of questions, choosing the answers from the second column.

(Answers: 1, fish; 2, bread; 3, ice cream; 4, carrots.)

3. Extend the activity by having students look back at the food chant on page 2. Have them read a line from the chant and predict which foods are good sources of protein, fat, or carbohydrates. Check the answers by looking in a handbook of nutrition.

Activity 4: Read a Graph

1. Copy the graph, "Protein in a Serving of Rice, Beans, and Milk" on the board. Have students read the title of the graph and find the vertical and horizontal axes.

2. Read the sentences in the Language Focus box. Have students point to each of the foods on the bar graph as you read the sentence about that food.

3. Read the Study Strategy box aloud, and discuss how the use of a bar graph is helpful in making comparisons. (You can actually see the differences among the items being compared.)

4. List the following foods on the board with the grams of protein in each:

Food	Protein
half cup cooked lima beans	8
slice of whole wheat bread	3
medium egg	6

Have students get into small groups. Give each group a copy of AM 1/7. Ask them to follow the model and make a bar graph for these foods and their grams of protein. Circulate to assist less proficient students.

5. Have groups compare their graphs and resolve discrepancies.

Study Strategy:

Making Bar Graphs

A bar graph helps you compare data or information.

Language Focus:

Giving Measurements

A serving of rice has 2 grams of protein.

A half cup of beans has 15 grams of protein.

A cup of milk has 8 grams of protein.

4. Read a Graph

Groupwork. Study the graph and answer the question below.

This bar graph makes it easy to compare the amount of protein in different foods. Which food has the most protein?

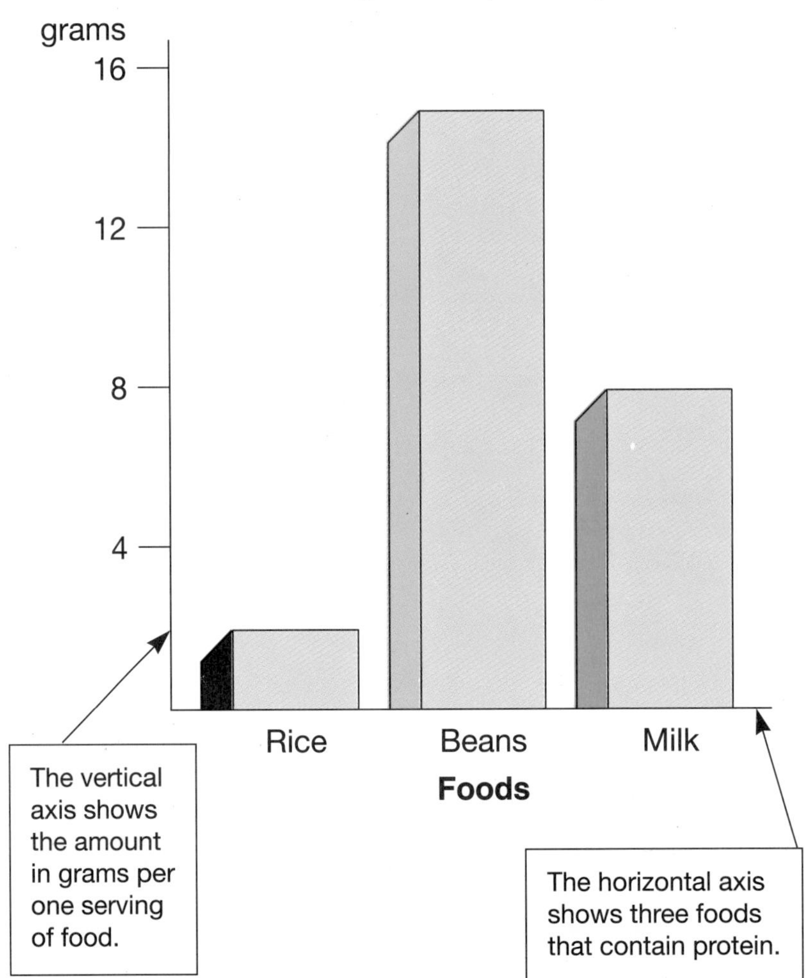

5. Make a Graph

Groupwork. Use the labels to make three bar graphs.

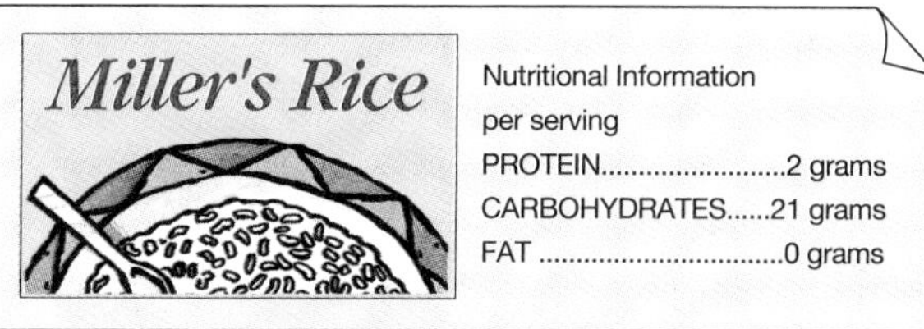

Miller's Rice
Nutritional Information
per serving
PROTEIN........................2 grams
CARBOHYDRATES......21 grams
FAT ....0 grams

DOCTOR'S PEANUT BUTTER
NO SALT
Nutritional Information
per serving
PROTEIN.........................9 grams
CARBOHYDRATES........5 grams
FAT ....17 grams

Len's YOGURT
Nutritional Information
per serving
PROTEIN......................10 grams
CARBOHYDRATES......14 grams
FAT ....4 grams

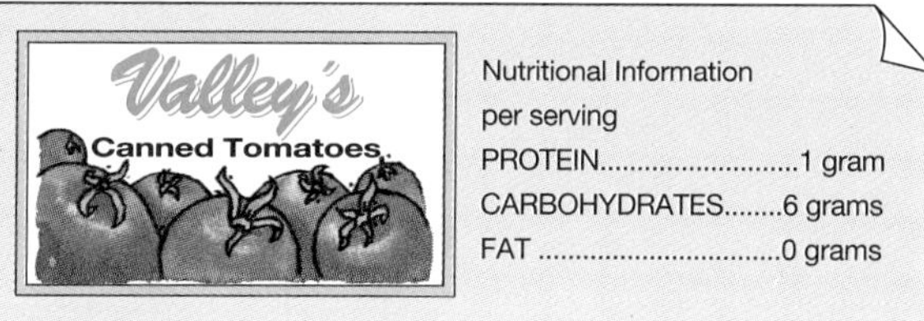

Valley's
Canned Tomatoes
Nutritional Information
per serving
PROTEIN..........................1 gram
CARBOHYDRATES........6 grams
FAT ....0 grams

Protein
Per Serving

grams

Rice | Peanut Butter | Yogurt | Canned Tomatoes

Foods

Carbohydrate
Per Serving

grams

Rice | Peanut Butter | Yogurt | Canned Tomatoes

Foods

Fat
Per Serving

grams

Rice | Peanut Butter | Yogurt | Canned Tomatoes

Foods

Activity 5: Make a Graph

1. Have students work in groups of 3–4 to make the bar graphs. Give each group three copies of AM 1/8. Make sure they write the title of the graph and label the horizontal and vertical axes.

2. Let students figure out how to do the task. You can act as consultant, stepping in when they have specific questions.

3. Let groups read the labels on the rice, peanut butter, yogurt, and canned tomatoes, and add the nutritional information to the graphs.

4. Have groups compare their three bar graphs with those of another group and clear up any discrepancies.

Activity 6: Compare and Contrast

1. Have students look at their bar graphs while you ask the questions in the first Language Focus box. Elicit the answers from students.

2. Pass out one copy of AM 1/9 to each group and have them ask and answer questions to complete the first chart (comparing two foods).

(Answers: more protein, yogurt; more carbohydrates, rice; less fat, rice.)

3. Model the questions in the second Language Focus box and let students answer. Then have students work in groups to complete the second chart (comparing four foods).

4. Put two groups together to compare charts. Discuss any differences.

(Answers: most protein—yogurt, least protein—rice, most carbohydrate—rice, least carbohydrate—peanut butter, most fat—peanut butter, least fat—rice and canned tomatoes.)

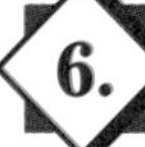

6. Compare and Contrast

Language Focus:

Comparing Two Things

Q: Which has more protein, rice or yogurt?
A: Yogurt.

Q: Which has less fat, rice or peanut butter?
A: Rice.

Groupwork. Ask questions about the foods on your bar graphs.

Q: Which has *more protein*, *rice* or *yogurt*?
A: *Yogurt*.

Nutrient	rice	yogurt
more protein		✓
more carbohydrate		
less fat		

Q: Which food has *the most protein*?
A: Yogurt.

Nutrient	rice	yogurt	peanut butter	canned tomatoes
the most protein		✓		
the least protein				
the most carbohydrate				
the least carbohydrate				
the most fat				
the least fat				

Language Focus:

Comparing Three or More Things

Q: Which has the most protein?
A: Peanut butter.

Q: Which has the least protein?
A: Rice.

7. Synthesize

Classwork. Choose packages of food at home or in a store. Read the labels. Find the amount of protein, carbohydrate, and fat per serving. With your classmates, make three bar graphs. Then compare the nutrients in the different foods.

Protein
Per Serving

grams

Foods

Carbohydrate
Per Serving

grams

Foods

Fat
Per Serving

grams

Foods

Americans cook 17 percent of all meals in the microwave.

Activity 7: Synthesize

1. Bring in a labeled package of food for each student, or have students bring in nutritional labels collected from packages at home.

2. Make sure that each student has a food or label to work with. Put the students in groups of four to make bar graphs of their foods. Give each group three copies of AM 1/8. Have them title these *Protein per Serving, Carbohydrates per Serving* and *Fat per Serving.* Make sure they write the names of the foods on the horizontal axis and the number of grams on the vertical axis. Each student should add the information about his or her food on each graph.

3. When the graphs are completed, have the students in each group take turns telling each other about their food. Write these questions on the board to help them: *How many grams of each nutrient does it contain? How does it compare with other foods on the graphs?*

4. Have each group present one of its graphs to the class.

5. Display the graphs, and use them to compare the foods, e.g., *Which food has more protein, tuna fish or kidney beans? Which food on this graph has the most fat?*

6. After the groups make their presentations, give each student a copy of AM 1/10, Teamwork Evaluation Chart. Have students write their teammates' names and put a check mark next to the activities in which each teammate took part.

Activity 1: Predict

Materials:
different kinds of food such as potato chips, pretzels, potatoes, milk, cheese, butter.

1. Put the foods on the table. Have groups of students predict which foods have a lot of fat, which have some fat, and which have little or no fat.

2. Distribute copies of AM 1/11 to each group or have students copy the chart on page 20. Let students write their predictions on their chart; then have the groups compare predictions. Have them keep their charts for use in the next activity.

Activity 2: Investigate

Materials:
brown paper bag, scissors, foods from Activity 1, table lamp

1. Students can work in groups to test their predictions. Have them follow the steps in the book. Circulate among the groups to answer any questions. When students rub the foods on the brown paper, they should use a little "elbow grease," pressing down hard while rubbing.

2. Have groups paste, tape, or staple their squares of brown paper in the appropriate places on their charts from Activity 1. Let them compare their results with the predictions they made, and let groups compare charts.

How much fat?

Too much fat in your diet may be bad for your health. In this section, you will do an investigation to find out which foods contain a lot of fat.

1. Predict

Classwork. Most nutritionists say that too much fat is bad for your health. Which foods have a lot of fat, some fat, or little or no fat? Make predictions.

Materials: different kinds of food, such as carrots, potato chips, pretzels, potatoes, milk, cheese, butter

A lot of fat	Some fat	Little or no fat
		carrots

2. Investigate

Groupwork. Follow these steps to test your predictions about the foods in activity 1.

Materials: one brown paper bag, scissors, foods from activity 1

Steps:
1. Cut a brown bag into two-inch squares.
2. Write the name of a food on each square.
3. Rub each food on the square with its name. For liquids, put several drops on the square.
4. Let the squares dry.
5. Hold each square up to a light. Can you see a greasy spot? If so, the food has some fat in it.
6. Paste the squares on a chart. Share your chart with the class.

A lot of fat	Some fat	Little or no fat

Steps:

1.
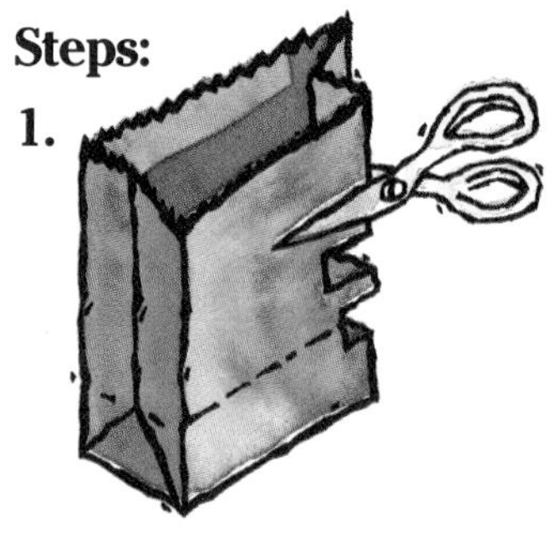

2.

3.

4.

5.

How did the potato get to North America?

Five hundred years ago, potatoes didn't grow in North America, but today they are an important food crop. Where did the potato come from? How did it get to North America? Find out in this section.

Classwork. These places were important in the history of the potato. Find them on the map.

- South America
- Andes Mountains
- Colombia
- New England
- Italy
- North America
- Spain
- France
- England
- Portugal
- Ireland

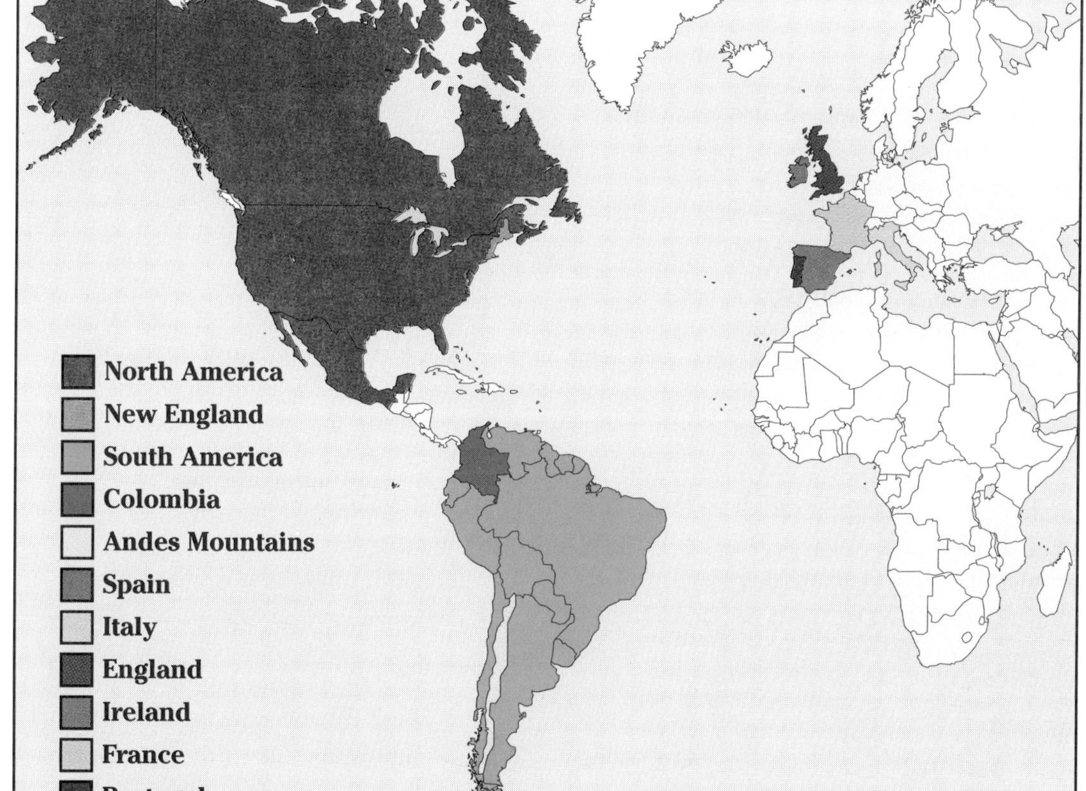

Activity 1: Locate

Optional materials: a potato in a closed paper bag

1. (Optional) Before students open to this page, show them the closed bag with the potato inside. Tell them there is something to eat in the bag. Have them ask yes/no questions to guess the food. *(Is it a vegetable? Is it popular in the United States?)* They should not use a name of a food in their questions. Pass the bag around and have students feel it and make guesses. Finally, let a volunteer open the bag and show the potato to the class.

2. Elicit information about potatoes. *(Are potatoes popular in students' native countries? What are some ways to cook potatoes? Where do potatoes come from?)*

3. Write the following questions on the board: *How many kinds of potatoes are there? Which state in the United States produces the most potatoes? What percentage of the United States potato crop is used for potato chips? Potatoes are a good source of which nutrients?* Have groups of students predict answers and write them on the board. Then have the class read the potato facts on page 22 to check their predictions.

4. Read the instruction line on page 21 aloud. Have students get together in groups of three and look at the map in one book. Read the name of a place on the list at the top of the page and have a student in each group find and point to the place. Other students can help. Look quickly to check their answers. Have other students repeat the process with other places.

5. With less proficient students you may want to repeat this activity, using a wall map.

6. Tell students that 500 years ago potatoes grew only in the Andes Mountains. Have them speculate how the potato got from the Andes to North America.

Activity 2: Shared Reading

1. Before class, go through the reading and circle any words that might be new to your students. Decide which, if any, of these words cannot be understood from the context of their use in the reading. Introduce these words in context-rich sentences, e.g., *People died when they ate the poisonous plants.* Have students use context to guess the meaning of each word.

2. On the board, make a chart like the one below. Together, read the first paragraph of the article on page 22 and then read the note next to "Andes" in the chart on the board. Point out that when you take notes, you write only the most important information, and you don't have to write complete sentences. Distribute AM 1/12 or have students copy the chart on another piece of paper. They can then finish the article on their own, taking notes as they read.

How Did the Potato Get to North America?

Country/Region	*Potato History*
Andes	Potatoes here 500 years ago
Spain	
France	
England	
Ireland	
North America	

Sample completed chart:

How Did the Potato Get to North America?

Country/Region	*Potato History*
Andes	Potatoes here 500 years ago
Spain	Spanish explorers took potatoes to Spain, mid 1500s
France	Potato taken to France; people wouldn't eat it; thought it poisonous
England	Drake took potato to England from Colombia. Potatoes fed to animals in England
Ireland	Got potato from England; became important food
North America	Irish settlers took potato to North America, early 1700s

(Continued on page 23.)

2. Shared Reading

How did the potato get to North America?

Five hundred years ago, potatoes grew in the Andes region of South America. They were an important food for the people who lived in these high mountains. In other parts of the world, however, people didn't know about potatoes.

The Spanish invaded South America in the mid-1500s. They learned of potatoes and took some back to Spain. By 1570, white potatoes were growing in parts of Spain. By 1580, people in Portugal and Italy were also growing potatoes.

From Spain, potatoes traveled to France. In France, however, people were afraid to eat this new vegetable. They thought it was poisonous. Louis XVI, the King of France, tried to convince French people to eat potatoes. He even served them at the palace. But for many years, the French still refused to eat potatoes.

Potatoes reached England in a different way. In 1586, the English explorer Sir Francis Drake stopped in Colombia. There he probably picked up some potatoes and took them back to England. At first, the English refused to eat potatoes, too. Instead, they fed them to their pigs and chickens.

From England, the potato traveled to Ireland. The potato grew well in the poor soil of Ireland, and soon it was an important source of nutrients for Irish people.

In the early 1700s, Irish settlers brought the potato to North America. By 1750, many people in New England were growing and eating potatoes.

Digging and harvesting potatoes in Inca times.
—Poma de Ayola manuscript

Potato Facts

One hundred and sixty kinds of potatoes are grown in the United States today. Idaho is the biggest producer of potatoes in the United States. About 15 percent of the U.S. potato crop goes into potato chips. Potatoes have no fat. They are good sources of Vitamin C, niacin, and potassium. They are also a good source of carbohydrates.

3. Draw

Pairwork. How did the potato get from South America to North America? Draw its route. Use the map on page 21.

4. Draw Inferences

Pairwork. Who said it—someone from Spain, France, or England? Match the statement on the left with the country on the right.

Circle your answer.

1. "You can't eat that. It might kill you." a. Spain
2. "I won't eat it. Give it to the animals." b. France
3. "I'll try it." c. England

The average
time an American
family
spends eating
dinner is
32 minutes.

5. Design

Pairwork. Choose one activity.

a. Help Louis XVI. Think of a way to convince people in France to eat potatoes.

b. Think of a food you like. Design a poster or advertisement to get your classmates to try this food.

Activity 2: Shared Reading *(continued)*

3. Have students compare charts and discuss differences.

4. For follow-up, have groups of students write sentences about the history of the potato. Have them make some of the sentences true and some of them false. Have the groups exchange sentences and determine which sentences are false.

5. Have groups of students write questions to test their knowledge of potato history. Let the groups exchange tests and find the answers in the article.

Activity 3: Draw

1. Give pairs of students a piece of tracing paper. Have them draw the route of the potato over the map on page 21. Have them use the map as they take turns telling about the history of the potato.

2. Have students take turns giving you information to draw or trace with your finger the route of the potato on a map.

Activity 4: Draw Inferences

1. Have students read the instruction line. Then have them match the quotations with countries.

(Answers: 1. b; 2. c; 3. a.)

2. Have students write dialogues and roleplay potato-eating scenes in different countries.

Activity 5: Design

Have students work in pairs to choose an activity and present their work to the class. Have a stack of magazines and food-store flyers available for b.

Activity 1: Report

Students can look at the picture of a hot fudge sundae and answer the questions. If a number of students have eaten hot fudge sundaes, take a poll to find out what the most popular part is.

Activity 2: Compare

This activity introduces similes, comparisons of things that are not usually thought of as alike, using the word *like* or *as*. Read the introduction and have students complete the sentence in different ways. *What else is the whipped cream (or the sauce, or the ice cream) like?*

(In the drawing of the earth and in the poem on page 25, *strata* refers to different layers of the earth. [It is a technical term used by earth scientists and is the plural of the Latin word *stratum,* meaning layer.] The center of the earth is the *core* in the poem.)

Activity 3: Shared Reading

1. Using context-rich sentences and the picture on page 24, introduce vocabulary you believe will be new to the students, including *tap, vein, delve, strata, goblet.*

How do you eat a hot fudge sundae?

When you look at a hot fudge sundae, you might see ice cream and hot fudge sauce. But when you read a poem about a hot fudge sundae, you might see something else—something very different. Find out what it is in this section.

1. Report

Classwork. Have you ever eaten a hot fudge sundae? What part did you like best?

2. Compare

Classwork. The poet Jonathan Holden looks at a hot fudge sundae and sees the world. What do you see when you look at the parts of a hot fudge sundae?

The whipped cream is like the clouds in the sky.

The ________________ is like the ________________.

3. Shared Reading

Listen to this poem. Then read it aloud several times.

How to Eat a Hot Fudge Sundae

Start with the
clouds. Eat
the clouds. Eat through
to the ground. Eat
the ground until you tap
the first rich vein. Delve
from strata to strata
down to the cold lava
core. Stir
the lava, pick up
the whole goblet, drink
straight from the goblet
until you've finished the world.

—*Jonathan Holden*

4. Identify

Pairwork. What words does the poet use to describe the parts of a hot fudge sundae?

whipped cream	*clouds*
ice cream	______
hot fudge sauce	______

5. Write

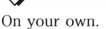

On your own.

1. Choose a food you like. Describe it.

   What shape is it? round, thin, flat
   What color is it? red

2. Ask a partner to use your words to draw a picture of something that is not a food.
3. Use your words and your partner's idea to write a poem.

Name of food: PIZZA
Descriptive words: round, thin, red, flat,
Partner idea: Like a spaceship

Activity 3: Shared Reading *(continued)*

2. Read the poem aloud. Then have the class read it aloud in different ways. Some suggested ways to read it are:

- Have groups take turns reading a sentence.
- Read and act out the poem, using a spoon and a goblet.
- Read together, while one student points to the parts of the sundae in the picture.
- Have pairs take turns reading a sentence to each other.

3. Discuss the poem with the class. Ask, *Do you think the poet likes hot fudge sundaes? Why do you think so?*

Activity 4: Identify

Students can work in pairs to find the words the poet uses for the parts of a sundae. They can check their answers with another pair.

Activity 5: Write

1. Let students work on their own to choose a food that they like. Then have them write, on their own paper, a list of words that describe it, without giving the name of the food. (If desired, the name of the food can be written on the reverse side of the paper.)

2. Have students exchange their lists, so each has another student's list. They should then read the new list of descriptive words and draw a picture of something the words might describe that is **not** a food.

3. Less proficient students can then write a simple poem about the object they have drawn. Or, if the names of the foods are on the reverse side of the paper, more proficient students can write their poem comparing the two, as the poet did with the sundae and the earth.

4. Have students choose a way to "publish" their poems. They might want to put them together in a class booklet or post them in the classroom for others to read.

Activity Menu

Read and explain the activities to the class. Then have students individually or in small groups select a project for a class or homework assignment. Projects can later be displayed in the classroom as they are shared with the class.

Activity Menu

Choose one of the following activities to do.

1. Make a Food Display
Cut pictures of food from different magazines. Paste the foods into the correct groups in a Food Guide Pyramid. Then label the foods and display your pyramid.

2. Check Out a Vending Machine
Find a vending machine in your area. List the foods in the vending machine. Write the foods in the correct groups in a food guide pyramid. Does the vending machine provide food from all groups? Report what you learned to the class.

3. What's the Difference?
Take a trip to the grocery store and read some food labels. Compare the amount of fat, protein, and carbohydrate in a serving of these foods. Tell your classmates what you learned.

- whole milk, lowfat milk, and skim milk
- regular yogurt and nonfat light yogurt
- ice cream, sherbet, and ice milk
- butter and margarine
- cottage cheese and cream cheese

4. Supermarket Smarts
Predict answers to the questions below. Then visit a supermarket to check your predictions.

1. How many kinds of breakfast cereal can you buy in a supermarket?
2. How many kinds of fruit are available?
3. What kinds of foods are next to the cash register?
4. What international foods are available?

5. A Meal in a Sandwich

Invent a new kind of sandwich with food from all groups in the Food Guide Pyramid. Give your sandwich a name. Draw or cut pictures of the food in your sandwich. Then make a poster to advertise your sandwich. Include the name of your sandwich on the poster.

6. What's for Lunch?

Can you find these foods in the school cafeteria?

- a food that is high in protein but low in fat
- a food that is high in fat
- a food that costs less than 50 cents
- the cheapest source of carbohydrate
- the most expensive source of protein
- the sweetest food

7. Eating Around the World

Tell your classmates about the food in your native country.

Describe what people eat on a typical day. Present this information to your classmates in a short oral report or on a small poster with pictures.

8. Make a Food Database

Collect data on the nutrients in a variety of foods. Then follow your teacher's instructions to make a food database. Use your database to evaluate your diet or to plan healthy meals.

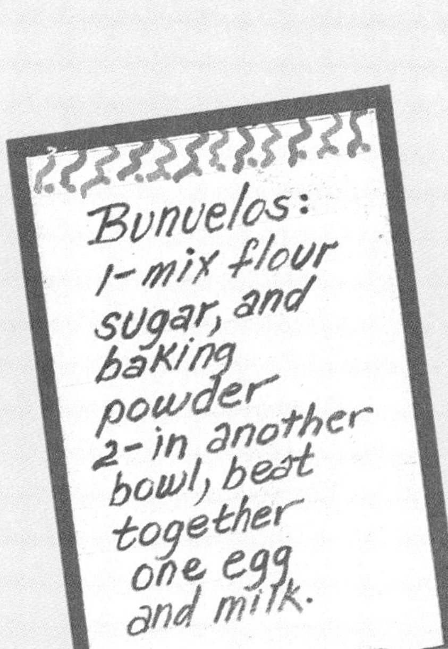

9. You Are the Chef

Choose a favorite dish. Tell your classmates how to make this dish. List the ingredients and write the instructions. Exchange instructions with a classmate. At home, follow the instructions to make this dish. Bring the food to class and share it with your classmates.

10. Food Customs

People in different parts of the world learn different table manners, or polite ways to eat. Tell about table manners in your native country. List things you should and shouldn't do at a meal. Then interview someone from the United States. Find out what they think you should and shouldn't do at the dinner table. Here are a few questions to get you started:

- *Is it polite to eat everything on your plate or in your dish?*
- *Is it polite to eat with your hands?*

Read on . . .

Read the poems to the class. Then the class can read the poems in a variety of ways:

- Have them read aloud chorally with you.
- Individuals or groups can read a stanza or a line.
- Some students can pantomime the actions while more proficient students read the poems aloud.

How to Eat a Poem

Discussion questions: *What is the poem being compared to? Why is the poem easier to eat? Why do you think Eve Merriam talks about "eating" a poem?*

Watermelons

Discussion questions: *Why are watermelons called Green Buddhas? What is the smile? What are the teeth?*

Read on...

95 percent of American families say they ate their last dinner at home.

How to Eat a Poem

Don't be polite,
Bite in.
Pick it up with your fingers and lick the juice that
may run down your chin.
It is ready and ripe now, whenever you are.

You do not need a knife or fork or spoon
or plate or napkin or tablecloth.

For there is no core
or stem
or rind
or pit
or seed
or skin
to throw away.

—Eve Merriam

Watermelons

Green Buddhas
On the fruit stand
We eat the smile
and spit out the teeth.

—Charles Simic

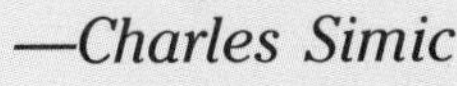

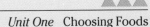

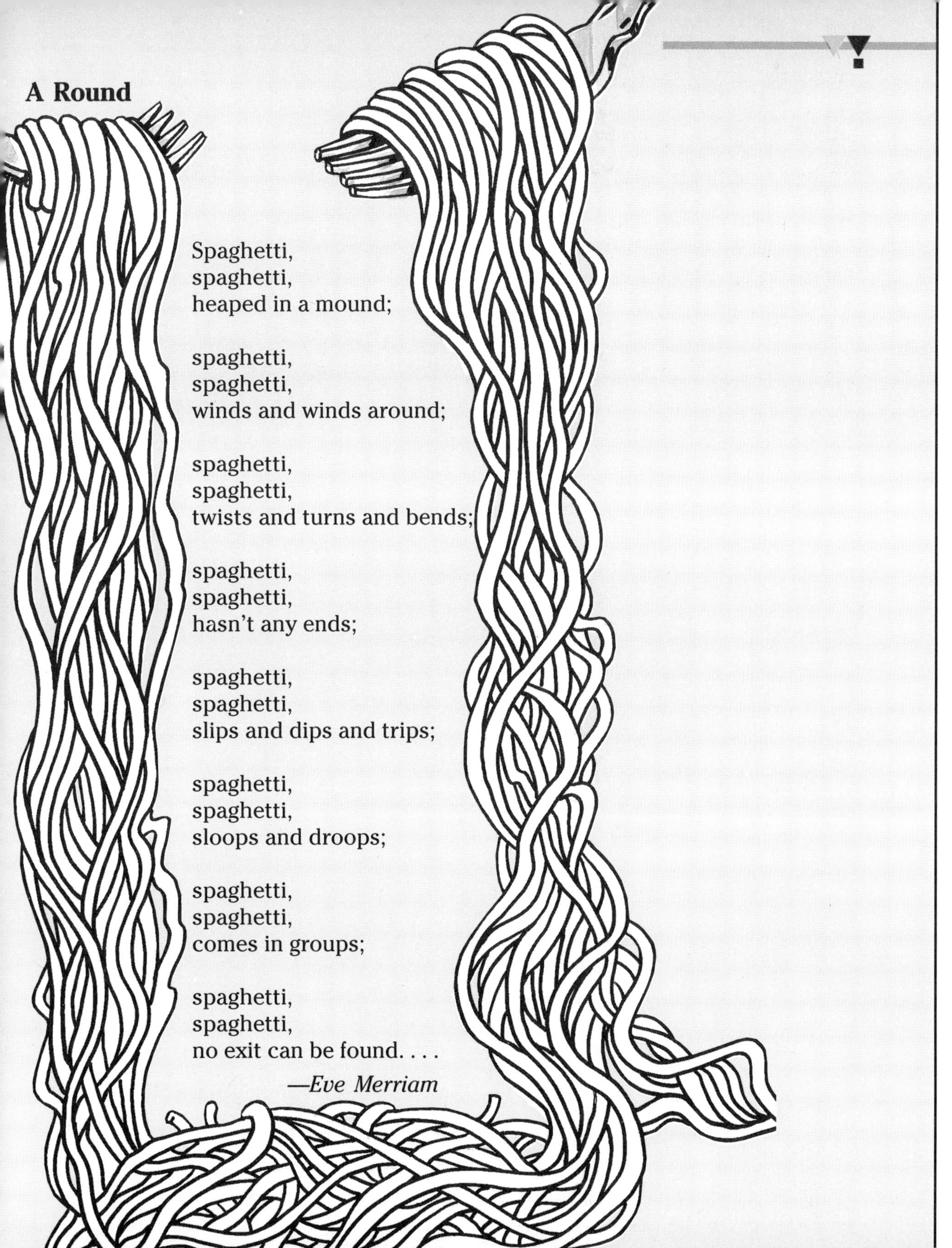

A Round

Spaghetti,
spaghetti,
heaped in a mound;

spaghetti,
spaghetti,
winds and winds around;

spaghetti,
spaghetti,
twists and turns and bends;

spaghetti,
spaghetti,
hasn't any ends;

spaghetti,
spaghetti,
slips and dips and trips;

spaghetti,
spaghetti,
sloops and droops;

spaghetti,
spaghetti,
comes in groups;

spaghetti,
spaghetti,
no exit can be found. . . .

—*Eve Merriam*

Student text page 29

A Round

Discussion questions: *Why does Eve Merriam repeat the word* spaghetti? *How does she describe this food? What words in the poem tell about the problems you have with eating spaghetti? Why can "no exit be found"?*

Encourage students to express their opinions about the poems.

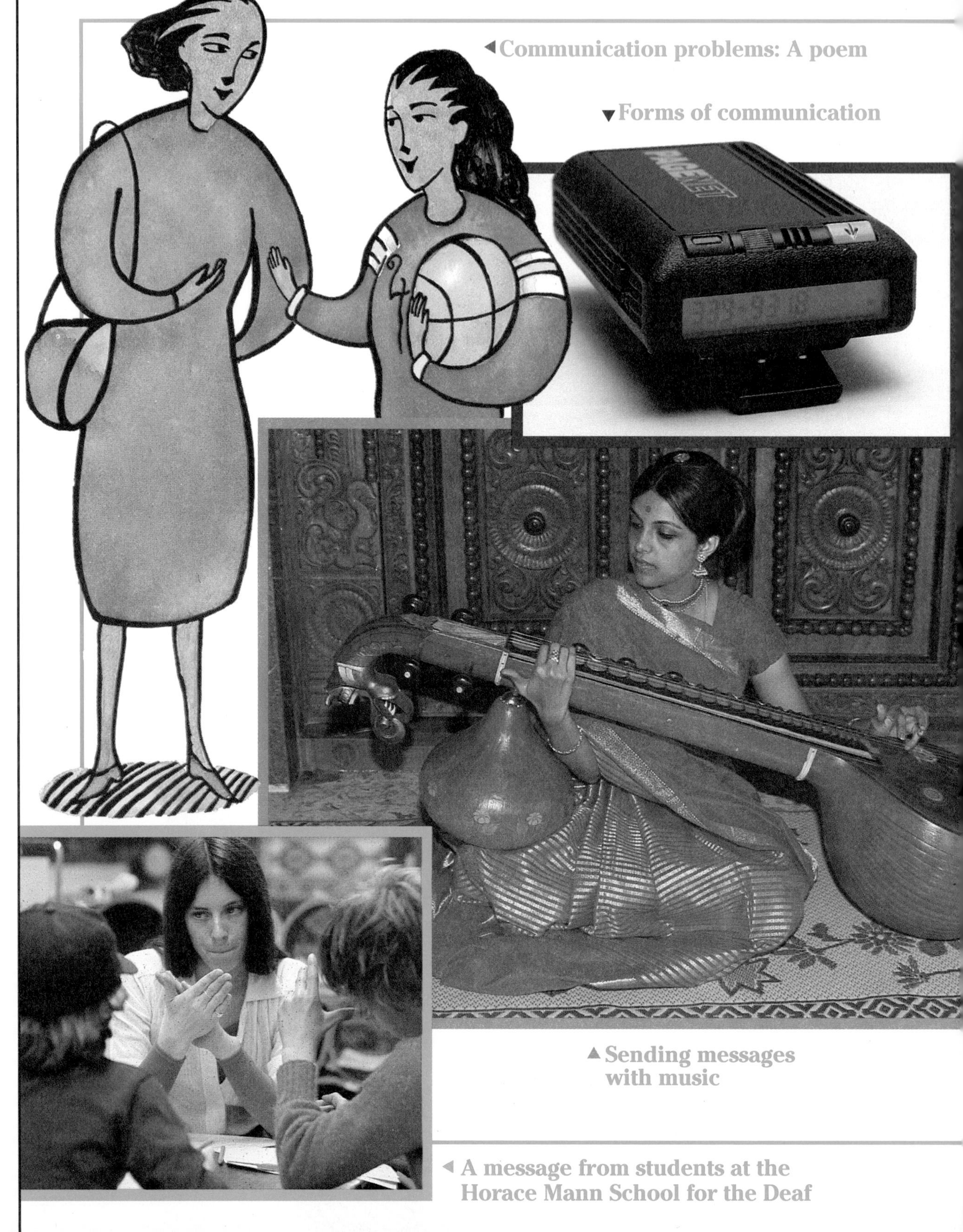

◀ Communication problems: A poem

▼ Forms of communication

▲ Sending messages with music

◀ A message from students at the Horace Mann School for the Deaf

SENDING MESSAGES

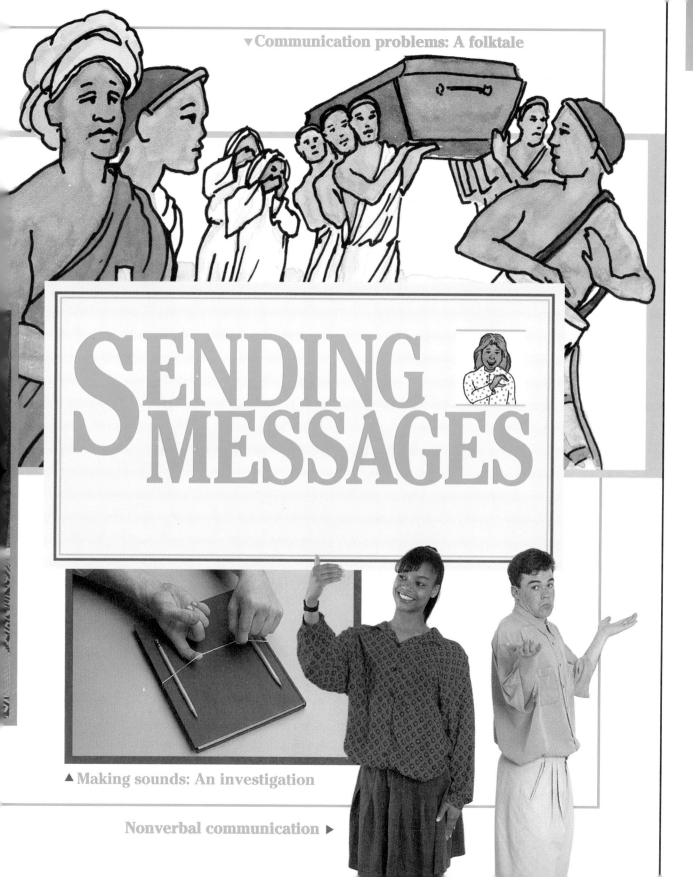

▼Communication problems: A folktale

▲Making sounds: An investigation

Nonverbal communication ▶

Forms of communication

In this section, you will explore ways that people communicate.

Study Strategy:

Brainstorming

Brainstorming is a good way to collect ideas. When you brainstorm, you write down every idea that you think of.

1. Identify

Classwork. What are some ways that people communicate?

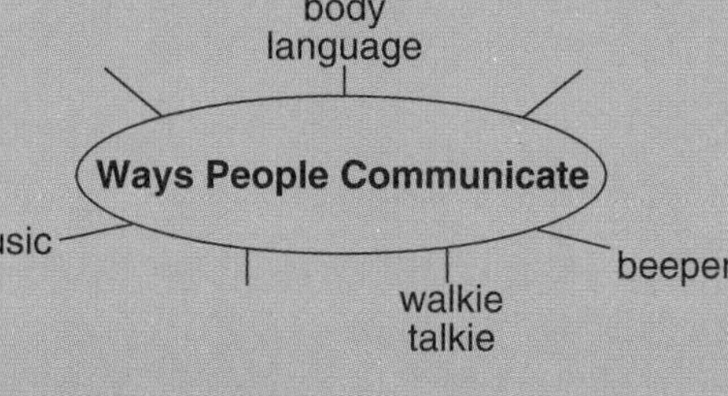

2. Evaluate

Pairwork. Choose one form of communication and write about it in a chart.

Form of Communication: *telephone*	
Advantages +	**Disadvantages** –
You can talk to someone far away.	*It costs money.*
You don't have to leave home.	*You can't see the person.*

Activity 1: Identify

1. Copy the cluster diagram on the board. Together identify the forms of communication shown in the pictures, and add them to the cluster diagram.

2. Have students add their own ideas to the cluster diagram. Explain to students that they are "brainstorming," or writing down every idea that they can think of.

3. Have students classify the forms of communication on the cluster diagram. For example, have them group them in the following ways: fast ways to communicate/slow ways to communicate; communicating by talking/communicating without talking; communicating with words/communicating without words.

Activity 2: Evaluate

1. Together read the chart evaluating communication by telephone. Elicit definitions of advantages (good things) and disadvantages (bad things or problems). Have students suggest other advantages or disadvantages of this form of communication.

2. Draw the evaluation chart on the board or on a transparency. Have the class work together to evaluate another form of communication. Write their ideas on the chart.

3. Have students work in pairs to evaluate a form of communication. They should make an evaluation chart on another piece of paper and add their ideas. Then have the pairs take turns reporting their ideas to the class.

Read the introduction aloud and then have students suggest some ways that people communicate without using words (e.g., signs, body language, sign language, etc.).

Activity 1: Identify

1. Work together to identify the symbols shown on this page. First let students identify the symbols they know. Model the question in the Language Focus box, asking them about the symbols they know. Ask, *What does this symbol mean?* Then let them ask you about any unfamiliar symbols, using that question.

2. Ask where they might see each of these symbols.

3. Have volunteers draw other symbols on the board and ask their classmates what they mean.

4. Make a chart like this on a large piece of chart paper:

Symbol	What does it mean?

Hang the chart in the classroom and have students add symbols to it as they come across them at school or outside of school.

Activity 2: Design

1. Have the class study the symbol shown here and guess what it means. Then have them match the symbol with one of the ideas on the list at the bottom of page 34. Encourage them to think of other ways they could communicate this information in a symbol.

2. Working in groups, students can choose one of the ideas in the list and design a symbol to communicate this information. Have them display their symbols, and let the class guess what they mean.

3. If you or the students can think of symbols to identify places or activities in your classroom, have students design these symbols. For example, they could design a symbol to identify a reading corner of the classroom. They could design symbols for groupwork and pairwork. You could hang these symbols on a wall and point to them at appropriate times.

Language Focus:

Asking What Something Means

Q: What does this symbol mean?
A: It means "you can't smoke here."

Nonverbal communication

In this section, you will investigate ways that people communicate without using words.

1. Identify

Classwork. What do these symbols mean?

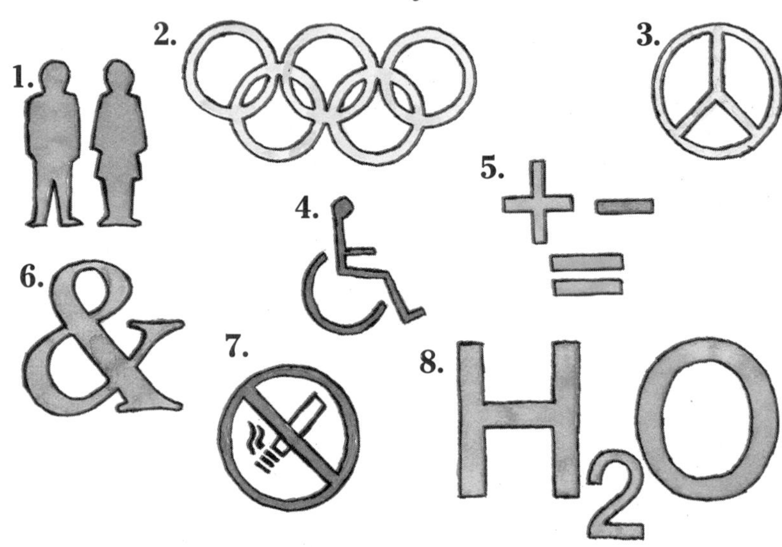

Symbols communicate important information.

2. Design

Groupwork. Design a symbol to communicate information. Choose one of these ideas, or think of your own.

You must wear shoes here.

This is an ESL classroom.

Don't put bottles in this trash can.

No eating here.

Friendship.

Love.

Danger.

3. Match

Classwork. What information are these people communicating? Match the people with the ideas on the right.

Body language communicates important information.

I have a question.
Look at that.
I'm angry.
Hi!
I'm sad.
Come here.
I'm worried.
It's this big.
I don't know.

Activity 3: Match

1. Read the instruction line and caption aloud, and let students study the first picture. Then have them read the list of expressions in the column at right and choose an expression to match the picture. People from different cultures use different body language, so some of these examples may be unfamiliar to students. Encourage them to guess.

2. Let the class work together to match the remaining pictures and ideas in the list.

3. Body language consists of both facial expressions and body movements. Have students note which people are using facial expressions to communicate, and which are using mostly body language.

(Answers: 1. I'm angry. 2. I'm sad. 3. I'm worried. 4. I have a question. 5. I don't know. 6. It's this big. 7. Hi. 8. Come here. 9. Look at that.)

Activity 4: Compare and Contrast

1. To prepare students for this activity, show a video clip of a scene from a soap opera or other drama without the sound (or use pictures cut from magazines). Ask them to look for examples of body language. Play a very short segment, and then let volunteers demonstrate any body language they noticed. Have the class suggest what the body language means.

2. Body language varies from culture to culture. If possible, pair students from different cultures to do this activity. Give each pair a copy of AM 2/1 or have them copy the chart at the bottom of page 36. Let them use body language to communicate the information in the chart. They should then answer the question in the chart by checking yes or no.

3. Have pairs report what they learned. Make sure that students understand that there is no right or wrong way to use body language, but that the differences might cause communication problems.

Activity 5: Draw

1. Bring in some cartoons, and have students identify the body language that the cartoon characters are using.

2. Have students look at the "face" drawn here. Does the person look angry, happy, or sad? What helps students know how the person feels?

3. Show how the "angry" face is drawn, using the eyebrows, eyes, and mouth in the first row of the chart. Then have pairs work together to draw three more faces, using the eyebrows, eyes, and mouth in each row. Once they have drawn the faces, have them tell what information the person's face is communicating.

(Answers: I'm sad; I'm worried; I'm happy.)

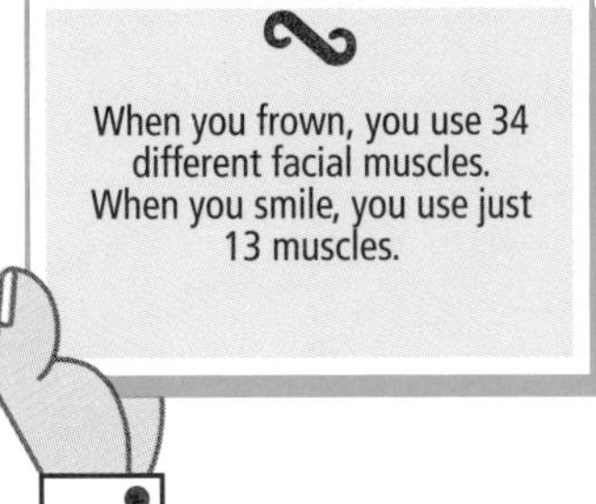

When you frown, you use 34 different facial muscles. When you smile, you use just 13 muscles.

4. Compare and Contrast

Pairwork. Take turns using body language to communicate these ideas.

Did you use the same body language?

	YES	NO
1. I'm tired.	______	✓
2. I'm happy.	______	______
3. I understand.	______	______
4. I'm listening.	______	______
5. Goodbye.	______	______
6. That smells bad.	______	______
7. Yes.	______	______
8. No.	______	______

Tell your classmates if you used the same or different body language.

5. Draw

Pairwork. Draw three faces. Use the mouth, eyes, and eyebrows in each row below. Then tell what information each person is communicating.

Example: 

Artists use special techniques to show the body language of cartoon characters.

Row	Information	Eyebrows	Eyes	Mouth
1	*I'm angry*			
2	______			
3	______			
4	______			

Communication problems: Younde Goes to Town (a folktale)

In this section, you will read a story about a man named Younde. When Younde travels to a faraway town, he meets people who speak a different language. Younde can't understand their language, and they can't understand his language. You can imagine the kinds of problems he has.

1. Think-Pair-Share

a. Think about a time when you didn't understand someone.

- Where were you?
- What did you do?
- How did you feel?

b. Tell your story to a partner. Listen carefully to your partner's story.

c. Get together with another pair. Tell your partner's story.

2. Learn New Words

Classwork. Study the pictures and captions on pages 38–40. Use information in the pictures to define these words:

Picture #1: village *a small town*

Picture #2: donkey ________

Picture #3: herd ________

Picture #4: tremendous ________

Picture #5: unusual ________

Picture #6: funeral procession ________

Study Strategy: Using Pictures

Pictures can help you understand a story and learn new words.

Student text page 37

Introduction: Have students look over the section and suggest what it is about. Read the title of this section. Point to the two people in the bottom picture on page 39. Say, *These people have a communication problem.* Ask them to list possible reasons for this problem. Read the introduction aloud. Have students suggest some of the problems Younde might have on his trip.

Activity 1: Think-Pair-Share

Part a. Read aloud the questions and tell students they will have two minutes to think about them.

Part b. Encourage students to get together with someone they don't know well. Tell them they each have one minute to tell their stories and answer their partner's question. They must listen to their partner's answers carefully, because they will have to retell his/her story later. At the end of one minute, ask the students to shift, and time another minute while the partner tells her/his story.

Part c. Put pairs of students together to form groups of four. Each student tells the group about his/her partner's story.

Activity 2: Learn New Words

1. Have students read the list of words. Ask if they know any of these words. Write any ideas on the board.

2. Have students look at the first picture on page 38 and read the caption. What do they think a village is? What do they know about the village from this picture? Then encourage students to guess the meaning of each word on the list, using the remaining pictures for information. Provide help as necessary, using context-rich sentences, (e.g., *The event was unusual; in fact, nothing like it had ever happened before.)*

Activity 3: Preview

1. Draw the Know/Want to Know/Learned chart on the board or on a transparency. Have students look again at the first picture and caption. Ask them to tell what is happening in the picture. You or a volunteer can list information about the story in the Know column of the chart on the board. Encourage students to make inferences based on the pictures. For example, is Younde old or young? Why do they think so? For each of their sentences about the pictures, have them think of things they want to find out. List these as questions in the Want to Know column.

2. You can have the class work together to list ideas about the remaining pictures or put the students in groups and have each group add their ideas about one of the pictures to a chart. Then have the groups share ideas.

Activity 4: Shared Reading

1. Read the background information with the class. Have a volunteer find Ghana on a world map. Explain that folktales would be told by parents to their children. Those children would then grow up and tell the stories to their children.

2. Play the tape or read the story to the students to have them just listen to enjoy it.

3. Then have students read the story by themselves.

4. Have students return to the Know/Want to Know/Learned chart. In the Learned column, have the class or small groups answer the questions in the Want to Know column. Check small group answers together.

5. The articles *a* and *the* are not used in some languages. Students often have difficulty learning how to use them correctly in English. Have students read the box on the bottom left of page 40 and then count the *the*'s on the page. This exercise will call their attention to a word they frequently overlook.

3. Preview

Classwork. Use the pictures and captions on pages 38–40 to answer the questions in a Know/Want to Know chart.

Answer these questions before you read the story.

Answer this question after you read the story.

Know	Want to know	Learned
What do you know about the story from the pictures?	What do you want to know?	What did you learn?
Younde lives in a village.	*Where is the village?*	

Study Strategy:

Making a Know/ Want to Know Chart

Making a Know/ Want to Know chart is a good way to get ready to read.

4. Shared Reading

Background

Younde Goes to Town is a folktale from Ghana, West Africa. Folktales are stories told aloud by each generation to the next.

Younde was a farmer. He lived in a village in the hills.

Younde Goes to Town

Once in the country of Akim, in the hills far from the coast, there was a man named Younde. He was a simple man who farmed and hunted like the other people in his village. He often heard about the big town of Accra by the ocean, but he had never seen it. He had never been farther from his village than the river.

But one day Younde had to go to Accra. He put on his best clothes and took his knife and put it in his belt. He wrapped some food in a cloth and put it on his head and started out. He walked for many days, and the road was hot and dusty. After a while, he was out of his own country, and people didn't speak his language any more. He came closer and closer to Accra. There were many people and donkeys on the road, all going to town or coming back from town.

Then he saw a large herd of cows grazing by the edge of the road. He had never seen so many cows in his life. He stopped and looked at them in wonder. There was a little boy herding the cows, and he went up to him and asked, "Who is the owner of these cows?"

But the boy didn't understand because Younde spoke Akim and the boy knew only the Ga language. So the boy replied, "Minu," which meant "I don't understand" in the Ga language.

"Minu! What a rich man he must be to have so many cows!" Younde said.

He continued his way into the town. He was very impressed with everything he saw.

He came to a large building and stopped to look at it. It was made of stone, and it was very high. When a woman came by, Younde spoke to her.

"What a tremendous house!" he said. "What rich person can own such a building?"

But the woman didn't understand Younde because he spoke Akim and she spoke the Ga language. So she replied to him:

"Minu," which meant "I don't understand" in the Ga language.

"Minu! That man again!" said Younde.

Younde was overcome. No one in his village was as wealthy as Minu. As he went farther into town, he saw more wonders. He came to the market. It covered a space larger than all the houses in Younde's village. He walked through the market and saw women selling things that were rare in his village, like iron pots and iron spoons.

One day Younde took a trip to the big town of Accra. There were many people and donkeys on the road.

On the road to Accra, Younde met a boy with a large herd of cows.

Near Accra, he saw a tremendous house.

Younde went to the market in Accra. There he saw many unusual things.

"Where do all these things come from?" Younde asked a little girl.

She smiled at him.

"Minu," she replied.

Younde was silent. Everything was Minu. Minu everywhere.

Younde finished his business in Accra, wrapped food in his cloth and started home. When he came to the edge of town, he saw a great procession and he heard the beating of drums. He came close and saw it was a funeral. Men were carrying a coffin and women were crying.

"Who is this person who has died?" Younde asked one of the men.

"Minu," the man answered.

"What! The great Minu is dead?" Younde said. "Oh, poor Minu! He had to leave all his wealth behind. He has died just like an ordinary person!"

Younde continued home, but he couldn't get the tragedy of Minu from his mind.

"Poor Minu!" he said over and over again. "Poor Minu!"

The word used most often in English is *the*. How many times is the word *the* used on this page?

On his way home, Younde saw a funeral procession.

5. Role Play

a. Pairwork. Choose one of these characters from the story. Find the conversation between Younde and this character in the story. Write it as a dialogue.

Characters: *woman* *little girl* *man*

Example:

Younde: *Who is the owner of all these cows?*
Little boy: *Minu.*
Younde: *Minu! What a rich man he must be to have so many cows!*

b. Pairwork. Practice reading the dialogue aloud.

c. Pairwork. Share ideas about the story with your partner. Here are some questions you might think about:

- Did you like the story? Why or why not?
- Why did Younde have a communication problem?
- Younde didn't understand the word *Minu.* What did he think it meant? What did it really mean?

6. Classify

On your own. Find words in the story to answer the questions.

What did Younde see?	What did Younde hear?	How did Younde feel?
donkeys	*Ga language*	*impressed*

> ***Study Strategy:***
> ***Classifying***
> Classifying, or grouping, words helps you to learn and remember them.

Activity 5: Role Play

Part a. Have students identify the characters in the story. Explain that Younde (pronounced YOON-day) is the main character—the story is about him. Ask who Younde talks to first in the story (the little boy). Have them find this conversation in the story. Together write this conversation as a dialogue (see the example on this page). Students can practice reading the dialogue aloud, using plenty of expression and body language.

Part b. Working in pairs, students can choose one of the other characters in the story. Have them find Younde's conversation with this person in the story and rewrite it as a dialogue. Assist less proficient students with this activity. They can then practice reading the dialogue, adding appropriate body language. Have the pairs perform for the class.

Part c. Give students a specific amount of time to share ideas about the story (2 minutes). To get started, pairs can discuss the questions listed in the book. Then have the pairs summarize their discussion for the class.

Activity 6: Classify

1. In this activity students classify words in the story. Give each student a copy of AM 2/2 or have students copy the three column chart at the bottom of page 41. Read the questions in the chart and the sample answers aloud. Before looking back at the story, ask students if they can think of other words to add to the chart.

2. Working on their own, students can look back over the story to find other words to add to each category.

3. Have pairs compare answers. Have them show where in the story they found each of their answers. Then make a class master chart on the board, adding everyone's answers.

(Possible answers: What did Younde see? donkeys, many people, large herd of cows, little boy, large building or house, market, iron pots, iron

(Continued on page 42.)

Activity 6: Classify *(continued)*

spoons, little girl, procession, drums, coffin; What did Younde hear? Ga language, beating of drums, women crying; How did Younde feel? impressed, overcome)

4. Have students make inferences to answer the questions. Some of the things that Younde saw, heard, and felt are not directly stated, but they can be inferred. For example, at the end of the story, Younde seems to be sad.

5. Call attention to the Study Strategy box: Classifying, so students see the rationale for this activity.

Activity 7: Make a Chart

1. To prepare students for this activity, look over the chart together. Read the questions aloud, and let students read the sample answers, telling about the little boy in the story. Then have students copy the chart, or give them copies of AM 2/3. Caution them not to write in the book.

2. Have students work in pairs to complete their charts.

3. Model retelling the story, using the information about the little boy in the chart. *(The little boy was in a field near the road. He was taking care of some cows. Younde asked, "Who is the owner of all these cows?" The boy answered, "Minu," which meant "I don't understand." But Younde didn't understand the boy. He thought Minu owned all of the cows.)* Then have pairs practice telling about the people in the story.

4. For additional practice, put the students in groups of four. Number the students in each group—1, 2, 3, 4—corresponding to the characters in the chart. Each student in a group should retell the part of the story with their character.

Activity 8: Write

1. *Part a.* Tell students that Younde met another person on his trip. They can read about this person in the chart.

2. Using the information in the chart, let students tell this new scene in the story.

(Continued on page 43.)

7. Make a Chart

Pairwork. In the story, Younde talked to four people. Write about these people in a chart.

	(1) little boy	(2) woman	(3) little girl	(4) man
Where was the person?	*near the road*			
What was the person doing?	*taking care of cows*			
What did Younde ask?	*"Who is the owner of these cows?"*			
What did the person answer?	*"Minu."*			
What did Younde think?	*Minu owned all of the cows.*			

Use the chart to retell the story.

Language Focus:

Asking for Information

- Where was the person?
- What was the person doing?
- What did Younde ask?
- What did the person answer?
- What did Younde think?

8. Write

a. Classwork. Use the information in this chart to tell about another person Younde met.

	Person: *an old man*
Where was the person?	*in the market*
What was the person doing?	*selling donkeys*
What did Younde ask?	*"Who owns all these donkeys?"*
What did the person answer?	*"Minu."*
What did Younde think?	*Minu owned all of the donkeys.*

b. Add quotation marks to each speaker's words in this new scene from the story.

In the market, Younde saw an old man selling donkeys. The man had large donkeys and small donkeys. He had more donkeys than there were in the whole village of Akim.

Who owns all these donkeys? Younde asked the man.

Minu, said the man.

Really? Minu owns all of these donkeys? Younde asked.

c. Pairwork. Imagine another person Younde met. Write your ideas in a chart.

	Person: ______
Where was the person?	
What was the person doing?	
What did Younde ask?	
What did the person answer?	
What did Younde think?	

d. Pairwork. Use the ideas in your chart to write a new scene for the story. Then share your scene with the class.

Language Focus:

Reporting What Someone Said

- "Where do all of these things come from?" Younde asked a little girl.
- "What a tremendous house!" Younde said.

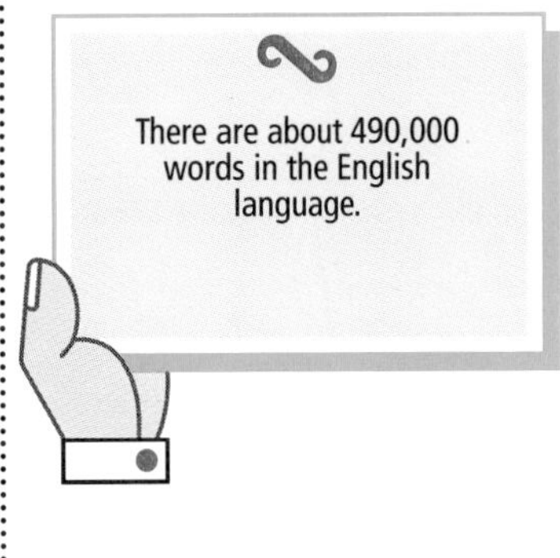

There are about 490,000 words in the English language.

Activity 8: Write *(continued)*

3. *Part b.* Write this sentence on the board: *"What a tremendous house!" Younde said.* Then read the information about using quotation marks in the Writing Strategy box.

4. Have students look back at the story to find examples of sentences with quotation marks. Have volunteers write these sentences on the board.

5. Ask one student: *Did you like the story about Younde?* Let the student answer. Then write your question and the student's answer on the board using quotation marks. *("Did you like the story about Younde?" the teacher asked. "Yes, I did," Jaime answered.)* Let students take turns asking and answering, while someone writes their conversation on the board using quotation marks.

6. Read the new scene from the story aloud. Then let students work on their own to add quotation marks. Students can self-check by comparing their work with a completed version on the transparency.

Part c. Working in pairs, students can add a new scene to the story. Model the activity by having the class work as a group to complete the chart, telling about another person Younde met. Less proficient students may need some suggestions such as a fisherman, a man selling shoes, a farmer. Then let students work in pairs to complete the chart about a different person.

Part d. Give students time to write their new scene. Encourage them to use quotation marks where appropriate. Assist less proficient students with this task. Students might want to read their scenes aloud or illustrate them and put them together to make a booklet.

Activity 1: Quickwrite

1. Read the Introduction. Then read the instructions aloud. Review or introduce quickwriting. Model quickwriting by writing about a time when someone didn't listen to you. Write on the board so that students can watch you write. Write without stopping. If you get stuck, write, *I'm stuck* or *I can't think of anything to write.* Remind students that quickwriting is a way to collect ideas. They shouldn't worry about correct grammar or punctuation. If they can't think of a word in English, they should use a word from their native language.

2. Give students two minutes to quickwrite. Then let them get together in pairs to tell something they thought of while quickwriting.

Activity 2: Shared Reading

1. Before reading the poem, have students look at the picture and tell about the two people. *What is the girl wearing? What is she holding?* Find out what students know about basketball. *How many people are on a basketball team?* (5) *What equipment do basketball players use?* Together read the first line of the poem and have students suggest what it means.

2. Play the tape or read the poem aloud. If you are reading the poem, change your voice to differentiate the mother's and daughter's lines.

3. Let pairs of students practice reading the poem as a dialogue. Then ask them to add body language as they read. Have volunteers perform for the class, reading the poem as a dialogue with accompanying body language. Let the rest of the class identify the body language and tell what it reveals about the speakers.

Communication problems: That's Nice (a poem)

Sometimes people don't listen when you talk to them. This is just what happens in the poem *That's Nice.*

Study Strategy:

Quickwriting

Quickwriting is a good way to collect ideas. When you quickwrite, you try to write without stopping.

1. Quickwrite

On your own. Write about a time when someone didn't listen to you. What happened? How did you feel?

2. Shared Reading

Pairwork. Listen to the poem. Then take turns reading a line.

That's Nice

I made the team!
Really?
Yes, and I'm the youngest player.
That's nice. Did you clean your room?
Yes. The coach said I'm the fastest on the team.
Is your homework done?
No, I thought I'd shoot some baskets first—
to practice.
Practice what?

—*Stephanie Todorovich*

Share Ideas

Classwork. What's your reaction to the poem? Share ideas with your classmates and teacher. Here are some other questions to think about:

a. Do you think the two people have a communication problem? Why or why not?

b. How do you think the basketball player feels at the beginning of the conversation? At the end? Why?

c. What questions would you ask the basketball player?

Sequence

Pairwork. Put the lines in this conversation in the correct order. Then read the conversation aloud.

____ Next month.
____ Do you know anyone on the Baylor team?
____ Who are you going to play on the 15th?
____ That's wonderful! When's your first game?
__1__ I made the team!
____ No, I don't.
____ On the 15th.
____ The team from Baylor High School.
____ What day next month?

What words helped you to know the order of lines in the dialogue?
Do these two people have a communication problem? Why or why not?

Activity 3: Share Ideas

1. Find out if students liked the poem. If so, what did they like about it?

2. Make sure to allow plenty of "wait time" during discussions to give students a chance to collect their thoughts. Instead of doing this as a class activity, you could also have groups of three work together to answer the questions. Each person in a group can report the group's answer to one of the questions.

Activity 4: Sequence

1. Have students look at the pictures with this dialogue and suggest what it is about. Tell students that the lines in this conversation are mixed up. They need to put the lines in an order that makes sense. Have them find the first line, which is marked with the number 1. Then distribute copies of AM 2/4 or have students copy the dialogue on another piece of paper. (Caution them not to write in the book.)

2. Working in pairs, students should put the lines in order, writing numbers on the lines on their charts to show which line is second, third, etc. Once they have the lines in order, they can practice reading the conversation aloud. Have volunteers read the dialogue aloud so that the rest of the class can compare ideas.

(Answers: 3, 8, 6, 2, **1**, 9, 5, 7, 4.)

3. As a class, discuss the questions below the conversation.

4. Extend the activity by having pairs rewrite the poem *That's Nice* so that a communication problem no longer exists.

Activity 5: Question and Answer

1. *Parts a–d.* In this activity, students can practice keeping a conversation going. Model the activity by writing the question on the board: *What did you do last weekend?* Have a volunteer answer the question in writing on the board. Read the answer and write a question to get more information. Extend the conversation for several exchanges.

2. Have each student write the question on a piece of paper. Put the students in pairs and have them exchange papers and write answers. They should then exchange papers again and write new questions. Have them continue for several minutes.

3. *Part e.* Have students change partners and try the activity, this time having a spoken conversation.

5. Question and Answer

Pairwork. Follow these steps to practice having a conversation.

a. Write this question on a piece of paper.

What did you do last weekend?

b. Give your paper to a partner. Your partner answers the question on the paper.

What did you do last weekend?
I went to the movies.
What did you see?

c. Read your partner's answer. Write a question about the answer.

d. How long can you continue the conversation? Try to fill up the page.

e. Change partners. Try the activity again, but this time try talking instead of writing.

6. Write

a. Groupwork. Who said it? Match these quotes with the people in the pictures.

"I failed the test," *she said to her friend.*

"Can I go to a movie tonight?" ______

"I have a new girlfriend," ______

"I have a new boyfriend," ______

"I think I love you," ______

"I lost my homework," ______

Two friends

Two friends

Mother and daughter

Teacher and female student

Boyfriend and girlfriend

b. Choose one of the quotes. Continue the conversation. Write your ideas.

c. Share your conversation with another group.

Activity 6: Write

1. *Part a.* Write *quote* on the board and ask students if they know what it means. Elicit or explain that it is a short form of *quotation.* Call attention to the quotation marks around each quote and point out that they go around only the part of the sentence that gives the words that a person is actually saying. You may want also to point out the use of the comma and question mark before the second quotation mark in this kind of sentence.

2. Together read the first quote and match the speaker to one of the people in one of the photographs.

3. Together extend the first conversation. Write on the board, *"I failed the test," she said to her friend.* Ask what her friend might reply and write volunteers' ideas under the first sentence. For example, *"Are you sure?" her friend asked.*

4. *Part b.* Have students work in small groups to match the quotes to people in the pictures. Give each group a copy of AM 2/5 or have them write on another piece of paper. Then have them choose one of the quotes and write a continuation of the conversation.

5. *Part c.* Students can exchange papers with another group and then roleplay the scene for the class.

As an introduction to this section, use a plastic or metal ruler to demonstrate the concept of vibration. Hold a ruler by one end on top of a desk and have the rest of the ruler extend over the edge. Gently bend the extended edge down and release it. Ask students, *What happened?* (The ruler moved quickly up and down; this movement is a vibration. The vibration produced a sound.)

Activity 1: Predict

1. Stretch a small rubber band between your fingers and pluck it. (The rubber band must be held tightly in order for you to hear a sound.) Read the caption aloud: *When you pluck a rubber band, it vibrates or moves back and forth.* These vibrations produce sounds.

2. Put the students in groups of four. Distribute a copy of AM 2/6 to each group or have them copy the chart at the bottom of page 48. Have them study the three pictures and circle their predicted answers in the "Prediction" column of the chart.

Making sounds

You hear a sound when something vibrates or moves back and forth. In this section, you will investigate vibrations and the sounds they produce.

1. Predict

Groupwork. Study these pictures and answer the questions in the chart.

When you pluck a rubber band, it vibrates or moves back and forth. These vibrations produce sounds.

A

B

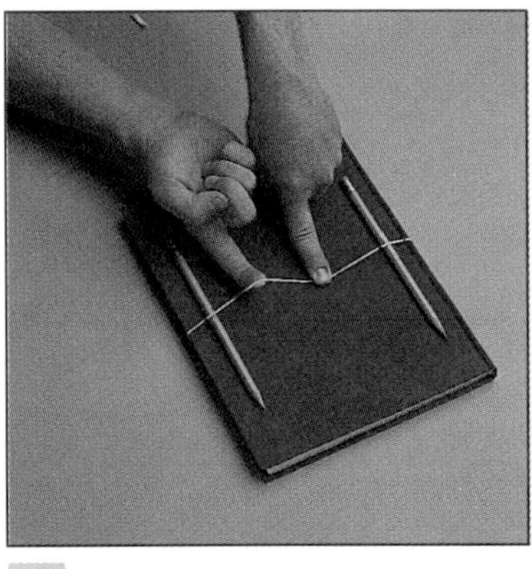

C

	Prediction	Actual
Which rubber band vibrates faster?	A or B	A or B
Which vibrations produce a higher sound?	A or B	A or B
Which rubber band vibrates faster?	A or C	A or C
Which vibrations produce a higher sound?	A or C	A or C

2. Investigate

Groupwork. Follow these steps to test your predictions.

Materials: a book, a large rubber band, two pencils

Steps:

1. Put the rubber band around the book.
2. Put a pencil under the rubber band on each side of the book.
3. Pluck the rubber band in the middle. Listen to the sound it makes.
4. Use one hand to stretch the rubber band just a little. Pluck it with the other hand.
   - Does the rubber band make a higher or lower sound than before?
   - Is the rubber band tighter or looser than before?
   - Does the rubber band vibrate more quickly or more slowly than before?
5. Release the rubber band. Pluck it in the middle again. Listen to the sound again.
6. Press down on the middle of the rubber band. Pluck the rubber band on one side of your finger.
   - Does the rubber band make a higher or lower sound than before? ______
   - Is the part of the rubber band that vibrates shorter or longer than before? ______
   - Does the rubber band vibrate more quickly or more slowly than before? ______
7. Record the results of your investigation in the chart in Activity 1.

Steps:

1. 2.

3.

4.

5.

6.

Activity 2: Investigate

Materials:
a book, a large rubber band, two pencils

Keep students in groups of four and give each group a rubber band, book, and two pencils. Have one student read the steps aloud while another follows the directions. The third student will check that the group's experiment matches the numbered illustrations. Circulate to answer any questions, but allow students sufficient time to discuss each step and reach consensus. The fourth member of the group can record their answers in the "Actual" column of AM 2/6.

(Answers: B, B, C, C.)

Activity 3: Synthesize

1. Students are now ready to combine ideas to form a new whole. Write *tighten, higher, shorten,* and *quickly* on the board and elicit the opposites of each: *loosen, lower, lengthen, slowly.* For less proficient students, you may wish to demonstrate these concepts, using a rubber band, your hands, etc.

2. Explain the exercise. In each numbered sentence, students are to match one of the words in the first pair in parentheses with one of the words in the second pair in parentheses. Then they will match the other word in the first pair with a word in the second pair. Do the first item with the class. Write *tighten* on the board, and read, *When you tighten the rubber band it vibrates. . . .* Ask the class which words from the second set should follow; elicit *more quickly.* Then read the complete sentence, *When you tighten the rubber band it vibrates more quickly.* Do the same with the other pair (*loosen, more slowly.*) Then give groups a few minutes to complete the exercise by writing on AM 2/7 or on another piece of paper the choices that belong together.

(Answers: 1. tighten, more quickly; loosen, more slowly. 2. tighten, higher; loosen, lower. 3. shorten, more quickly; lengthen, more slowly. 4. shorten, higher; lengthen, lower; 5. quickly, high; slowly, low.)

Activity 4: Apply

1. Introduce the activity by asking students to name musical instruments that use vibrating strings to make sounds (e.g., guitar, violin, cello, piano). Ask students to look at the guitar. Ask, *What are the strings and sounding box similar to in our experiment?* (The rubber bands and the book.)

2. Put students in groups again and have them read the information together and decide on their answers to the question. Have groups give their answers; then have a volunteer read the explanation at the bottom of the page.

Language Focus:

Describing Cause and Effect

- When you pluck the rubber band, it vibrates.
- When the rubber band vibrates, you hear a sound.

3. Synthesize

Groupwork. Tell what you learned from this investigation.

1. When you (tighten/loosen) the rubber band, it vibrates (more quickly/more slowly).
2. When you (tighten/loosen) the rubber band, you hear a (higher/lower) sound.
3. When you (shorten/lengthen) the rubber band, it vibrates (more quickly/more slowly).
4. When you (shorten/lengthen) the rubber band, you hear a (higher/lower) sound.
5. When the rubber band vibrates (quickly/slowly), you hear a (high/low) sound.

4. Apply

Groupwork. Read the information below and answer the question.

A guitar is a musical instrument made with stretched strings and a sounding box. The strings and the sounding box vibrate to produce sounds.

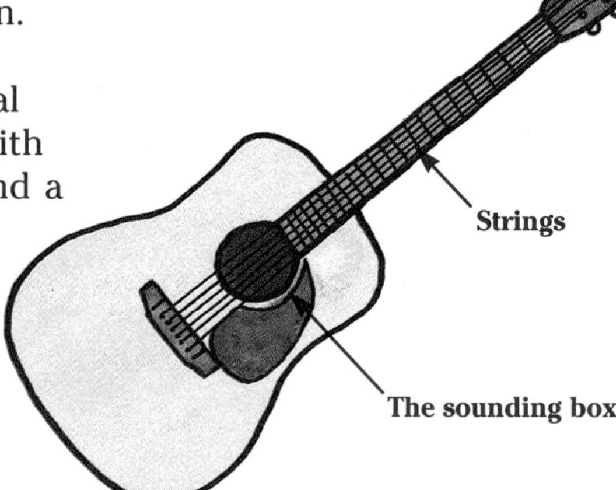

How can you make high notes and low notes on a guitar?

Answer to Activity 4: *To make high and low notes, you can tighten and loosen the strings on a guitar. You can also use your fingers to make the strings shorter or longer.*

Sending messages with music

Music is an important form of communication. In this section, you will read about different kinds of musical instruments and how they make sounds.

1. Quickwrite

On your own. Listen to this music. What does it make you think of? How does it make you feel? As you listen, write your ideas.

2. Preview

Groupwork. Study the pictures on pages 52–53. Then read the questions below and write your guesses.

What vibrates when you play a violin?

Our Guess ____________________ **Text Information** ____________________

What vibrates when you play a flute?

Our Guess ____________________ **Text Information** ____________________

What vibrates when you play a drum?

Our Guess ____________________ **Text Information** ____________________

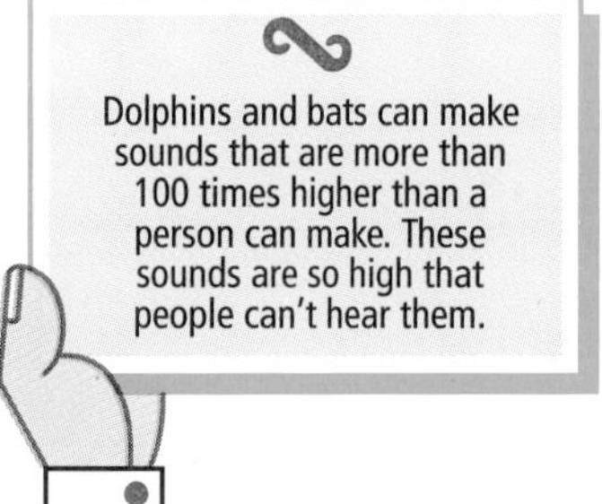

Dolphins and bats can make sounds that are more than 100 times higher than a person can make. These sounds are so high that people can't hear them.

Activity 1: Quickwrite

1. Read the introduction to the class. Ask, *How is music a form of communication? What does music communicate?* Write student ideas on the board and discuss them with the class.

2. Review the procedure for quickwriting that students learned earlier in this unit (page 44). Read the directions for the activity aloud. Tell students they—and you—will quickwrite for two minutes after they have heard the music. Then play the musical selection on the tape. Time the students for two minutes as they and you write the images and feelings suggested by the music. (Writing as fast as you can along with the students provides a stimulus for them, too, to write as fast as they can.)

3. Have students get together in pairs to tell their partners something they thought of during the quickwrite.

Activity 2: Preview

Have students work in groups for this activity. Distribute a copy of AM 2/8 to each group or have students copy the questions and answer spaces on another piece of paper. Ask, *What vibrated on the guitar?* (The strings and the sounding box.) Now have them turn to pages 52 and 53 and look at the pictures of the violin, the flute, and the drum. Have them record their answers in the "Our Guesses" answer spaces on the activity master or their paper. Caution them not to read for the answers at this time.

Activity 3: Shared Reading

1. Have students read the selection and note any vocabulary words they need to know.

2. Using the pictures and working as a class, define unfamiliar vocabulary.

3. Play the tape or have students read the selection a second time.

4. Have students return to their groups to record the text information that answers the questions in Activity 2 on page 51.

5. Tell groups to check to see if their predictions were correct.

3. Shared Reading

Read or listen to check your guesses.

Making Music

A guitar is called a stringed musical instrument because it is made with strings stretched over a sounding box. Both the strings and the sounding box vibrate when the strings are plucked. Musicians know just how tense and how long to make the different-sized strings in order to create the high notes and low notes, or the pitch of music. Other stringed instruments include the violin, piano, and ukulele.

Violin **Piano** **Ukulele**

Wind instruments make musical sounds in a different way. A wind instrument is basically a hollow tube with a mouthpiece. When a musician blows into the mouthpiece, the air inside the tube vibrates. The length of vibrating air inside the tube is called the air column. By changing the size of the air column, the musician can make high and low notes. For example, making the air column shorter produces higher notes. Pipe organs, flutes, bugles, and saxophones are different kinds of wind instruments. They all depend upon vibrating air columns for their sounds.

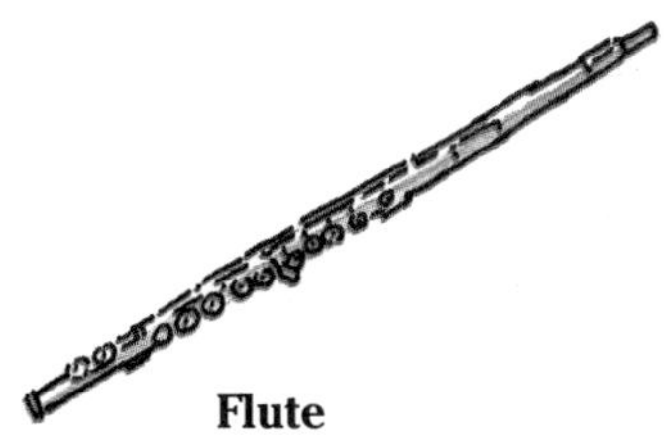

Flute

Pipe organ

Drums of different sizes and shapes are still another kind of musical instrument. Hitting a thin surface of a drum causes the surface to vibrate and produce sound. Hitting a drum hard makes a loud sound. Hitting it lightly makes soft sounds.

Drum

4. Take Notes in a Chart

Pairwork. Look back at the reading and take notes in a chart.

> ***Study Strategy:***
>
> ***Taking Notes in a Chart***
>
> When you take notes, write only the most important words.

Paragraph	Main Idea	Details and Examples
#1	the strings and sounding box vibrate on a stringed instrument	violin, piano, ukele
#2		
#3		

Activity 4: Take Notes in a Chart

1. This activity reviews the text information that students recorded in Activity 2 and restates it as the main idea of paragraphs 1, 2, and 3. Have students read the example for paragraph 1 on the chart on page 53. Ask, *In paragraph 1, what is the main (most important) idea?* (The strings and sounding box vibrate on a stringed instrument.) Ask, *What details and examples of stringed instruments are there?* (Violin, piano, ukelele.)

2. Have students work in pairs. Distribute a copy of AM 2/9 to each pair or have them copy the chart at the bottom of the page. (Caution them not to write in the book.) Have students complete the chart. Remind them of the study strategy: write only the most important words.

3. Have each pair compare notes with another pair and resolve discrepancies.

Activity 5: Test Your Knowledge

1. With a student, model asking for and giving information. Ask, *What vibrates when you play a violin?* The student answers, *The strings and sounding box.* Then have the student ask you another question about the chart. Answer it.

2. Put students in pairs, and have them practice asking and answering questions about all the instruments they have read about.

Activity 6: Match

1. *Part a.* Clarify the terms *cause* and *effect* for students by a demonstration. Stretch a rubber band across your thumb and little finger. Pluck the rubber band. Ask students, *What happened?* (It vibrated.) Explain that what happened—*it vibrated*—is an *effect.* Ask them what a *cause* is (something that produces/makes an effect).

2. Write on the board, *When you pluck a stretched rubber band, it vibrates.* Tell students to match the causes and effects to make similar sentences.

Part b. Play the tape or read the answer and have students listen and check their own answers.

(Answers: 1. When you play a stringed instrument, the strings and sounding box vibrate. 2. When you play a saxophone, the air column vibrates. 3. When you pluck the strings on a guitar, they vibrate. 4. When you hit the surface of a drum, it vibrates. 5. When you hit a drum lightly, it makes soft sounds. 6. When you play a piano, the strings and sounding box vibrate.)

Language Focus:

Asking for and Giving Information

Q: What vibrates when you play a violin?
A: The strings and sounding box.

5. Test Your Knowledge

Pairwork. Use the chart to practice asking and answering questions.

Example: Q: What vibrates when you play *a violin* ?

A: *The strings and sounding box.*

6. Match

a. On your own. Match the causes on the left with the effects on the right.

CAUSE	EFFECT
1. When you play a stringed instrument,	a. they vibrate.
2. When you play a saxophone,	b. it vibrates.
3. When you pluck the strings on a guitar,	c. it makes soft sounds.
4. When you hit the surface of a drum,	d. the strings and sounding box vibrate.
5. When you hit a drum lightly,	e. the air column vibrates.
6. When you play a piano,	

b. Compare answers with a classmate.

7. Apply

a. Groupwork. How do these instruments make sounds? What vibrates? Write your ideas in a chart.

Instrument	What Vibrates?
maracas	____________
'ud	____________
fujara	____________
sistrum	____________
sitar	____________
horn	____________

b. Share your group's ideas with the class.

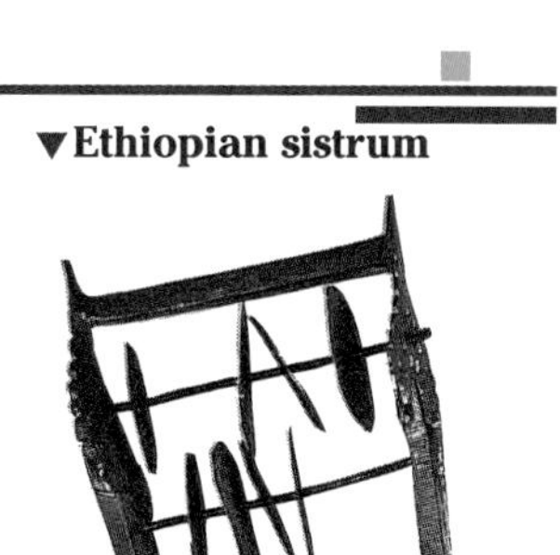

▼ Ethiopian sistrum

▲ Slovakian fujara

◀ Turkish 'ud

▼ Tibetan horn

▲ Indian sitar

▲ South American maracas

Activity 7: Apply

1. *Part a.* In this activity, students apply what they have learned about types of instruments and the way they vibrate. First ask students to name the places where they can find these instruments. (Turkey, Ethiopia, etc.) Ask volunteers to find these places on a world map.

2. Have students work in small groups. Give each group a copy of AM 2/10, or have them copy the chart at the top of page 55. (Caution them not to write in the book.) Circulate among the groups. Help less proficient students to make analogies: *What kind of instrument is the 'ud? What instrument is it like?*

Part b. Have each group report one answer to the class. Groups should also report any different answers that they had.

3. As an extension activity, ask students to bring in pictures of musical instruments and cassette tapes of music from their native countries. In short oral presentations, they can show a picture or drawing of the instrument, tell how it produces sounds, and then play the tape for the class to enjoy.

Introduction: Have students sit quietly and listen for a minute to the sounds around them. Have them note any sound they hear. You might want to open the clssroom door to let in some sounds. After a minute, collect everyone's notes on a master list of sounds on the board. At the top of the list write, *Hearing impaired (or deaf) students can't hear these sounds.* Have students look back at their cluster diagram from pages 32–33 (ways people communicate). Have them determine which of these ways hearing-impaired people can use to communicate. Read the title of the section and the introduction aloud.

Activity 1: List

1. Read the italicized caption aloud and let students study the picture. Then read the instruction line and question aloud. Using the pictures or background knowledge, students can suggest ideas while you or a student lists them on the board.

2. Tell students they will find out if their predictions are correct as they read this section.

Activity 2: Match

1. Write the word *gesture* on the board. Use gestures to communicate these ideas: come here/hi. Elicit from students that a gesture is movement of a part or parts of the body, especially the hands, to communicate information. It's a type of body language. What other gestures do they use to communicate information?

2. Read the caption aloud. Model the following example of sign language and ask if students can guess what it means: closed fist with index finger pointing to a person = you.

3. Have students look at the six words in the margin of page 56 and at the six numbered pictures of sign language. Read the first item (hello) and have students guess which example of sign language means hello.

4. Have students work in small groups to match the words and signs. Encourage students to practice making each sign.

(Continued on page 57.)

A message from students at the Horace Mann School for the Deaf

People who can't hear have special ways to communicate. In this section, you will read about some of these special ways.

1. List

Classwork. Read the question below and list your answers.

The students at the Horace Mann School for the Deaf in Allston, Massachusetts wrote the articles on the following pages. How do you think students at this school communicate?

2. Match

Groupwork. Match these gestures with the words on the left.

Many hearing-impaired (deaf) people use sign language to communicate. This language uses gestures instead of speech. Some signs look like what they represent. Others do not.

hello	watch
bird	flower
police officer	flag

1

2

3

Answers to Activity 2: *1. Police Officer; 2. Bird; 3. Watch; 4. Hello; 5. Flag; 6. Flower.*

3. Speculate

Pairwork. How do these devices help hearing-impaired people to communicate? Writer your guesses in a chart.

These special devices help hearing-impaired people to communicate.

> ***Language Focus:***
> ***Making Guesses***
> - I think it helps hearing-impaired people to ______ .
> - Maybe it helps hearing-impaired people to ______ .

TDD

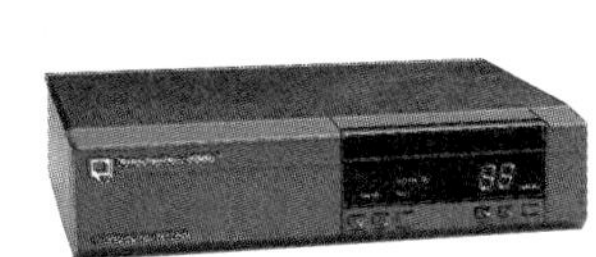

Closed-caption decoder

Vibrating clock

Device	**My Guess**	**Text Information**
TDD	______	______
	______	______
Closed-caption decoder	______	______
	______	______
Vibrating clock	______	______

Activity 2: Match *(continued)*

5. Have volunteers take turns forming one of the six signs shown here. Have each group report what it thinks the sign means.

Activity 3: Speculate

1. Have students look at the pictures of the three devices on page 57. Explain that these devices help hearing-impaired people to communicate.

2. Model the activity by together looking at the TDD and predicting how it might help hearing-impaired people to communicate. Tell students they should write their ideas in the first column.

3. Let students get together in pairs. Give each pair a copy of AM 2/11, or have them copy the chart at the bottom of page 57. They should work together to write one prediction for each device.

4. Have pairs report their predictions to the class. Tell pairs to retain their charts for use in the next activity.

Activity 4: Shared Reading

1. Play the article on the tape or read it aloud while students listen with books closed. Then form the same pairs that made predictions about the devices pictured on page 57. Each partner should read the article silently, writing on another piece of paper any unfamiliar words. They can then work together to define the words. Circulate and help the pairs with any words they are unable to define, using context-rich sentences wherever possible.

2. Have students listen to or read the article again and complete the chart they started in the previous activity, filling in the "Text Information" column. Remind them to list only the important words, using the Study Strategy on page 53, "Taking Notes in a Chart."

4. Shared Reading

Read this article. Add information to the chart on page 57.

Devices That Help the Deaf

How does a deaf person know when his doorbell is ringing or when someone is calling her on the phone? Can a deaf person watch television? Wake up with an alarm clock? A hearing person can do all of these, but deaf people need special devices to help them.

Most hearing children don't know about the little tricks deaf people use. Here's a description of some of them.

A TDD, or a Telecommunication Device for the Deaf, helps deaf people talk on the telephone. When the phone rings, a light flashes. The person picks up the phone, puts on the TDD, and types and reads the conversation. Doorbells that flash a light when someone pushes the bell are also popular.

A closed-caption decoder makes it possible for a deaf person to watch TV. Many shows are closed-captioned for the hearing impaired. Words appear at the bottom of the screen and the person reads what's being said.

Hate waking up to a blaring alarm? Deaf people use vibrating clocks. The alarm shakes the pillow. It feels like an earthquake, but it makes us jump out of bed!

All of these devices help deaf people. There are many others that deaf people use at home, school, and work.

—By students at the Horace Mann School for the Deaf

5. Identify

Pairwork. Identify these devices.

a. When a hearing-impaired person turns on this device, he or she can read a telephone conversation.
What is this device? ______________________

b. When this device goes off, it shakes the pillow.
What is this device? ______________________

c. When someone pushes this device, a light flashes.
What is it? ______________________

d. When you turn on this device, words appear on a TV screen.
What is it? ______________________

6. Design

Groupwork. These devices help hearing people to communicate. Redesign one of these devices for hearing-impaired people to use.

When someone wants to talk to you, they can call your beeper. When they dial your number, your beeper makes a noise. This tells you to call your home or office for a message.

Many buildings have smoke alarms. When there is a fire, the smoke causes a bell to ring. The bell warns you to leave the building.

Activity 5: Identify

1. In pairs, students can identify the four devices, using the information provided. They can refer back to the article if necessary. Give each pair a piece of paper and have them write the letters

a.

b.

c.

d.

on it. They can write the name of each device next to the appropriate letter.

2. Put pairs together to form groups of four and have them compare answers and talk about the way the devices are used.

Activity 6: Design

1. Read, or have a student read aloud the instruction line. Ask a student volunteer to read the first italicized caption (for the beeper). Discuss who uses beepers. Then have other volunteers read the italicized captions for the smoke alarm, automobile horn, baby monitor, and answering machine, and briefly discuss each one. (The last three are on page 60.)

2. Discuss briefly why these devices are not useful to hearing-impaired people. Then have groups work together to redesign one of these devices so that it will work for the hearing-impaired. Try to ensure that not all groups choose the same device to redesign. One member of each group should write up the redesign.

3. Have groups report their work to the class. You may wish to post the various redesigns on the class bulletin board.

Activity 7: State an Opinion

1. Write on the board: *opinion = what you think about something.* Ask students to give examples of opinions. To get them started, use examples from the classroom. (For example, *This is the best class in the school. Maria's dress is very pretty.)*

2. Read the instruction line aloud. Have students work in groups to discuss the question and form an opinion. Groups should give reasons for their opinion and reach consensus.

3. Have each group join another group. Let them compare opinions and give their reasons.

Cars have horns. When the driver presses the horn, it makes a noise.

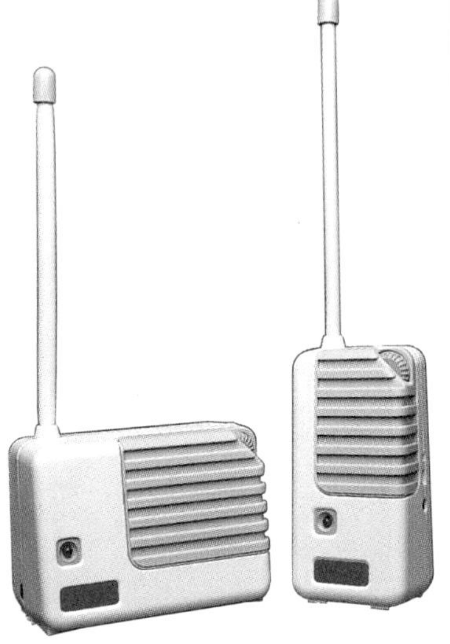

With a baby monitor, parents can sit in another room and hear every sound in the baby's room.

You can attach an answering machine to your telephone. When someone calls you, the answering machine records their message. When you get home, you can listen to the messages.

Language Focus:

Stating an Opinion

- We think hearing people should learn sign language.
- We don't think hearing people should learn sign language.

7. State an Opinion

Groupwork. Many deaf people use sign language to communicate. Do you think hearing people should learn sign language, too? Why or why not?

Opinion: ______________________

Reasons: ______________________

____

____

8. Shared Reading

An editorial is a special kind of newspaper article. It states the author's opinion about something. In this editorial, students from the Horace Mann School for the Deaf give opinions about learning sign language.

Teaching Sign Language in Schools

We think hearing people should learn sign language as a separate class in school. Why? So that some day soon, all people in our country will be able to talk with deaf people.

If hearing people learned sign language, it would be easier for deaf people to communicate. We could communicate better with waiters in restaurants, clerks in stores, doctors, even hearing kids on the playgrounds.

Hearing people would quickly see the benefits. The most important is that they could make friends with deaf people. Many hearing people who know sign language say they like to sign with deaf kids and adults.

We know many hearing people who are curious to learn sign language. In the future, if more hearing people knew sign, maybe a hearing person could become an interpreter for the deaf world.

We recommend that all schools offer sign language as an option for their students. It would make a big difference for all people.

—By students at the Horace Mann School for the Deaf

Activity 8: Shared Reading

1. Bring in several editorial pages from city, community, and school newspapers. Ask students to read the titles of the articles and guess what the opinion is about. Inform students that newspaper readers can write to the newspaper to express an opinion and their letters are often printed in the paper.

2. Read the introduction to the class. Before they look at this article, ask them to predict the opinion of hearing-impaired people on this issue. Do they think deaf people want hearing people to learn sign language or not? More proficient students can give reasons for their answers.

3. Go through the reading and find words that might be new to your students. Of these words, decide which, if any, cannot be understood from context. Introduce these words in context-rich sentences. Have students use context to guess the meaning of each word. For example, *The curious child asked many questions.*

4. Have students read the article silently. For additional practice, play the tape.

Activity 9: Take Notes

1. On the board or a transparency, make a chart like the one on page 62. Ask the question for paragraph 1: *What is the opinion of students at the Horace Mann School for the Deaf?* (Hearing people should learn sign language as a separate class.) Write the answer on the chart. Elicit the study strategy for taking notes on a chart (write only important words).

2. Have students work in groups of four. Provide each group with a pencil and a copy of AM 2/12, or have a group member make a copy of the chart on page 62. Each person in the group will take a turn asking a question and then write down the answer. (Note that the first question has already been answered; students should start with the question for paragraph 2.) Groups should reach consensus on the wording of the answers, referring to the editorial on page 61 as needed.

3. Have groups compare charts.

(Possible answers: Par. 2: easier for deaf people to communicate. Par. 3: hearing people could make friends with deaf. Par. 4: hearing person could become an interpreter. Par. 5: Conclusion: schools should offer sign language as option.)

Activity 10: Write

1. Review what an editorial is. You may want to "recycle" the sample editorials you used for Activity 8. Read the instruction line aloud.

2. *Part a.* Recall or introduce the strategy of brainstorming. Tell students that they should write down all their ideas and choose the best one later. Have students work in groups of four. Allow sufficient time for them to think and answer the question: What should students learn at school? They may use the examples to start, but should also generate their own list. Their education in their native country could be a frame of reference.

(Continued on page 63.)

9. Take Notes

Groupwork. Look back at each paragraph in the reading and take notes in a chart.

Title: Teaching Sign Language in School	
Paragraph 1 Introduction	What is the opinion of students at the Horace Mann School for the Deaf?
Paragraph 2	What is their first reason?
Paragraph 3	What is their second reason?
Paragraph 4	What is their third reason?
Paragraph 5 Conclusion	What do they say again?

Language Focus:* *Giving Reasons

- If hearing people learned sign language, it would be easier for deaf people to communicate.
- If hearing people learned sign language, deaf people could communicate more easily.

10. Write

Groupwork. Follow these steps to write an editorial for your classmates to read.

a. What should students learn at school? Brainstorm a list of ideas.

What should students learn at school?
to speak a foreign language
to play a musical instrument
history of different countries

b. Choose one idea on your list. Think of reasons to support your opinion. Write your ideas on a tree diagram.

Students should learn to speak a foreign language
- They could help visitors in the U.S.
- They could read books in other languages.
- They could watch foreign movies without subtitles.
- They could speak to people from different countries.

c. Organize your ideas in a chart. In box 1, write your opinion. In boxes 2–4, write your best reasons. In box 5, restate your opinion.

Title: ____________________

1. Introduction — We think students should learn ____________ at school.

2. Reason

3. Reason

4. Reason

5. Conclusion

d. Use your chart to write an editorial for your classmates to read.

Activity 10: Write *(continued)*

3. *Part b.* Draw a tree diagram on the board. Have students look at the example on page 63. Ask, *Which sentence in this tree diagram is the main idea?* (Students should learn to speak a foreign language.) Have students read the other sentences in the diagram. Ask, *What question do these sentences answer?* Prompt if necessary, *Who? When? Why?* Explain that reasons tell why. Then have students read the instruction line. Tell them to choose an idea for which they have many reasons. Have them write their main idea and the reasons in the appropriate places on a tree diagram. Circulate to assist students with this task.

4. *Part c.* Provide each group with a copy of AM 2/13, or have them make a copy of the chart on page 63. Have groups write down their opinion and reasons, using their tree diagram.

5. *Part d.* Have one person in each group write the editorial. The other members of the group will help him or her. Encourage the group to follow the model on page 61. Tell them to use five paragraphs, with the first paragraph stating an opinion, and the others providing reasons. The final paragraph should be a conclusion. More proficient students can add additional support sentences for the reasons given in each paragraph. Group members should check the finished editorial for correct ideas, organization, spelling, etc.

6. Publish their writing by posting editorials in the classroom or in the newspaper format of an editorial page.

Activity Menu

Read and explain the activities to the class. Then have students individually or in small groups select a project for a class or homework assignment. Projects can later be displayed in the classroom as they are shared with the class.

Activity Menu

Choose one of the following activities to do.

1. Identify Body Language
Collect pictures of people using body language. Take photographs or cut pictures from magazines. Post your pictures on a classroom wall and ask your classmates to tell what information the body language communicates.

2. Make a Display
Choose a phrase that describes an emotion, such as *I'm sad* or *I love you*. See how many ways you can communicate this idea. Translate it into other languages. Use symbols or music. Find or write poetry. Share the results of your investigation.

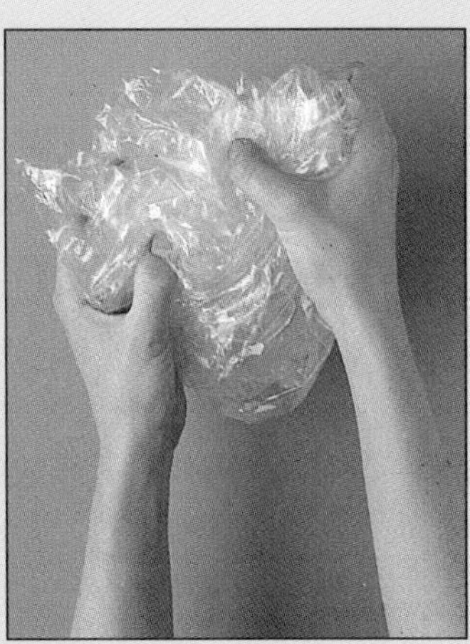

3. Look for Symbols
Look for symbols around your school and neighborhood. Photograph or draw each symbol. Write a caption for each symbol telling what it means. Use your pictures and captions to make a wall display.

4. Create Sound Effects
Storytellers use sound effects to make a story seem more real. For example, to make the sound of a fire, you can crumple a plastic wrapper. To make the sound of waves on the shore, you can put dried peas in a metal bowl and slowly roll the bowl back and forth.

Reread the story *Younde Goes to Town.* What sounds do you hear in the story? Find a way to make these sounds and then tell the story with your sound effects.

5. Play a Musical Scale

Materials: large and small drinking glasses, water, pencil.
Put different amounts of water into each glass. Using the pencil, gently strike each glass near the top. The tone that you hear depends on the length of the water column in the glass. Adjust the amount of water in the glasses so that you can play a musical scale. Then figure out a way to write down a song for this instrument.

6. Greeting Card Messages
Some people use greeting cards to send messages. You can find these cards in a drugstore or stationary store. Do a survey of greeting cards in a nearby store to find answers to these questions:

- What categories or groups of greeting cards does the store have?
- Which category of cards has the largest selection?
- How are the cards alike? Different?
- Which card do you like best? Why?

7. A Clothing Message
Choose pictures of people wearing different types of clothing. What information does their clothing communicate? Is it possible to get an incorrect message from clothing? Give an example.

8. Research a Communication Device
Choose a communication device that interests you. Look for information about this device in the library. Find out its history and how it works. Tell your classmates what you learned.

9. Investigate Map Symbols
Study a map of your area. Make a list of the symbols used on your map. Look at the map legend to learn the meaning of each symbol. Present the results of your research to the class.

10. Study Animal Communication
Choose an animal to observe. What sounds does it make? What body language does it use? Draw a picture of the animal and write down your observations. Then write a summary of your ideas, telling how this animal communicates. Present your ideas to the class.

65

Read on . . .

Can We Talk?

1. Put a K-W-L (Know/Want to Know/Learned) chart on the board. Tell students to copy the chart on a piece of paper. Ask them what they know about dolphins. Write their answers under *Know*. Elicit questions about the reading by asking students, *What do we want to know about dolphins?* Prompt students by telling them to look at the title and the picture. Write their questions under the *Want to Know* column (e.g., *Can dolphins communicate with people?*). Leave the *Learned* column blank until after the reading.

2. Read *Can We Talk?* to the class. Then have students work in small groups to find the answers to questions posed about the reading. Groups should record answers in the *Learned* column.

3. As an alternate activity, begin by asking students what they know about dolphins: *Why are dolphins known to be very intelligent animals?* Then read the selection to the class. After the reading, have students describe the dolphins' typewriter. *How does it look? How does it work? Why did scientists design such a typewriter? Would students like to communicate with the dolphins too?*

Read on . . .

Can We Talk?

It may not be your typical typewriter. But it's just the right type, for a dolphin.

Researchers at Walt Disneyworld's EPCOT Center have designed a giant "typewriter" for Toby and Bob, two bottlenose dolphins. With it, they hope to be able to communicate with the two animals.

The typewriter is the same size as a minivan. It has 60 "keys" that are actually hollow tubes. Each tube is labeled with a different 3-D symbol. When the dolphin pokes its snout into that tube, it triggers a response.

For example, if Toby chooses symbols for "Give stick to Toby," the trainers will offer the stick. Toby can use it to open a container holding food or toys.

The trainers hope Toby and Bob will learn word symbols in a year. After that, they want to train the duo to string words together to form sentences.

So who knows? Maybe one day you'll see these dolphins in a . . . secretary pool!

Deaf Donald

Deaf Donald met Talkie Sue

But  was all he could do.

And Sue said, "Donald, I sure do like you."

But  was all he could do.

And Sue asked Donald, "Do you like me too?"

But  was all he could do.

"Goodbye then, Donald, I'm leaving you."

But  was all he did do.

And she left forever so she never knew

That  means I love you.

—*Shel Silverstein*

Student text page 67

Deaf Donald

1. Recall with students what *deaf* means. Ask students how deaf people communicate. See if they remember any of the signs from the lesson.

2. Read the poem to the class. Then have students read lines individually or in groups. Have them include the signing in their reading. Let them practice several times to read and sign easily. Elicit reactions to the poem. *What feelings are expressed by Donald? by Sue? How do students feel after reading the poem?*

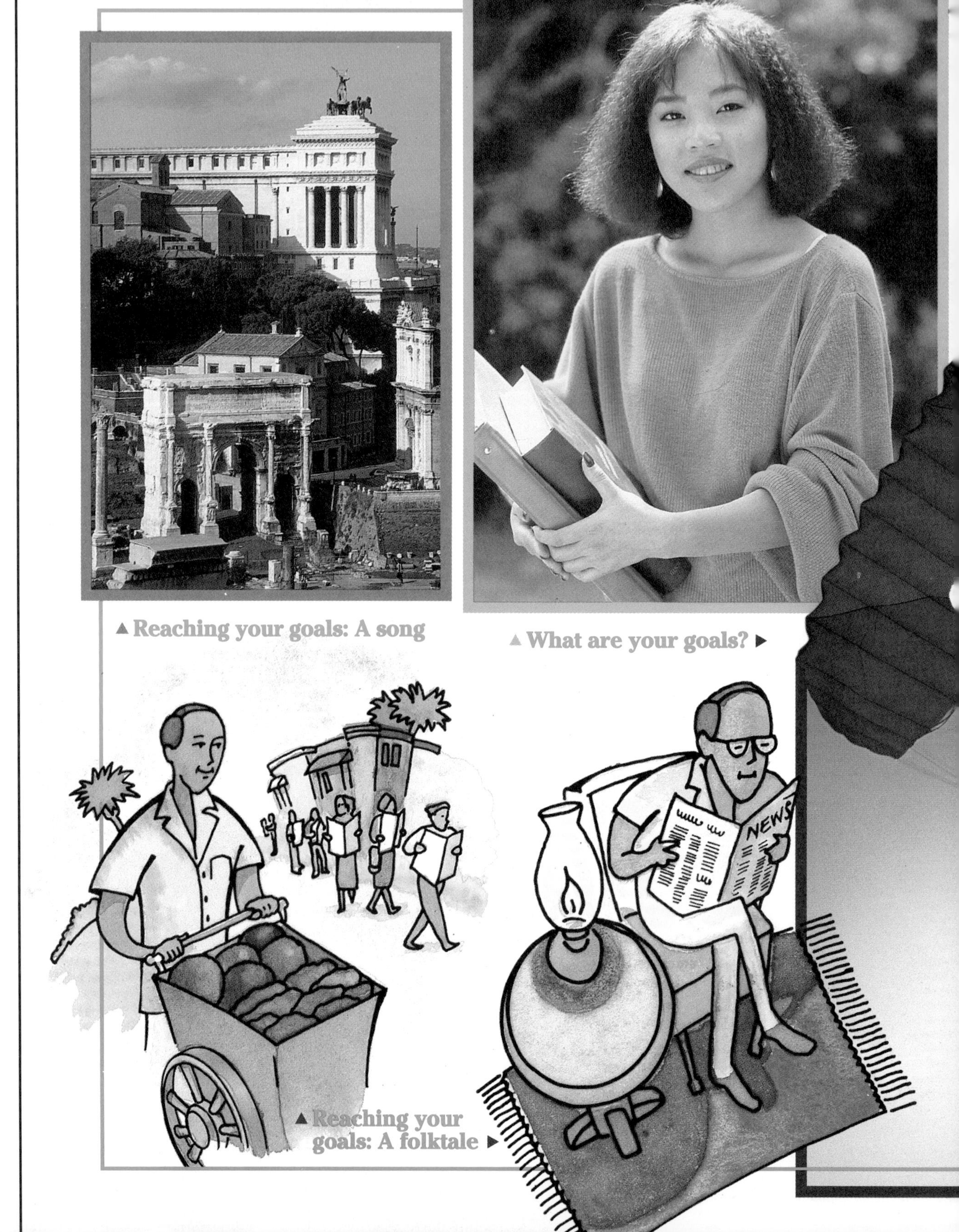

▲ Reaching your goals: A song

▲ What are your goals? ▶

▲ Reaching your goals: A folktale ▶

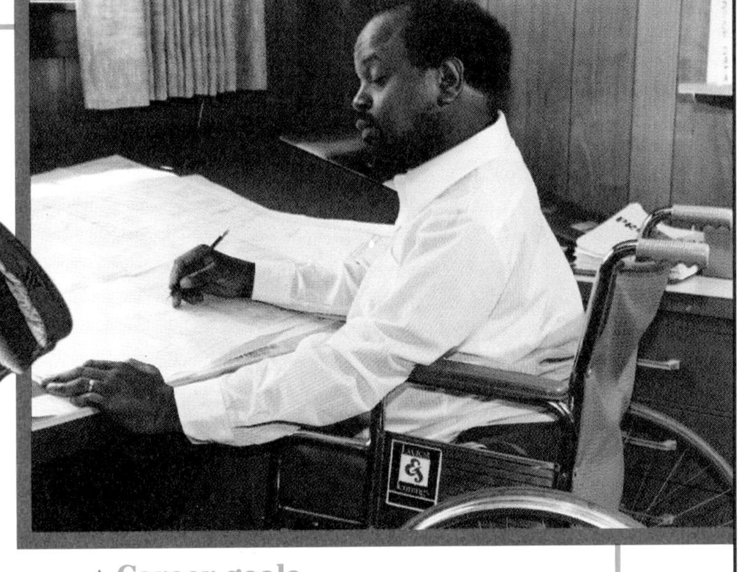

▲ Career goals

SETTING GOALS

▼ Goals of the U.S. government

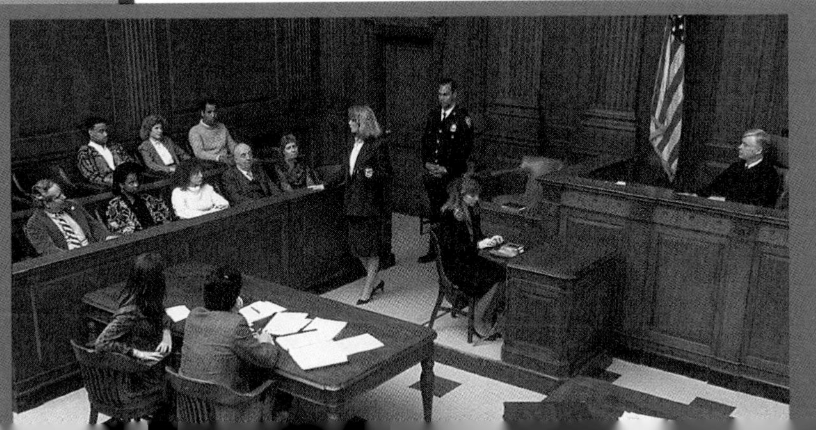

Liliana DaSilva is a junior in high school.

I plan to go to college after high school. I want to work as a computer programmer after college. Someday I'd like to travel around the world.

François Cerneus is a high school sophomore.

I want to get good grades in school this year. I would also like to become a good basketball player. I hope to become a doctor. Someday I'd like to get married and have a family.

What are your goals?

A goal is something you want to achieve in the future. In this section, you will look at different kinds of goals and read about a person with 127 goals.

1. Identify

Listen and read these captions.
What are these students' goals?

Language Focus:

Stating Goals

- Liliana **plans** to go to college after high school.
- She **wants** to work as a computer programmer after college.
- Some day she **would like to** travel around the world.

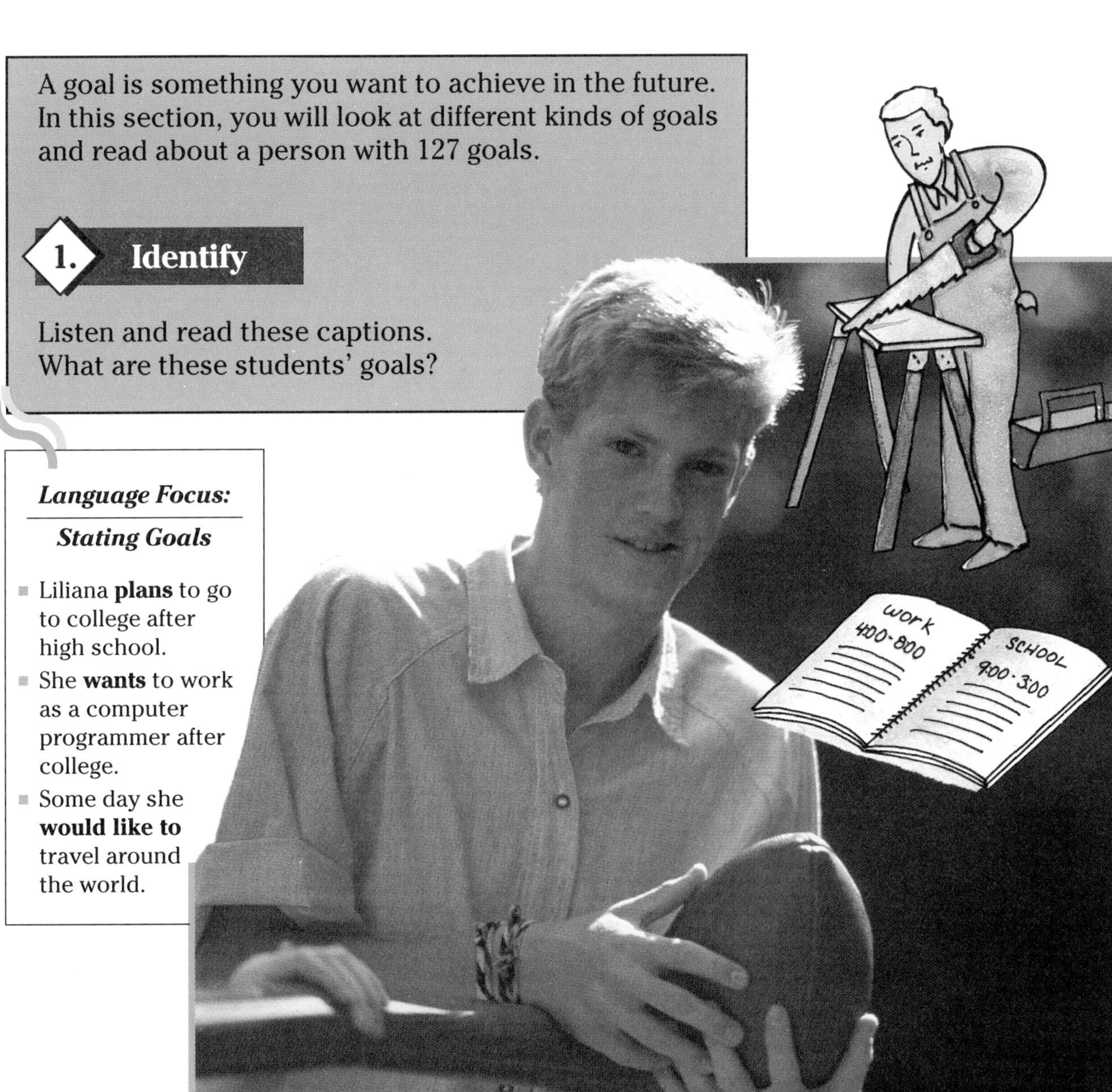

Robert Thomas is a high school senior.

I plan to get a job next year. I'd like to work as a carpenter. I also hope to go to college part-time.

Student text pages 70–71

Read the title and the introduction ("A Goal is something. . . .") aloud. On the board write, *Goal = something you want to achieve or do in the future.* Explore the concept by asking, *Who sets goals?* Write students' responses on the board, e.g., *students, teachers, parents, etc.* Then tell students that you will say a goal and they are to guess whose goal it is. The answers can be student, parent, or teacher. Use these goals:

I plan to learn English. (student)

I want to buy a home for my family. (parent)

I want my students to write in paragraphs. (teacher)

I'd like to travel around the world. (student, teacher, and parent—all three are possible.)

Ask students for examples of other goals that people might have (e.g., find a job, finish school, have a family, etc.). Discuss with students the fact that goal-setting never ends; it is a lifetime activity.

Activity 1: Identify

1. Name and identify the three high school students pictured here: Liliana DaSilva, a junior; François Cerneus, a sophomore; Robert Thomas, a senior. Tell students to listen to the tape or to you as you read the captions. They should follow along in the book and point to each person as that person speaks.

2. Have students use the pictures to restate each person's goals. Ask, *What are Robert Thomas's goals?* etc.

Activity 2: Interview

1. Draw the chart from page 72 on the board or on a transparency. Model the activity by asking a student, *Do you want to go to college after high school?* Check the student's answer in the appropriate column. Have the student ask you a question. Answer to model the short answer form, *Yes, I do/No, I don't. Maybe.*

2. Pass out copies of AM 3/1 to each student or have them copy the chart at the top of page 72. First they should list the ten goals of the three students on the chart.

3. Have students ask their partners questions about the goals and check the appropriate answers.

4. Have each student report his/her partner's *yes* answers, following the example in the text: Min wants to go to college after high school.

Activity 3: List

1. By this time, students should be clear on the concept of goals. Using the sentence openers, give students enough time to think of their own goals. Then have them list their goals on a piece of paper. Tell them to keep their list for future use.

2. Have students share some of their goals with a partner.

3. As an expansion activity, have students bring in pictures cut from magazines or draw pictures to illustrate their goals. Provide them with newsprint to make a collage illustrating goals of the entire class. Display the collage in the classroom.

4. Using their lists of goals, students can give a short oral presentation about their goals and when they hope to achieve them.

Activity 4: Analyze

Have students study the pictures of John Goddard and his goals. As students guess his goals aloud, you or a volunteer can write their ideas on the board. Assist students with correct vocabulary for the pictures.

2. Interview

Pairwork. List the students' goals from Activity 1. Then ask a partner about them.

Do you want to . . . ?	Yes	No	Maybe
go to college after high school			✓
work as a computer programmer			
travel around the world			

Report your partner's YES answer to the class.

Example: *Min wants to go to college after high school.*

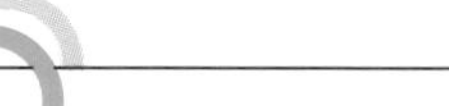

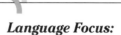

Language Focus:

Asking For and Giving Information

Q: Do you want to go to college after high school?
A: Yes, I do. (No, I don't./Maybe./I'm not sure.)

3. List

On your own. What are your goals? List several ideas.

I want to __________

I hope to __________

I'd like to __________

4. Analyze

Classwork. The pictures on the next page give information about John Goddard's goals. What do you think his goals are?

5. Shared Reading

My Life's List

When John Goddard was fifteen years old, he made a list of things that he wanted to do during his lifetime. By the time he finished, there were 127 goals on his list.

Some of Goddard's goals involved travel and exploration:

- *Explore the Amazon (a river in South America).*
- *Visit every country in the world.*

Other goals dealt with learning new things:

- *Play the flute and violin.*
- *Fly a plane.*
- *Type 50 words a minute.*
- *Make a parachute jump.*

Some of his goals were intellectually demanding:

- *Write a book.*
- *Compose music.*

Other goals were physically demanding:

- *Broad jump fifteen feet (4.6 meters).*
- *Climb the Matterhorn (a mountain in Switzerland).*
- *Ride an elephant, a camel, an ostrich, and a bucking bronco.*

John Goddard was serious about his list of goals. Over the next 50 years, he reached 108 of the goals on his list. And he is still working to reach the remaining 19 goals.

Activity 5: Shared Reading

1. Have students read *My Life's List* silently. Remind them to use the pictures for new vocabulary. When they have finished reading, encourage them to ask questions about other new vocabulary. Write: *What does _____ mean?* on the board. Ask them to use the correct question format when asking about vocabulary. Define any new words for students. Play the tape for additional practice.

2. Ask students about the organization of the reading. *What information do we get in paragraph 1?* (introduction: John Goddard at 15 wrote a list of 127 goals for his life.) *What information is in paragraph 2?, paragraph 3?, paragraph 4?, and the conclusion?*

3. Ask students what else they would like to know about John Goddard. If possible, provide them with additional materials on Goddard or other people known for their goals.

Activity 6: Classify

1. *Part a.* Have students work in pairs. Tell them they will classify John Goddard's goals. Ask students to read the categories in the book. Ask them what kind of words they see in the pairs: easy-difficult, fun-boring, etc. (opposites). Can they think of any other categories for Goddard's goals? Have them write these on a piece of paper. (Caution them not to write in the book.)

2. Have two students model the Language Focus dialogue on agreeing and disagreeing:

A: *I think that making a parachute jump is dangerous.*

B: *I agree.*

A: *I think writing a book is fun.*

B: *I don't think so.*

Encourage students to use these expressions as they categorize goals.

3. *Part b.* Have one pair write their category chart on the board. Ask subsequent pairs to agree or disagree with it by saying: *We agree (disagree) with ____ and ____ We think. . . .*

Activity 7: Identify

1. *Part a.* Read the direction line aloud. Have students read the examples in the text on page 74. For less proficient students, do another example. On the board, write: *Goal:* and *What should you do to reach this goal?* Write *fly a plane* under *Goal.* Elicit advice for the goal by asking students what they should do.

2. Have students work in pairs to write a goal and give advice for reaching it.

3. *Part b.* Students can report back to the class by writing their work on the board or on a transparency. Reports should be open-ended so that other students in the room can write additional advice for any student's goals.

Language Focus:

Agreeing and Disagreeing

Agreeing

A: I think making a parachute jump is dangerous.

B: I agree. (So do I./I think so too.)

Disagreeing

A: I think writing a book is fun.

B: I disagree. (I don't think so./ I'm not sure about that.)

6. Classify

a. Pairwork. Classify John Goddard's goals. Use these categories or think of your own.

Dangerous	Not Dangerous
make a parachute jump	*play the flute*

Fun	Boring

Easy	Difficult

b. Share your work with the class.

7. Identify

a. Pairwork. Choose one of the goals on page 73. What should you do to reach this goal? Write your ideas.

Examples:

Goal:	**What should you do to reach this goal?**
Type 50 words a minute	*Take a typing course* *Practice a lot*

Goal:	**What should you do to reach this goal?**
Climb the Matterhorn	*Get in good physical condition (Exercise a lot!)* *Save money to pay for the trip* *Learn about mountain climbing*

Language Focus:

Giving Advice

- You should take a typing course.
- You should practice a lot.

b. Share your ideas with the class.

8. Write

a. On your own. Add to your list of goals. Think of goals for each of these categories. (Some goals may fit in more than one category.) Share your chart with a classmate.

Goals				
Travel	**Learning New Things**	**Intellectual**	**Physical**	**Personal**
visit Russia	*learn to speak Russian*	*graduate from a university*	*become a good swimmer*	*make some new friends* *get married*

b. Choose one of your goals. Tell what you are going to do to reach this goal.

Goal	What are you going to do to reach this goal?
Learn to speak Russian	*Practice speaking with a Russian person* *Take a course in Russian* *Study hard* *Listen to tapes* *Read books in Russian* *Memorize words*

Language Focus:

Describing Future Plans

- I'm going to take a course in Russian.
- I'm going to listen to language tapes.

c. Write about one of your goals. Tell what you are going to do to reach your goal.

One of my goals is to ____________________.

To reach this goal, I am going to ____________________.

I am also going to ____________________

and ____________________.

Another thing I can do to reach my goal is to

____________________.

If I do all of these things, I might reach my goal.

Activity 8: Write

1. *Part a.* Ask students to look again at page 73. Have them recall how the reading was organized. Ask them to define *intellectual, physical,* and *personal.* Provide help if necessary.

2. Have students should look back at their lists from Activity 3, page 72. Distribute copies of AM 3/2, or have students copy the chart at the top of page 75. Ask them to write their goals from page 72 on the chart, and add other goals for each category.

3. Have students share charts with their classmates.

4. *Part b.* Model this activity by writing the example on the board, following the T-list form in the text. Then use it to report to the class, using future tense sentences: *I'm going to learn to speak Russian. I'm going to practice speaking with a Russian person.* etc.

5. Distribute copies of AM 3/3 or have students write in T-list form on another piece of paper. Tell them to list a goal at the left and ways to reach it at the right. Have them recall ideas from Activity 7 if they have difficulty thinking of goals.

6. Have each student report this information to the class.

7. *Part c.* Have students write about their goals, using the ideas on their T-list. They should model their sentences on those in the text, completing them on their own paper and writing them in a short paragraph (Caution them not to write in the book.) Remind them to indent the first line of the paragraph.

Read the introduction aloud. Have students find Haiti on a world map. Ask, *What language do Haitians speak?* (French) Tell students to find the capital city of Haiti. *What is it?* (Port au Prince) Ask students, *What do we call the place where the story happened?* (setting) Write on the board: *setting = where the story happened.*

Activity 1: Preview

1. *Part a.* Draw a K-W-L chart on the board or on a transparency. Under the Know column write *What do you know about the story from the pictures?* Under the Want to Know column write *What do you want to know?* Under the Learned column write *What did you learn?*

2. Have students study the chart in the text on page 76. Ask a volunteer to come to the board and write the sentences given in the Know column. *(Bouki was in a city. . . .)* Invite another student to write down the questions related to these ideas in the Want to Know column. *(Why was he in the city, etc.)* Remind students that the Learned column will be filled in after they have read the story. Continue eliciting sentences and questions for the other three pictures on page 77. Have volunteers add these ideas to the chart on the board.

3. *Part b.* Ask students, *What do you think Bouki's goal is?* Have them write down their prediction, and then invite them to share ideas with the class.

Reaching your goals: A folktale

Stories about foolish people exist in many cultures. In Haiti, people tell stories about a foolish man named Bouki. In the story in this section, Bouki tries to reach a goal. Read to find out what happens.

1. Preview

Study Strategy:
Using Pictures

Pictures can help you understand a story and learn new words.

a. Classwork. Use the pictures and captions on page 77 to make a K-W-L chart.

Answer these questions before you read the story.

Answer this question after you read the story.

Know	Want to know	Learned
What do you know about the story from the pictures?	What do you want to know?	What did you learn?
Bouki was in a city. *Many people were reading newspapers.*	*Why was he in the city?* *Why were they reading newspapers?*	

Study Strategy:
Making a K-W-L Chart

Making a K-W-L chart is a good way to get ready to read.

b. In the story on page 77, Bouki has a goal. What do you think his goal is? Make a prediction.

Bouki wants to ______________________________

____

____

______________________________.

2. Shared Reading

Bouki's Glasses

One day, Bouki was in the big city of Port-au-Prince. All around, he saw people reading newspapers. Now, there was one thing Bouki really wanted to do. More than anything, he wanted to read a newspaper. So after he sold his yams and coconuts, he went to a store that sold eyeglasses.

In the city, Bouki saw many people reading newspapers.

He tried on this pair of glasses and that pair. Finally, he found a pair that was just right. He bought the glasses and went outside. On the street he found a boy selling newspapers. He bought a newspaper and started home.

Bouki went to a store. He tried on many pairs of glasses.

That evening, Bouki and his wife had dinner together. After dinner, Bouki took his chair and put it near the oil lamp. He sat down and put on his new glasses. He leaned back and opened his newspaper. He looked at the paper a long time. He turned the pages. He turned the paper upside down. He turned it around. He turned up the lamp so there would be more light. At last, he said: "They cheated me! These glasses are no good! I can't understand a word of this newspaper!"

After dinner, Bouki sat down to read the newspaper.

He turned the newspaper upside down.

Activity 2: Shared Reading

Encourage students to use the pictures to help them understand any new vocabulary in the story. Have them read the story silently first. Then have them listen to the tape and read as they listen for additional practice.

Activity 3: Share Ideas

1. *Part a.* Do the discussion/comprehension questions as a class. Lead the discussion yourself or ask a more proficient student to be the discussion leader. Encourage all students to participate. If less proficient students don't volunteer ideas, ask them to repeat what another student just said, e.g., *Jae, I didn't hear that. Could you repeat what Min has just said?*

2. *Part b.* Read the instructions aloud. Give students time to think of different ways for Bouki to reach his goal. Write the question *What could Bouki do?* on the board. Have students do a chain drill to ensure whole class participation. Ask Student 1 the question and prompt an answer with could, e.g., *He could go to school.* Student 1 will then ask Student 2, and so on. Encourage a variety of answers.

Activity 4: Use Context

1. *Part a.* Have students read the Study Strategy box: Using Context. On a piece of paper, students will write the three sentences and add one of the words or phrases in red to complete the statement.

2. *Part b.* Working in pairs, students can compare their sentences and work out any differences. Have them underline the words of the context that helped them choose their answers. Then have them find sentences 1–3 in the story and write in the words the author used above their selected words.

(Answers: comfortable = just right; turned up = increased, made brighter; very bad = no good.)

3. Share Ideas

a. Classwork. What is your reaction to the story? Discuss ideas with your classmates. Here are some questions to think about:

1. Did you like this story? Why or why not?
2. What was Bouki's goal?
3. What did he to do reach his goal?
4. Did he reach his goal? Why or why not?
5. This story is a folktale. Folktales often show how a culture thinks a person should behave. In this way, folktales try to teach a lesson. What lesson do you think this folktale is trying to teach?

b. Classwork. Think about Bouki's goal. What could he do to reach his goal? Where could he go for help? Who could help him? Think of several possibilities.

> ***Language Focus:***
>
> ***Suggesting Possibilities***
>
> - He could go to school.
> - He could ____ .

4. Use Context

a. On your own. Read these sentences from the story. Choose a word to complete each sentence.

comfortable/uncomfortable

1. Finally Bouki found a pair of glasses that were ____________ . He bought them and went outside.

turned off/turned up

2. Bouki ____________ the lamp so there would be more light.

very good/very bad

3. "These glasses are ____________ ," Bouki said. "I can't understand a word of this newspaper!"

b. Pairwork. Compare sentences. Then answer these questions:

1. What words and ideas in the sentences helped you to choose a word?
2. Find the sentences above in the story on page 77. What words did the writer choose? Use context to guess the meaning of these words.

> ***Study Strategy:***
>
> ***Using Context***
>
> Use the words and ideas in the sentences before and after a new word to guess its meaning.

Make a Story Map

a. Pairwork. What happened in the story? Make a story map of *Bouki's Glasses.*

Story Title: ______________________

Setting:
(Where?)

Characters: ____________ ____________
(Who?) ____________ ____________

Initial Event:
(What happens first?)
Bouki saw people reading newspapers.

Goal Setting: ______________________
(What is the main character's goal?)

Attempt to Reach Goal:
(What does the main character do to reach the goal?)

Outcome: ______________________
(What happens in the end?)

b. Compare story maps with another pair.

Study Strategy:

Making a Story Map

A story map is a chart that shows the main elements of a story. Making a story map helps you understand a story.

Activity 5: Make a Story Map

1. *Part a.* Explain that a story map is a chart that shows the main elements of a story. Review definitions of the elements. Ask, *What is a title?* (the name of a story); *What is the setting?* (the place where the story happens); *What are characters?* (people in the story). Have students look at the Initial Event. Read this information aloud. Tell students that they will answer more questions about what happened in the story. Ask, *What questions will you answer?*

2. Have students work in pairs. Distribute one copy of AM 3/4 for each pair to complete, or have them copy the chart on page 79. Encourage students to use complete sentences in retelling the plot.

3. *Part b.* Have pairs compare story maps and resolve any differences.

Activity 6: Make a Timeline

1. *Part a.* Have students study the timeline. Ask them to find the single words that show Bouki's *actions (went, bought, had sat)*. Explain that these are past, or finished actions. Read the sentences describing past events in the upper Language Focus box aloud. *(Bouki **went** to Port au Prince)* and emphasize the verbs as you read. Then have students read the Study Strategy box, Making a Timeline.

2. Have students get into pairs and give each pair a copy of AM 3/5, or have them copy the chart on page 80. Tell them to follow the model and add three more things that Bouki did in the story. They may add actions anywhere on the timeline that is appropriate, but caution them to keep these events in the correct order.

3. *Part b.* Introduce students to transition words *after* and *then.* Explain that these words show when or in what order things happened in a story. Sometimes writers use *first, second,* etc.; other times they use words like *after* and *then.* Have students read the lower Language Focus box: Describing a Sequence of Events. Check their understanding of sequencing by asking, *What did Bouki do first?* (sold yams) *second?* (went to a store).

4. Have students retell the story to the class or to their partner. Be sure they are using *then* and *after* as they do this activity.

6. Make a Timeline

Language Focus:

Describing Past Events

- Bouki **went** to Port-au-Prince.
- He **bought** a newspaper.
- He **ate** dinner at home.
- He **sat** down with the newspaper.

Study Strategy:

Making a Timeline

Making a timeline helps you organize information.

Language Focus:

Describing a Sequence of Events

- **After** he sold his yams, he went to a store.
- He sold his yams. **Then** he went to a store.

a. Pairwork. Here are some things Bouki did in the story. Add three more things to the timeline.

Beginning

- went to Port-au-Prince
- bought a newspaper
- had dinner
- sat down with newspaper

End

b. Use your timeline to retell the story.

7. Write a Summary

a. On your own. Write a summary of the story *Bouki's Glasses*.

Bouki
wanted *to read a newspaper.* ______________
So, ______________
but ______________
In the end, ______________

b. Compare summaries with a partner.

Extend

Groupwork. Read the last paragraph of the story again. In writing, tell what Bouki did next. Share your writing with the class.

Study Strategy: Summarizing

When you summarize, you write the most important ideas only.

Activity 7: Write a Summary

1. *Part a.* On the board write: *summarize = write only the most important ideas.* Explain the definition and say, *What you write is called a* summary.

2. Tell students to write a summary of the story, using the sentence beginnings on page 81. They should write only main ideas. Caution them not to write in the book.

3. *Part b.* Have students read their summaries to a partner.

Activity 8: Extend

1. Read the instructions aloud. Have students work in groups of four. Ask one person in each group to read the last paragraph of the story to the group. Have another member of the group list ideas as they brainstorm what Bouki did next. (Review this strategy by telling students to write down all ideas as they are spoken. They will later choose one of them for the activity.) Tell groups to decide on one idea and write a new ending for the story in two to four sentences. Encourage them to use *so . . . but* and *In the end* in their sentences. Have the third member write down the new ending. Circulate to assist less proficient students with this task. The fourth member of each group can read the new ending to the class.

2. As an alternate activity, provide groups with newsprint. Have them write and illustrate a new ending for the story as directed above. Post the papers in the classroom and give students time to walk around, read and enjoy the new versions.

Read the introduction aloud. Ask students, *What does* give up *mean?* (quit, stop trying). Use the goal of learning a new language as an example. Ask students why they might give up learning a new language. Elicit the difficulties involved (e.g., remembering new vocabulary words, difficult spelling, people speak too fast, etc.).

Activity 1: Quickwrite

1. *Part a.* Review or introduce the strategy of quickwriting (see teacher notes for Activity 1 on page 44). Ask students to choose one of their goals to think about. Have them read the questions on page 82 to use as prompts for their writing. Tell them they have five minutes for the quickwrite. If feasible, quickwrite with the students to provide stimulus for their own quickwriting.

2. Time students for five minutes.

3. *Part b.* Have students share something about their goal with a classmate.

Activity 2: Match

1. *Part a.* Have students work in groups of three for this activity. Student 1 will read the first caption and all students will then take notes as the group brainstorms. Student 2 will read the second caption; after this is brainstormed, Student 3 will read the third caption. Get less proficient students started with the prompt, *What could the boy do?* (e.g., he could study harder, etc.).

2. Have each member of the group report the ideas for his or her picture. Have all groups report for picture one before reporting for picture two, and so on. Students can then see similarities in their advice.

(Continued on page 83.)

Reaching your goals: A song

It may seem difficult to reach some of your goals. You might want to give up, or stop trying. Instead of giving up, follow the advice in the song "You Can Get It If You Really Want."

1. Quickwrite

a. On your own. Choose a goal from your list on page 75. Quickwrite about this goal for five minutes. Here are some questions you might think about:

- Why is this goal important to you?
- Will this goal be difficult to reach? Why or why not?
- What problems might you have?

b. Tell a partner about your goal.

> ***Study Strategy: Quickwriting***
>
> Quickwriting is a good way to collect ideas. When you quickwrite, try to write without stopping.

2. Match

a. Groupwork. What advice would you give to these students? Write your ideas. Then share your group's ideas with the class.

"I tried to get good grades this year, but I didn't."

"I practice playing the guitar every day, but I still can't play very well."

"I want to study Arabic but it's very difficult. Maybe I should study something easier."

b. Choose one of these proverbs to give advice to each of the students above.

Proverbs

- If you don't succeed at first, try again. (Don't stop trying.)
- The harder the battle, the sweeter the victory. (The more difficult something is to do, the better you will feel when you do it.)
- Rome was not built in a day. (Be patient. It takes time to reach your goals.)

3. Shared Reading

Read this song aloud with your classmates.

You Can Get It If You Really Want

(*chorus*)
You can get it if you really want (3x)
But you must try, try, and try
Try and try
Till you succeed at last

Persecution you must bear
Win or lose you got to get your share
Got your mind set on a dream
You can get it tho' hard it may seem

Rome was not built in a day
Opposition will come your way
But the harder the battle you see
It's the sweeter the victory

—*Jimmy Cliff*

Rome

JIMMY CLIFF

Jimmy Cliff, born James Chambers in Jamaica in 1948, is one of the most well-known reggae performers. He performed at the New York World's Fair in 1964, then went to England and Brazil to record his music. After a brief movie career, Jimmy studied Islam in Africa. He continued recording through the '80's, when Bruce Springsteen recorded his version of Cliff's "Trapped." This new attention to Cliff earned him a role in the movie *Club Paradise* with Robin Williams.

Activity 2: Match *(continued)*

3. *Part b.* Read the proverbs aloud. Invite students to ask about unfamiliar vocabulary (e.g., *What does* battle *mean?*). Be sure students understand the meaning of the proverbs.

4. Have groups match each proverb to one of the pictures. Then have groups compare answers.

5. Proverbs are often similar across cultures. Ask if students have proverbs in their native languages that express the same ideas. Invite them to share these with the class by saying the proverb in their native language and then explaining it in English.

Activity 3: Shared Reading

1. Begin this activity by having students read for specific information about the songwriter. Put these questions on the board:

When was Jimmy Cliff born?
Where did he record his music?
What did he study in Africa?
Who recorded Cliff's song "Trapped"?
Which movie did Cliff play in?

Have students read the information on Cliff and answer the questions.

(Answers: 1. 1948, 2. England and Brazil, 3. Islam, 4. Bruce Springsteen, 5. *Club Paradise*.)

2. Define new vocabulary: *persecution, bear, opposition.* Have students read the song aloud. You could have them all do the chorus, but let individuals or pairs read single lines. Have them practice until they read easily and comfortably.

Activity 4: Share Ideas

1. *Parts a and b.* Ask a volunteer to read Part a aloud. Call on individual students to answer the question; write their answers in abbreviated form on the board. Then have another volunteer read Part b, the title of the song and the question. Elicit that *It* in the title means a goal. You may want to provide a restatement of the title: *You can reach your goal if you really want to.*

2. *Part c.* Ask the class for advice for Bouki, using ideas from the song. Write their contributions on the board. Encourage a variety of ideas that carry out the song's message.

3. Ask if any students are familiar with reggae music. Do they know where it originated? (Jamaica) Do they know any reggae songs? If possible, bring in tapes or other recordings of reggae music and play them for the class.

Activity 5: Write

1. *Part a.* Write the incomplete sentence on the board: *You can* _____ *if you* _____. Ask one or two volunteers for words or phrases to put in the blanks. Then have students look at the two sample sentences in the book. Give each student a piece of paper and ask them to write down at least three other ways to complete the sentence; they should write more if they can.

(Continued on page 85.)

4. Share Ideas

Classwork. What's your reaction to the song? Share ideas with your classmates. Here are some questions to think about:

a. What does the song mean to you?

b. Read the title of the song. What do you think the word *it* means?

c. Use the ideas in the song to give some advice to Bouki, the main character in the story on page 77.

d. The song "You Can Get It If You Really Want" is a reggae song. Have you ever heard any reggae music? What was it like?

5. Write

a. On your own. Complete this sentence in different ways.

You can ____________ *if you* ____________.

Examples:

You can *go to college* if you *study hard*.

You can *earn some money* if you *get a job*.

b. Choose one of your sentences. Write it in large letters on a piece of paper.

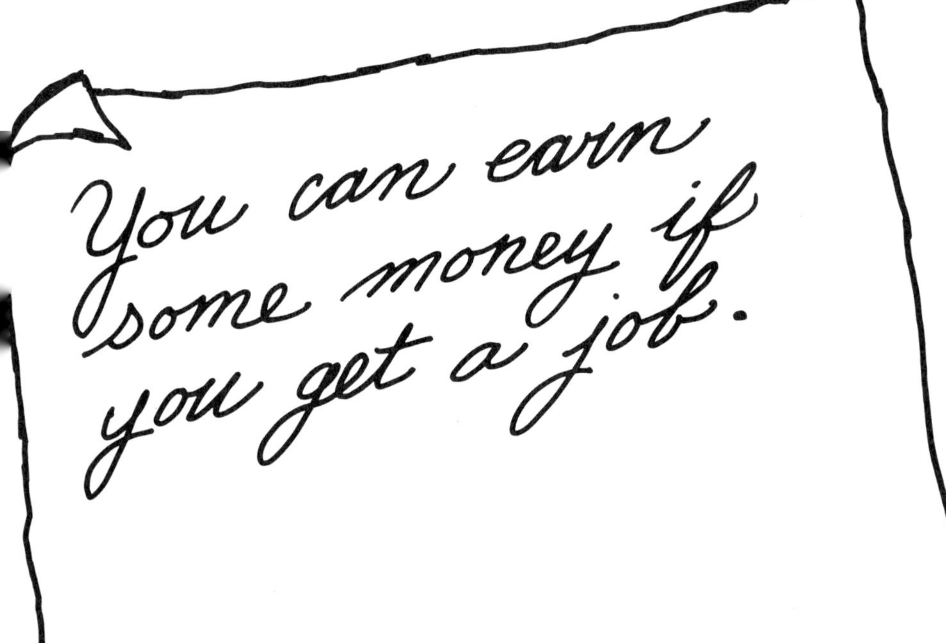
You can earn
some money if
you get a job.

c. Groupwork. Get together in groups of six or more. Follow these instructions:

- One student collects your group's papers.
- Together, read all of the sentences aloud.
- Change the order of the papers.
- Read the sentences aloud again.
- Experiment with the order of sentences.
- Choose the order that sounds best. Together, read the lines aloud as a poem. If you want, add a chorus.
- Read your poem to the class.

Activity 5: Write *(continued)*

2. *Part b.* Give each student another piece of paper. Tell students to pick their best sentence, the one that is most important to them, and write it in large letters on the paper, using the illustration on page 85 as a model.

3. *Part c.* Read, or have a proficient student read aloud the instruction line and the bulleted steps at the bottom of page 85. Answer any questions; then form groups of six or more students and have them follow the steps. Circulate to make sure students are following the directions. Have groups practice reading their poems together several times. Then have each group read its poem to the class. You may want to tape record the poems and play them back another day as a review and a reminder of goal setting.

Write *career* on the board, and ask students to define it. Provide help if necessary, writing one or more context-rich sentences on the board. Ask, *What is my career?* and elicit that your career is teaching. Ask how careers are connected with goal setting and elicit that choosing a career is setting one kind of goal, a career goal. Write *career goal* on the board.

If possible, bring in and show newspaper or magazine photos of famous people that your students would know, for example, a well-known athlete, the mayor of your city, a prominent rock musician, a TV actor. Try to find examples of different careers. Ask students to identify these people. Then ask them what career goals they think these people had.

Read the introduction aloud. Tell the class that this section may help them think about their own career goals.

Activity 1: Match

1. Have students look at the four pictures and read the names of careers under them. Ask students to tell what they know or can guess about each career (e.g., the jewelry designer makes rings, etc.).

2. Have students read the chart at the bottom of the page. Ask a volunteer to read aloud the example of the computer specialist and the job description. Then read aloud the second job description, *I make things with my hands.* Ask students which career they think matches this job description. Write suggested answers on the board. When someone says, *Jewelry designer,* agree, *Yes, the jewelry designer makes things with his hands.* Follow the same procedure with the third job description (sports reporter). When you come to the fourth description, briefly define *research* for the class if necessary. You may want to ask students to think about what kinds of research a transportation planner would do and what sorts of reports he would write.

Career Goals

Career goals identify the type of work you want to do. In this section, you will read about people in different jobs and think about your own career goals.

1. Match

Classwork. Match these careers with the job descriptions below.

Transportation Planner

Computer Specialist

Sports Reporter

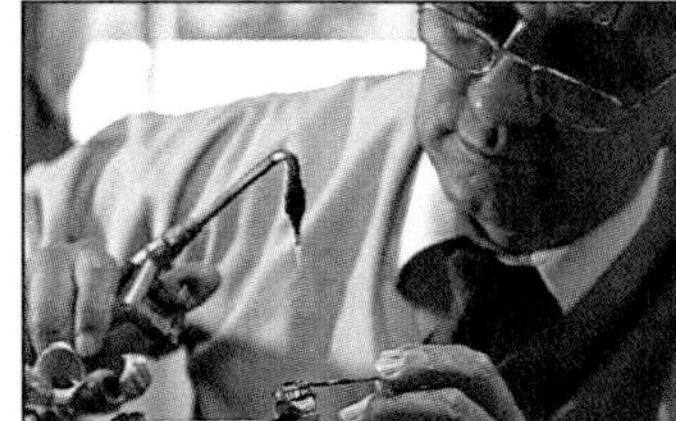

Jewelry Designer

Career	**Job Description** (What do you do in your job?)
Computer Specialist	"I teach people how to use their equipment. I also fix equipment."
______________	"I make things with my hands."
______________	"I interview people and write about special events."
______________	"I do research and write a lot of reports."

2. Jigsaw

Groupwork. Read one of the questionnaires below or listen to the interview. Take notes in a chart.

Career: ______________________________

Activities	Likes	Dislikes	Skills/Training	How to Prepare

Four people answered questions about their careers. Their answers are on these questionnaires.

Questionnaire #1: A Transportation Planner

1. What is your job?

   I work as a Transportation Planner.

2. What do you do in your job?

   I do a lot of research. I study the transportation needs of people—where they need to go and how. I use this information to predict where a town or city will need new roads, bus lines, etc. I also go to a lot of meetings to collect information. And I write a lot of reports, using a computer.

3. What do you like and dislike about your job?

   I like looking for ways to solve problems. I spend a lot of time writing and I like that. I also like working in an office and getting a good salary. Sometimes I have to work outdoors in cold weather (counting cars) and I don't like that.

4. What kinds of skills and training do you need?

   You should be able to think about all sides of a problem. You should also be able to write clearly.

   To get a job as a Transportation Planner, you should get a college degree.

5. What can students do to prepare for this career?

   They should study mathematics, science, and English. And learning to write clearly is important.

Activity 2: Jigsaw

1. You may do this activity as either a listening exercise or reading exercise. In either case, divide the class into four groups, and assign a separate occupation (transporation planner, computer specialist, sports reporter, jewelry designer) to each group. Give each group member a copy of AM 3/5 or have them copy the chart at the top of page 87 on a piece of paper.

2. For a listening exercise, have students close their books. Separate the groups as widely as possible, and play the appropriate interview to each group. (All four are on the tape, and they are brief enough to make this possible. They are recorded in the order in which they appear in the book.) Play the interviews quietly so the interview is heard by only the group to which that career has been assigned. Each student should first write the name of the career on the chart. Then, as they listen, they should take notes about activities, likes, dislikes, skills/training, and how to prepare for the career. They can prepare notes as a group and change their individual charts as necessary. Tell them that they can hear the interview again if they want to after the other groups have heard their interviews.

3. For a reading exercise, have each group read the appropriate interview on page 87 or 88, and fill out their charts individually. Again, tell them that they can compare notes as a group and check their answers.

4. With less proficient students, you may want to do the activity first as a listening exercise and then as a reading exercise so students can self-check their answers. They can still compare notes as a group.

Questionnaire #2: Computer Specialist

1. What is your job?

   I'm a Computer Specialist.

2. What do you do in your job?

   I spend a lot of time fixing computers and helping people. I teach them how to use their computers. Computers are always changing, so I have to read a lot of technical books and magazines.

3. What do you like and dislike about your job?

   I'm always learning something new—I like that. I also enjoy working with people. But sometimes I have too much work and I don't like that.

4. What kinds of skills and training do you need?

   It's helpful to have a degree in Computer Science. You should also be able to communicate well with people.

5. What can students do to prepare for this career?

   Take computer classes in high school. Use computers whenever possible. Get a college education.

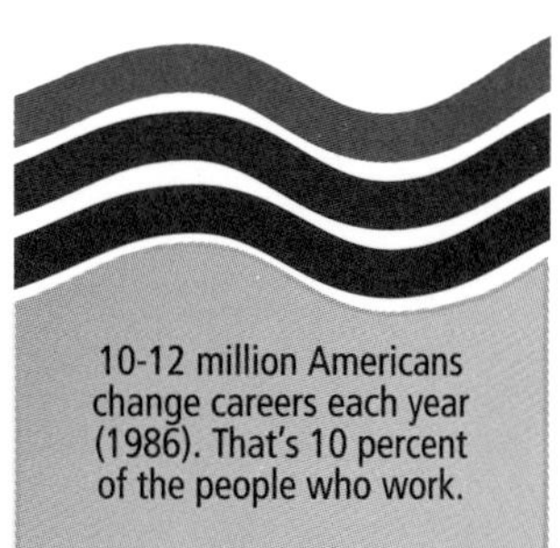

10-12 million Americans change careers each year (1986). That's 10 percent of the people who work.

Questionnaire #3: Sports Reporter

1. What is your job?

   I write about sports for a newspaper.

2. What do you do in your job?

   I go to sports games and write about them. I interview athletes and coaches. I spend a lot of time on the telephone talking to people and getting information. I also do a lot of typing.

3. What do you like and dislike about your job?

   I like playing with words.

   I have to do lots of different things. Every day is different. I like that.

   I don't like spending so much time on the phone.

   Sometimes I have to work on the weekends and I don't like that.

4. What kinds of skills and training do you need?

   You need good communication skills. A knowledge of sports helps, too. But most of all, you should be curious and observant.

5. What can students do to prepare for this career?

   Read as many books as you can. Learn to type. Keep a diary. Writing is a skill that you can learn.

Questionnaire #4: Jewelry Designer

1. What is your job?
   I'm a jewelry designer.
2. What do you do in your job?
   I spend a lot of time drawing my ideas for a piece of jewelry. Then I work with special tools and materials to make jewelry. I also have to sell my work and keep records of my sales and expenses.
3. What do you like and dislike about your job?
   I like almost everything about my job. I love making beautiful things. I like working by myself—I'm my own boss. I don't like keeping records, but it's an important part of the job.
4. What kinds of skills and training do you need?
   First of all, you need to be creative. You also need to study art and learn to use special tools and materials. And you have to be good with your hands.
5. What can students do to prepare for this career?
   Take art, math, and science courses. Draw a lot. Learn to use a computer.

3. Share Information

Groupwork. Get together with a new group of students. Find out about the three other careers. Take notes in a chart.

Career: ____________________

Activities	Likes	Dislikes	Skills/Training	How to Prepare

Activity 3: Share Information

1. Assign students to new groups, making sure that each new group includes students from each of the four original groups. Pass out new copies of AM 3/5 or have students make new copies of the chart and ask one another about each of the other careers. Students can use their chart from Activity 2 to tell about "their" career. Encourage students to ask questions about any vocabulary they don't understand.

2. As an alternative, you can play all four taped interviews to the new groups and have each student take notes on the careers he/she had not heard in Activity 2, or have them read all four interviews in the text to take their notes. In either case, the new groups should compare notes and check answers on the new careers.

Activity 4: Apply

1. *Part a.* Working individually, students use their charts to complete the matching exercise. Distribute copies of AM 3/6 or have students copy the chart on page 90 to record their answers. (Caution them not to write in the book.) Tell students to look over all the categories in order to determine the best career suggestion for the interests and abilities given.

2. *Part b.* Students compare answers with a partner.

3. *Part c.* Invite students to suggest other careers for these people, based on their interests and abilities (e.g., *"I enjoy writing but I don't want to work in an office."—novelist, textbook writer, etc.*).

4. Apply

a. On your own. Match these students' interests and abilities with a career. Use the information in your charts.

Careers: Transportation Planner, Computer Specialist, Sports Reporter, Jewelry Designer

Interests and Abilities	Career Suggestions
1. "I enjoy writing, but I don't want to work in an office."	*Sports Reporter*
2. "I like writing and working with numbers. My favorite school subjects are math and English."	________
3. "I like making things with my hands. I'd like to have my own business."	________
4. "I'm good at fixing things, but I also like working with people. I don't want to sit at a desk all day."	________

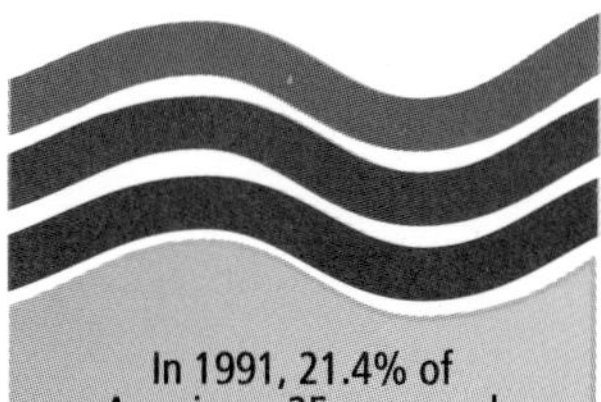

In 1991, 21.4% of Americans 25 years and older ahd completed four years of college or more.

b. Compare ideas with a partner.

c. Can you think of other careers for these people? Share your ideas with the class.

5. Self-evaluate

a. On your own. Which career might be good for you? Complete these checklists to find out.

Transportation Planner			
Are you interested in ______?	**Very interested (2 points each)**	**A little interested (1 point each)**	**Not interested at all (0 points each)**
doing research	✓	__	__
going to meetings	__	✓	__
writing reports	__	✓	__
using a computer	__	✓	__
working in an office	__	__	✓
SUBTOTAL:	*1* × 2 = *2*	*3* × 1 = *3*	*1* × 0 = *0*
TOTAL:	2 + 3 + 0 = 5		

Computer Specialist			
Are you interested in ______?	**Very interested (2 points each)**	**A little interested (1 point each)**	**Not interested at all (0 points each)**
fixing things	__	__	__
helping people	__	__	__
teaching	__	__	__
reading technical information	__	__	__
using a computer	__	__	__
SUBTOTAL:	__ × 2 = __	__ × 1 = __	__ × 0 = __
TOTAL:	__ + __ + __ = __		

Activity 5: Self-evaluate

1. *Part a.* Tell students that this activity will help them find out if any of the four careers they have been talking about might be good for them. Have them look at the first checklist, Transportation Planner, at the top of page 91. Say, *This chart shows the way one student evaluated her interest in some of the things a transportation planner does.* Guide the class through the checklist, showing how the "score" for each column was arrived at.

2. Write three columns on the board headed, Very interested (2 points), A little interested (1 point, and Not interested at all (0 points). Work through the same checklist (Transportation Planner) with an individual student. Ask, *Marta, are you interested in doing research? Please tell me if you are very interested, a little interested, or not interested at all.* Repeat Marta's answer, place a check mark in the appropriate column, and ask the class, *How many points is Marta's answer worth?* Continue asking the other questions, and have the class tell you the point value of each answer. At the end, have the class count the number of answers in the first column, and multiply by two. Have them count the number of answers in the second column and multiply by one, and then the number in the third column and multiply by zero. Have a volunteer add the column totals to get a final "score" for the student's interest in what a Transportation Planner does.

3. Tell students that they are to evaluate their own interests in each of the careers. Distribute copies of AM 3/7 and AM 3/8 or have students copy the four checklists on their own paper. (Caution them not to write in the book.) Circulate to make sure they are checking only one column for each activity; be ready to answer any questions and provide help as necessary.

4. *Part b (page 93).* Ask each student to report his or her career with the highest number. Tally the number of students who chose each career. Ask the class to comment on the results. Are they surprised? Why or why not?

Sports Reporter			
Are you interested in ________ ?	**Very interested (2 points each)**	**A little interested (1 point each)**	**Not interested at all (0 points each)**
going to sports games	__	__	__
interviewing people	__	__	__
talking on the telephone	__	__	__
working unusual hours	__	__	__
using a computer	__	__	__

SUBTOTAL: __ × 2 = __ __ × 1 = __ __ × 0 = __

TOTAL: __ + __ + __ = __

Jewelry Designer			
Are you interested in ________ ?	**Very interested (2 points each)**	**A little interested (1 point each)**	**Not interested at all (0 points each)**
working with your hands	__	__	__
drawing pictures	__	__	__
selling things	__	__	__
keeping business records	__	__	__
working by yourself	__	__	__

SUBTOTAL: __ × 2 = __ __ × 1 = __ __ × 0 = __

TOTAL: __ + __ + __ = __

92

b. Look at your total for each checklist. Which career has the highest number? Does this surprise you? Why or why not?

6. Collect Information

Classwork. Give a copy of this questionnaire to people in different careers. Use their answers to make a self-evaluation checklist.

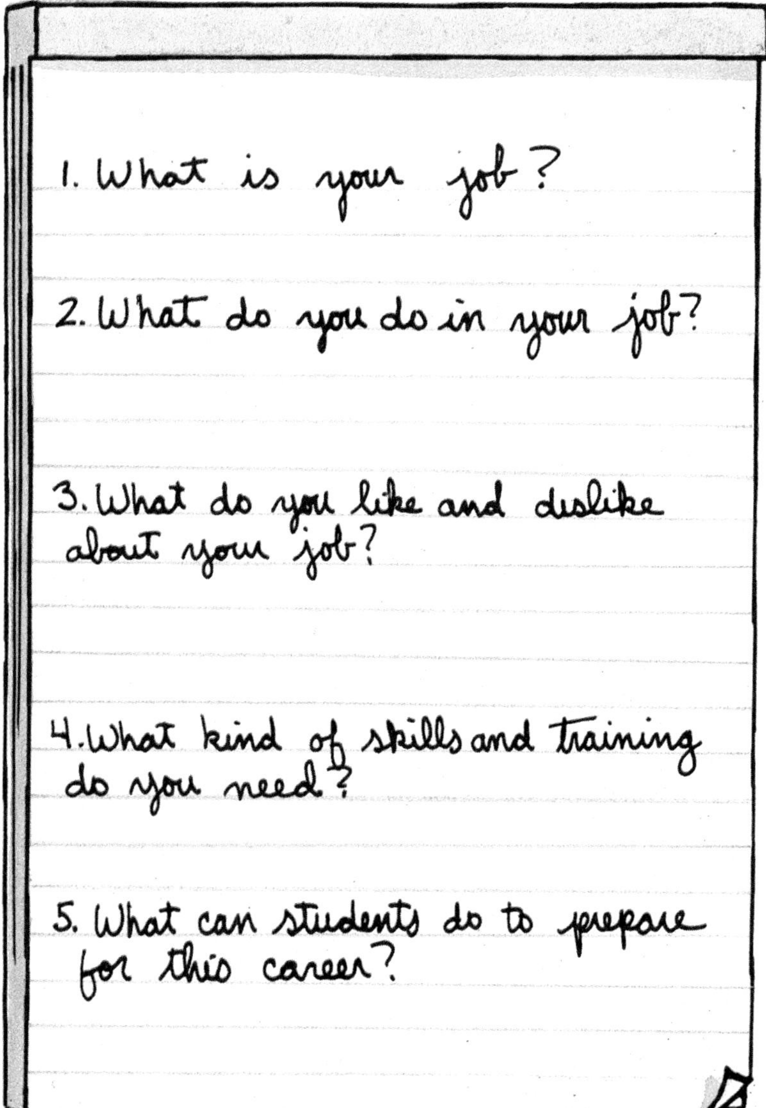

1. What is your job?
2. What do you do in your job?
3. What do you like and dislike about you job?
4. What kind of skills and training do you need?
5. What can students do to prepare for this career?

Activity 6: Collect Information

1. Distribute a copy of AM 3/9 to each student or have them copy the questionnaire on page 93. Read the instruction line aloud. Ask students to think of someone they know whose career is interesting. *Who is that person? What is that career?* Survey the class to ensure a sampling of different careers. Write the careers on the board. If students have trouble thinking of someone in a career, have the class brainstorm possible careers (nurse, pharmacist, store manager, chef, etc.). Suggest that they think of their family members and friends as resources.

2. Assign the questionnaire for homework. Students should have someone in an interesting career fill it out.

3. Have students bring back their completed questionnaires. Provide them with copies of AM 3/10 or have them make a copy of the form used in Activity 5, omitting the career name and the skills or job duties. Have them write the name of the career on the top of the chart. Then after reviewing the information in the questionnaire, they can determine five skills or job duties for this career. Assist less proficient students with this activity.

4. Collect the self-evaluation checklists. Compile a career resource booklet for the class for future reference.

5. As a follow up activity, have students select a career in the booklet and do a self-evaluation. Have them decide if that is the right career for them.

1. Begin this section by showing students pictures of people in government (e.g., the President, the Supreme Court, Congress, etc.). Ask, *What jobs do these people have?* Say, *These people are in government jobs.* Explore the concept further by asking students what *government* means. Write their ideas on the board as they say what government is and does. Ask who the leaders of government are in their native countries. Write down the names of presidents, monarchs, prime ministers, etc., and their countries. Then ask students what they know about the US government.

2. Read the introduction aloud.

Activity 1: List

1. *Part a.* Have students work in small groups. On a piece of paper have each group list their answers to the question: *Why do countries have governments?* Ask students to think of all the things a government does.

2. *Part b.* As groups share their ideas, have a volunteer make a master list of all the reasons why we have a government. Post the list in the classroom.

Activity 2: Match

1. Have students study the pictures. Ask, *Why does the government provide courts? schools? a military force? Why does it build roads?* Elicit whatever information students know about these services.

2. Read the directions and the goals aloud. Explain any unfamiliar vocabulary (e.g., *defend, attack, well-being, disputes*). Point out to students the use of the comma for apposition and parentheses for definition. Write on the board, *provides for the well-being (good living and working conditions) of people.* Say: *The authors thought you might not know the meaning of "well-being," so they gave you the definition in parentheses after the word.* Write, *provides ways to settle disputes, or*

(Continued on page 95.)

Goals of the U.S. government

Like individuals, governments have goals. In this section, you will read about the goals of the U.S. government and what it does to reach these goals.

a. Groupwork. There are more than 160 countries in the world. Each of these countries has a government. Why? List your ideas.

Why do countries have governments?

____

____

____

____

b. Share your group's ideas with the class.

Classwork. What can a government do to reach these goals? Match each picture with a goal.

GOALS

- defend the country from attack
- provide for the well-being (good living and working conditions) of people
- provide ways to settle disputes, or disagreements

Provide courts

Provide schools

Provide a military force

Build roads

3. Speculate

a. Groupwork. Think about the questions in the chart below. Guess answers to the questions and write them in the chart.

	My Guess	Text Information
How much money does the U.S. government spend each year?		
How many people work for the U.S. government?		
What are the goals of the U.S. government?		

b. Read or listen to the passage on pages 96–99. Look for answers to the questions above and write them in the chart.

Activity 2: Match *(continued)*

disagreements. Say: *Here the authors use a comma after the new word "disputes" and then they give you the meaning—disagreements.*

3. Read each goal again and ask which picture(s) match(es) it.

(Answers: defend the country from attack; provide a military force; provide for the well-being of people; provide schools and build roads; provide ways to settle disputes; provide courts.)

Activity 3: Speculate

1. *Part a.* Have students work in small groups for this activity. Pass out a copy of AM 3/11 to each group or have them copy the chart on page 95. Have students guess the answers to the three questions in the chart (e.g., How much money does the US government spend each year, etc.). Groups should reach consensus before they record their answers on the chart.

2. *Part b.* After the reading, have groups return to their charts and fill in the *text information* answers for each question.

(Answers: 1. The US government spends about one trillion dollars every year. 2. More than 3,117,000 people work for the government. 3. The goals of the US government are to: (1) make sure all people are treated equally; (2) promote peace within the United States; (3) defend the country against attack; (4) provide for the well-being of all people; and (5) protect our freedoms and make certain that our children have the same freedoms.)

Activity 4: Shared Reading

1. Have the students look at the illustration on page 97. Say, *This is the first page of the very first copy of the Constitution of the United States.* Ask, *What do you think the Constitution is? What does it say?* Write student comments on the board and discuss them.

2. Have students read the text on page 96 silently. Have them take note of any unfamiliar vocabulary as they read.

3. Have students turn to pages 98 and 99 and look at the pictures. Say, *You have just read five goals of the United States Government. What do these pictures tell you about how the government reaches these goals?* Elicit comments for each picture (e.g., the government builds highways, gives food coupons to poor people, keeps an army, etc.). Then have them read pages 98 and 99 silently, again taking note of unfamiliar vocabulary.

4. Put students in small groups. Have them work together to define unfamiliar vocabulary. Provide help as necessary.

5. Play the tape of the entire reading passage and have students follow along in their book as they listen.

4. Shared Reading

What are the goals of the U.S. government?

The U.S. government spends more than 1,000,000,000,000 (one trillion) dollars every year. It employs more than 3,117,000 people. It represents more than two hundred million people.

Why does the government spend so much money and employ so many people? To answer this question, just think about what the government has to do—what its goals are.

The goals of the U.S. government are stated in the Preamble (introduction) to the U.S. Constitution. The Constitution is a set of laws that define what the government can do. It also tells how the government should do these things. These laws were written more than 200 years ago when the United States became an independent country. The Preamble states that the goals of the government are to:

1. make sure all people are treated equally
2. promote peace within the United States
3. defend the country against attack
4. provide for the well-being of all people
5. protect our freedoms and make certain that our children have the same freedoms

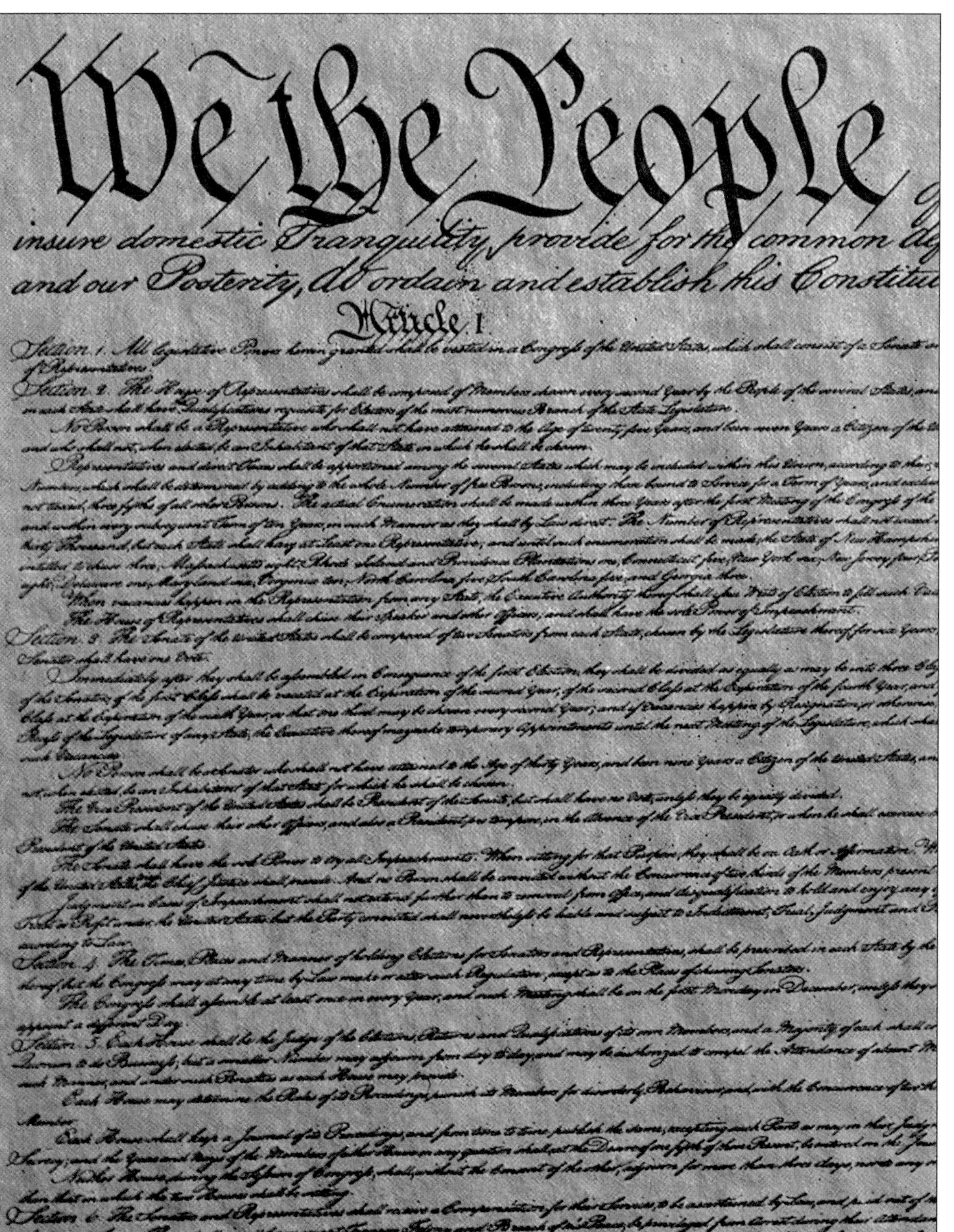

We the People

insure domestic Tranquility, provide for the common de

and our Posterity, do ordain and establish this Constitu

Article I

The U.S. Constitution.

97

And what does the U.S. government do to reach these goals? Here are a few examples:

- The U.S. government maintains a military force to defend the country. There are 2.1 million men and women in the U.S. Army, Navy, Marine Corps, and Air Force.
- It builds superhighways.
- It enforces laws that forbid discrimination, or unequal treatment, in public places such as restaurants and hotels.
- It provides loans for students who want to go to college. About five million students receive these loans each year.
- It provides food stamps to about 26 million people. People can use food stamps to buy food.

- It protects the right of people to protest, or express their disagreement with a law. If people think a law is unfair, they can express their disagreement peacefully.
- It provides a system of courts to settle disputes fairly and peacefully.
- It supports research into the causes and cures of disease.
- It makes sure that food is safe to eat.

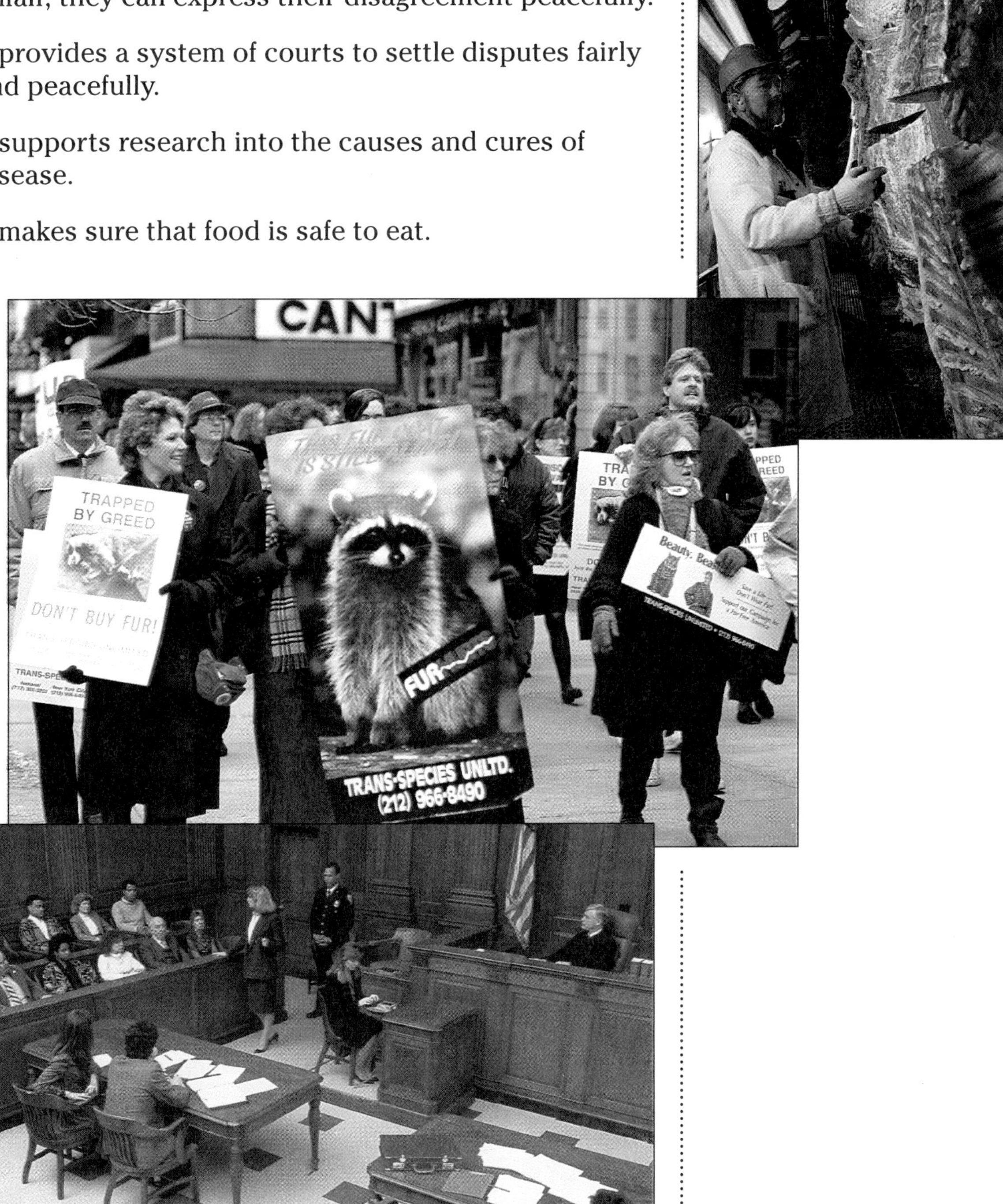

Activity 5: Match

1. *Part a.* Have students work in small groups. Provide each person in the group with a copy of AM 3/12 or have them copy the chart on page 100. Have groups read the 5 goals of the government at the top (to make sure all people are treated equally, etc.).

2. Demonstrate how to complete the chart by reviewing the example. Ask, *Why does the US government maintain (keep) a military force?* Elicit the answers: *to defend the country, to protect our freedoms.*

3. Instruct students to provide *why* questions for each of the other activities. Group members should agree on one or more of the goals that are fulfilled by this activity.

4. *Part b.* Using their charts, students can complete the sentences. Read the example aloud and call attention to the use of the gerund form (_____ ing) used after *by.*

(Answers: 1. providing a system of courts; 2. maintaining a military force; 3. providing foodstamps/providing loans for college students/making sure food is safe to eat; 4. enforcing laws that forbid discrimination; 5. maintaining a military force/providing a system of courts/enforcing laws that forbid discrimination.)

5. Have students work in pairs to compare their sentences.

5. Match

a. Groupwork. Match the activities of the U.S. government with one or more of its goals.

1. to make sure all people are treated equally
2. to promote peace
3. to defend the country
4. to provide for the well-being of all people
5. to protect our freedoms

Activities of the U.S. Government	to make sure all people are treated equally	to promote peace	to defend the country	to provide for the well-being of all people	to protect our freedoms
The U.S. government maintains a military force.			✓		✓
It provides loans for college students.					
It provides foodstamps.					
It provides a system of courts.					
It enforces laws that forbid discrimination.					
It makes sure food is safe to eat.					

b. On your own. Use your chart to complete these sentences.

1. One way the government promotes peace within the United States is by *providing a system of courts*.
2. One way the government defends the country is by _____________________.

3. One way the government provides for the well-being of people is by ______________________________ ______________________________.
4. One way the government makes sure people are treated equally is by ______________________________ ______________________________.
5. One way the government protects our freedoms is by ______________________________ ______________________________.

6. List

a. Groupwork. One of the government's goals is to provide for the well-being of all people. What do you need for your well-being (to live a safe, healthy, and good life)? List your ideas.

a job
a place to live
____
____

b. What can you do to provide for your own well-being? List your ideas.

____
____
____

c. What do you think the government should do to provide for the well-being of all people? List your ideas.

____
____
____

d. Share your group's ideas with the class.

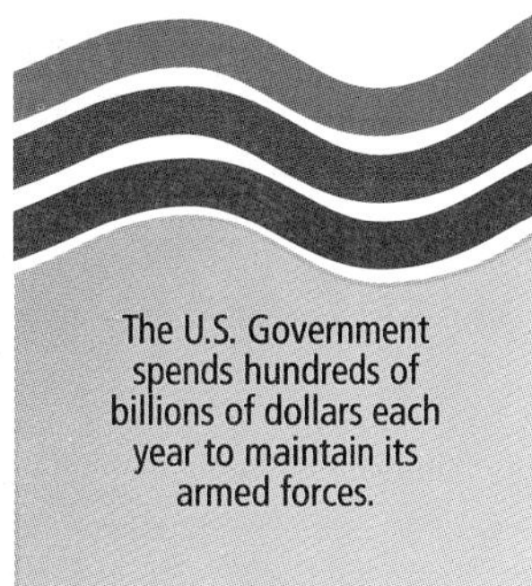

The U.S. Government spends hundreds of billions of dollars each year to maintain its armed forces.

Activity 6: List

1. *Parts a, b, and c.* Read aloud the instructions for part a, ending with the question, *What do you need for your well-being (to live a safe, healthy, and good life)?* Elicit the two sample answers. Then tell the class, *You may have many other answers to this question and to the other two questions. In this activity you're going to think and talk about the questions and their answers.*

2. Have students get into groups of three. Give each group a pencil and a copy of AM 3/13 or have them write on their own paper. (Caution them not to write in the book.) Tell them that one member of the group will read question a and will write down the group's ideas or answers. Then another group member will read question b and write down the group's ideas, and the third group member will read question c and write down the group's ideas.

3. *Part d.* Groups can share their answers in any one of a variety of ways: reading them aloud to the class, posting their completed questionnaires, or making illustrated posters on newsprint with their answers. A general discussion of the answers to parts b and c may help students think constructively about the government's and their own individual responsibility for their well-being.

Activity Menu

Read and explain the activities to the class. Then have students individually or in small groups select a project for a class or homework assignment. Projects can later be displayed in the classroom as they are shared with the class.

Activity Menu

Choose one of the following activities to do.

1. Make a Poster
Make a poster telling about one of your goals. Use pictures and words to explain what you are going to do to reach this goal. Choose a place in the classroom to display your poster.

2. Collect Pictures
Collect pictures of people in different occupations. Label the pictures and use them to make a wall display of career information.

3. Make a Career Alphabet
Write the letters of the alphabet in a vertical list. Identify a career that begins with each letter of the alphabet. Tell what people in these careers do.

A Architect—designs buildings
B Botanist—studies plants

4. Make a Plan
Work with a group of students. Together, choose a goal that you can reach in one week. Together, decide what you need to do to reach this goal. Decide what each person in your group will do. At the end of the week, tell the class what your group did. Include answers to these questions in your report to the class.

- What was your goal?
- Did you reach your goal?
- What did you learn from doing this project?
- What skills did you use to do your project?

5. Write a Story That Teaches a Lesson
Use a story map like the one on page 79 to write a new story. First, organize your ideas by completing the story map. Then use the map to write the story. Read your story to someone in your class.

6. Explore a Career
Look for books about careers in your school library or career center. Read about a career that interests you. Collect information in a chart like this:

Job Description	Salary	Skills and Training Needed

Use the chart to tell your classmates about this career.

7. Listen and Take Notes
Invite your school guidance counselor or career center director to speak to your class about careers. Before this person comes to your class, prepare a list of questions to ask. Take notes on the speaker's answers to your questions.

8. Investigate an Organization
Choose an organization that interests you. Read or talk to people about the organization. Find out about the organization's goals. Make a list of the goals and present them to your classmates.

Some suggested organizations:
- a school club
- a school sports teams
- a town or city organization

9. Collect Data
Go to the library. Find information about the number of people in different careers. Use the data to make a graph. Write about your findings.

103

Read on . . .

David Klein

1. Set the stage for the poem by asking students about the role that parents have in helping them with their goals. Their native culture will influence their opinions. Ask, *Do you think parents should plan your career for you? What if you don't want this career? Must you follow your parents' plans? What is expected in your first culture regarding marriage? Will your parents choose your husband or wife or will you? What happens if your parents don't agree with your choice? What happens if you don't agree with their choice? How important is it to marry someone from your own culture? from your religious background?*

2. Read the poem to the class twice. Ask students, *What problem does the poet have? What can he do about it?*

Read on...

David Klein

My parents' plans for me include
College,
Medical School,
Internship,
Residency,
Private practice.
They do not include Jennie,
Jennie, who makes me think of
Walks along the shore,
Quick kisses in the movies,
Frisbee-tossing in the park.
"You'll meet the right type of girl,"
  my mother says,
Not making the least attempt to be subtle.
"Somebody with a similar background,"
  my father says,
Not making the least attempt to be understanding.
The thought of Chinese-Jewish grandchildren
Terrifies them.
If I am going to be a doctor
And hold life and death in my hands,
Why can't I take charge of my own life
And hold the hand
Of the girl I love?

by Mel Glenn

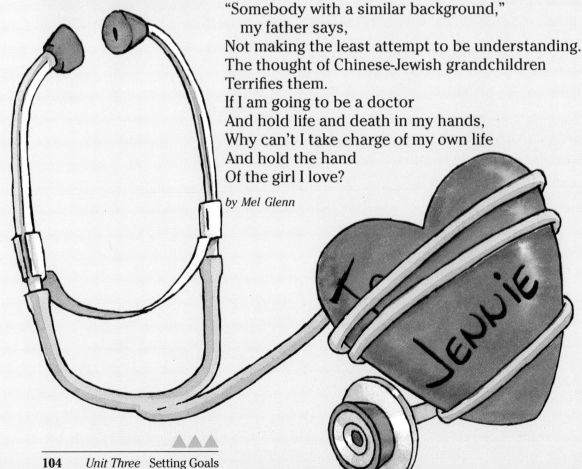

Homero E. Acevedo II

Homero E. Acevedo II is an executive with the American Telephone and Telegraph Company (AT&T). Mr. Acevedo has used his good education and his ability to communicate well in English and Spanish to become one of the youngest managers of the AT&T National Bilingual Center in San Antonio, Texas. There are lots of things we can learn from Mr. Acevedo.

Mr. Acevedo is very close to his family. Born in 1961, he is the youngest child. His family includes his late father, Homero, Sr., his mother, Maria, his two sisters, Annette and Angelique, and his twin brothers, Hugo and Hector.

When Mr. Acevedo was young, he was never lonesome with his brothers and sisters around. He especially remembers going down the stairs Christmas morning when his father made home movies and blinded him with bright floodlights.

His father and mother always encouraged him to get a good education, share with others, love others, work hard, and be all that he could be. They were also a good example for him. His parents were and still are his heroes. Some day, he hopes to have a beautiful family of his own.

Mr. Acevedo's parents gave him advice about how to handle teasing and prejudice. His father told him that if someone thought there was something wrong with him because he was Hispanic, then that person must not have been educated very well and should be ignored. So, that is exactly what he has done. He is proud of who he is.

Mr. Acevedo's dad taught him what goals are and helped him achieve some. One of his goals was to become an outstanding athlete. He did, and his favorite sports were soccer, baseball, and basketball. At one point, he played semiprofessional soccer. He loves Chicago teams, especially the Bears, Bulls, Cubs, and Blackhawks. Although sports are an important part of Mr. Acevedo's life, they never became his main goal.

The most important goal was to get a good education. Mr. Acevedo realized that a good education would open many doors for him in the future. In high school, he studied hard and made excellent grades. He then graduated from the University of Denver. While in college, he had a chance to study in Spain. By being one of the top academic students, he got to meet the king of Spain, Juan Carlos.

Mr. Acevedo knew that he needed to be ready to move to different parts of the country to advance in his career. He moved to New Jersey for training. He was in charge of testing a new billing system and a new computer system that would take care of eighty million residential customer accounts. This was a great responsibility.

After six months of testing the computer system, he was moved to San Antonio, Texas. There he is an operations manager in charge of the International Communications Service Center. Many office managers report to him. There are about 175 people in his department. He makes sure that everything runs smoothly.

Mr. Acevedo is able to communicate with people very well. He can speak and write fluent English and Spanish. He feels very lucky to know two languages and believes it has helped him be a successful executive. He says, "Anyone can be a success if they are secure with themselves, ready to move, and an achiever."

Student text page 105

Homero E. Acevedo II

1. Introduce students to the term *role model.* Write *role model = a person who is a good example for others* on the board. Have students look at the title of the reading and the picture. Tell them, *Homero E. Acevedo II is a role model for bilingual students. Can you guess why? Why do you think we are reading about him in the unit on goals?* Elicit students' guesses and opinions.

2. Read the selection to the students first. Then have them read it again silently. Write the separate words *Family Goals Career* on the board. Ask students to remember what they read about Mr. Acevedo in each of these areas. *In his life, how were these three things related? Why is Mr. Acevedo a good role model for bilingual students?*

▼ A changing population

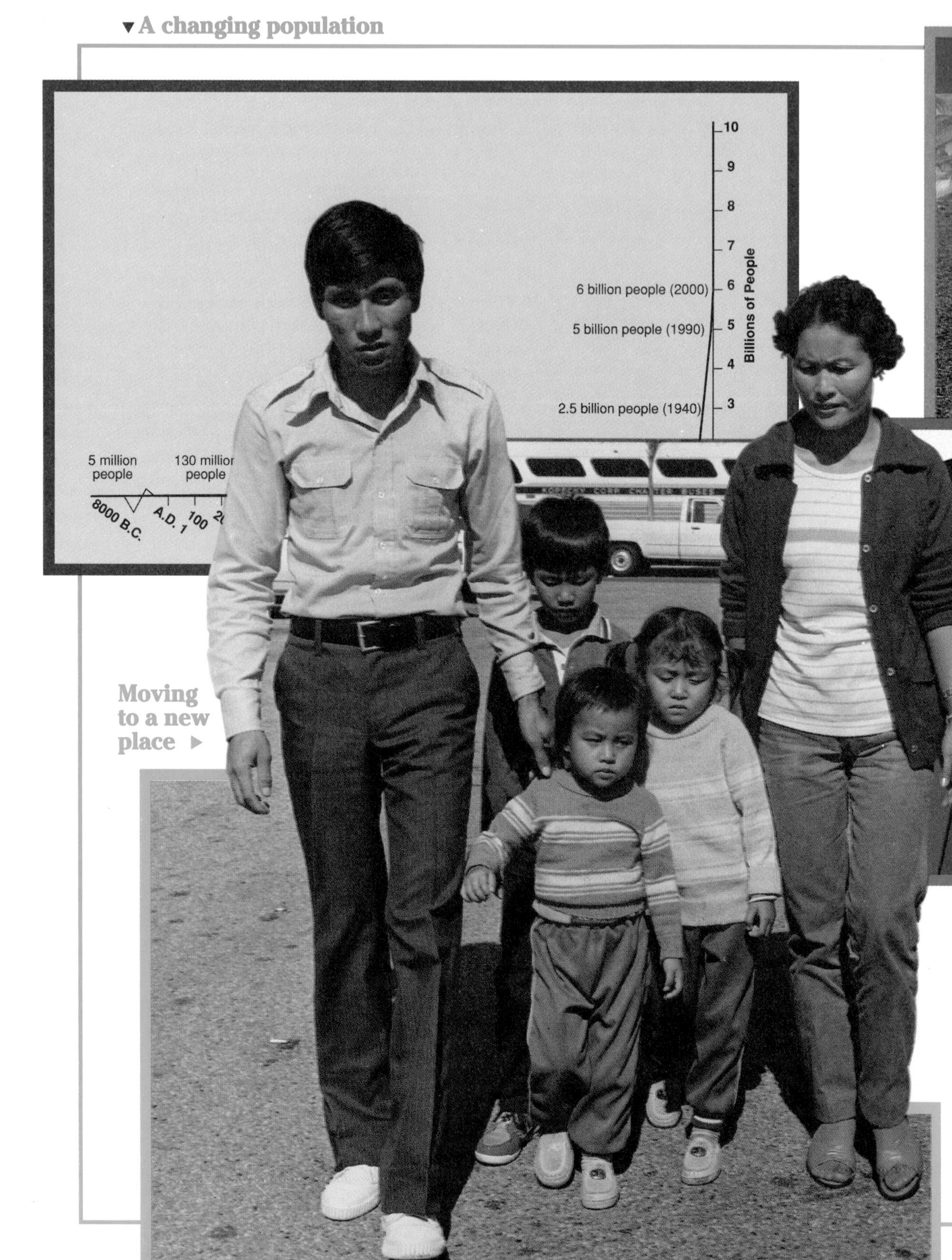

Moving to a new place ▶

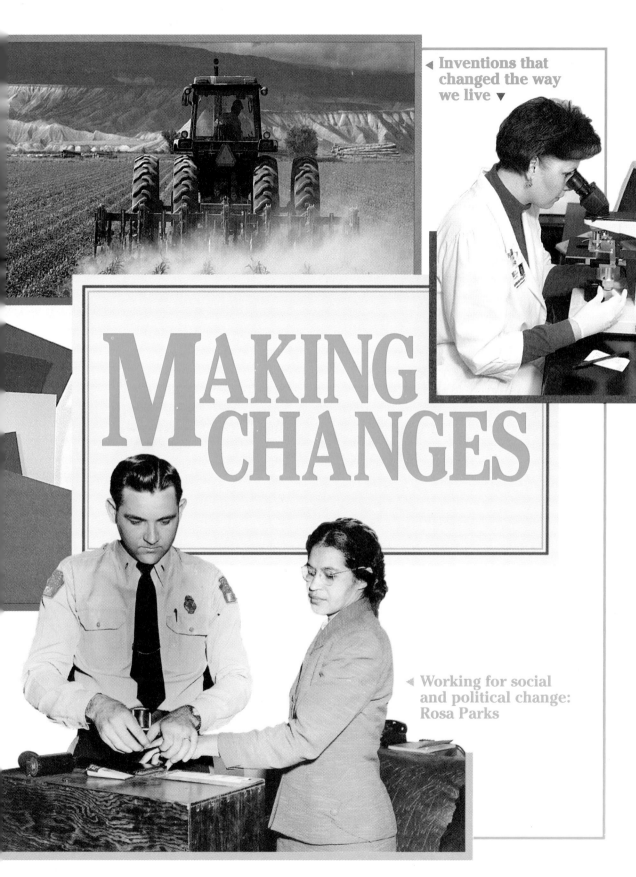

◂ Inventions that changed the way we live ▾

MAKING CHANGES

◂ Working for social and political change: Rosa Parks

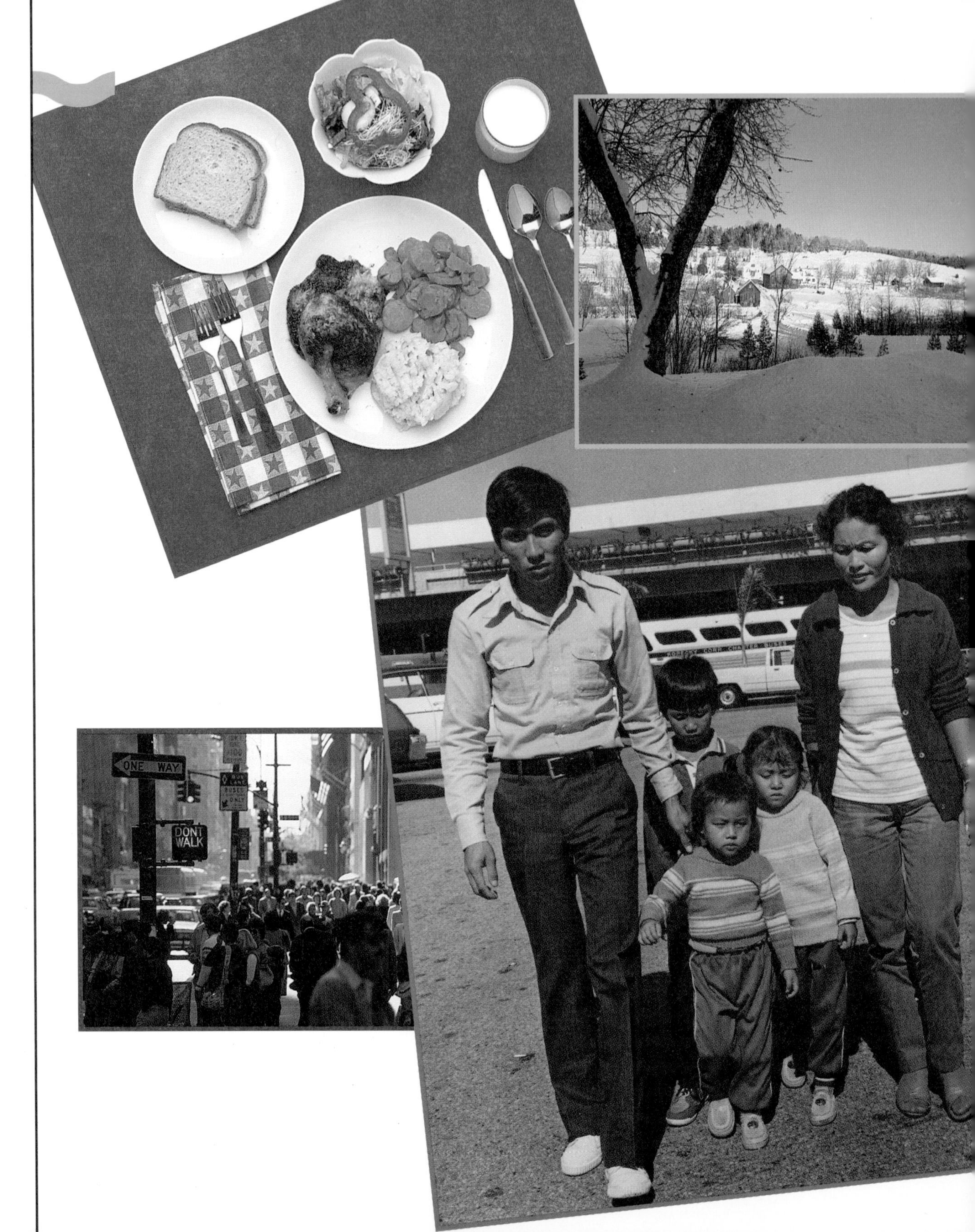
ONE WAY
DONT WALK

Moving to a new place:
An autobiographical account

An autobiography is a person's story of his or her own life. In the autobiographical account on pages 110–111, a young man tells how his life changed when he moved from Cambodia to the United States.

1. Identify

a. Classwork. Think about your first days in the United States. What was new or different for you? Share ideas with your classmates.

Example: *Everyone spoke English.*
It was very rainy.

b. Classwork. Ponn Pet moved to the United States from Cambodia. What do you think was new or different for him in the United States? List your ideas on the board.

Things that were different in the United States

the food

1. Introduce this section by asking students: *What is the story of a person's life called?* Write *biography* on the board. Then ask, *What is the story of a person's life written by himself or herself?* Add *auto* to make the word *autobiography.* Read the title and the introduction aloud or have a student read them. Explain that the young man who wrote this story is Ponn Pet. Ask students, *Who wrote the story of Ponn Pet's life?* (He did.)

2. Have students locate Cambodia on a world map. Ask, *Where is Cambodia?* (southeast Asia) *What is the nationality of the people?* (Cambodian) *What countries are near Cambodia?* (Viet Nam, Laos, Thailand) Ask if anyone knows the name of the language that Cambodians speak. If no one does, tell them it is Khmer.

Activity 1: Identify

1. *Part a.* Have the class brainstorm ideas about their first days in the United States. Ask, *What was new or different for you?* Have students read the examples in the text. (Everyone spoke English. It was very rainy.) Write their additional ideas on the board.

2. *Part b.* Read the instructions aloud. Have students look at the pictures for ideas. Write *Things that were different in the United States for Ponn Pet* on the board. Invite students to come to the board and write their ideas on the list (e.g., the food, the customs, etc.).

Activity 2: Take Notes in a Chart

1. Tell students that they will take notes in a chart as they read Ponn Pet's story. Have a volunteer read the Study Strategy box aloud. Discuss how writing information in a chart helps one to remember it. Then ask, *When you take notes in a chart, what do you write down?* Elicit that you write only the important words or phrases, not complete sentences. Distribute copies of AM 4/1 or have students copy the chart, *Changes in Ponn Pet's Life.*

2. Do the example with the class. Ask, *What is the climate in Cambodia?* (warm). *What is the climate in the United States?* (cold, according to Ponn Pet). *Are the climates the same or different?* (different).

Activity 3: Shared Reading

Introduce any vocabulary you think may be new to the students, for example, *immigrant, refugee, scary, costumes.* Then have students read the passage silently, taking notes on their charts as they read. When they have finished, play the tape or read the passage aloud and have students check their notes as they read.

(Continued on page 111.)

2. Take Notes in a Chart

On your own. As you read the story below, take notes in a chart.

Changes in Ponn Pet's Life

	In Cambodia	In the United States	Same or Different?
Climate	*warm*	*cold*	*different*
People			
Food			
Language			
Customs			

3. Shared Reading

> ***Study Strategy:***
>
> ***Taking Notes in a Chart***
>
> Taking notes in a chart will help you to organize information. This helps you remember it.

An Immigrant in the United States

I am a Cambodian immigrant refugee living in the United States. My family and I left Cambodia because of the war in the country where I was born. I can't believe that we are free in this country.

I was eight years old when I first saw different colored people. How strange, scary, and frightening to see white and black colored people, red and brown and yellow hair, blue, green, and brown eyes. I thought they had costumes on. My eyes had only seen brown-skinned people with black hair. The only pictures in books I had ever seen in my country were of Cambodian people who are of the brown race.

Everything was different here. The climate was so cold, and when I saw something white on the ground, I thought somebody went up in an airplane and dropped lots and lots of tiny pieces of paper down on the ground. It was the first time I saw snow. When I went to school, I couldn't speak English and the teacher didn't speak Khmer. I couldn't understand what to do. It was very difficult. Eating in the cafeteria at the beginning was so different. I had never seen or tasted milk and never eaten cheese or butter. I had never used a fork or a knife. There were about five other Cambodian kids in my room who had been in America longer, so they showed me how to use a fork and a knife. At first, I didn't like the foods—cheese, salad, pizza, and milk—so I threw them away. The foods I hated are some of my favorite foods now, like pizza, cheese, and milk.

American kids showed me how to play American sports and we became friends. Today, I feel very happy to be in America, a free country. The color of people doesn't scare me anymore. I think how silly it was to be afraid. Everyone is the same inside with the same feelings.

—*Ponn Pet*

4. Compare and Contrast

a. Groupwork. Compare charts from Activity 2.

b. Groupwork. Take turns writing a sentence about Ponn Pet's life in Cambodia and in the United States. Use your chart for ideas.

> *Ponn Pet used to live in a warm climate, but now he lives in a cold climate.*
> *He used to speak Khmer at school, but now he speaks English.*

c. Share your group's sentences with the class.

Language Focus:

Comparing the Past and the Present

- Ponn Pet used to live in a warm climate, but now he lives in a cold climate.
- He used to speak Khmer at school, but now he speaks English.

Activity 4: Compare and Contrast

1. *Part a.* Have students work in groups of four to compare their charts. Each group member can lead off with his/her information on a specific category: people, food, language, customs; then the others can discuss how their responses agreed or disagreed with that member. Not all charts need be the same. Some information that should probably be included follows. In Cambodia: People—brown race, black hair and eyes; Food—(not mentioned in reading); Language—Khmer; Customs—sit on floor, use spoons, chopsticks. In United States: People—different races, different skin, hair and eye colors; Food—pizza, milk, cheese, butter; Language—English; Customs—sit on chairs, use forks and knives. Same or Different: All different.

2. Introduce the structure *used to* + a verb. Write on the board, *Used to* + ____ *(verb) = an action done in the past but not now.* Write an example on the board, underlining the *used to* and the verb in each, for example, *Rajesh used to live in India.* Point out that Rajesh no longer lives in India. Add to the sentence on the board: *Rajesh used to live in India, but now he lives in the United States.* Explain that the first part of the sentence, up to the comma, tells about the past. The word *but* shows a contrast, because the rest of the sentence tells about the present. Add another sentence about yourself, for example, *I used to teach Spanish, but now I teach English.* Ask students to explain what this sentence means. Then elicit other *used to . . . but* sentences from the class.

3. *Part b.* Still working in their groups, on a single piece of paper, have each group member write a sentence about Ponn Pet's life in Cambodia and in the United States. Students should follow the models at the bottom of page 111, using *used to* and *but now. . . .*

4. *Part c.* Each member of the group can read his or her sentence to the class.

Activity 5: Write

1. *Part a.* Pass out copies of AM 4/2 or have them copy the chart at the top of the page. Have each student complete the chart comparing life in his/her native country and in the United States. As before, notes should be short and should include only important words.

2. *Part b.* Put students in pairs. Have partners share ideas from their charts. Encourage them to use the expressions *used to* and *but now* as they tell their partners about their lives.

3. *Part c and d.* Tell students that they will write a composition like Ponn Pet's about the changes in their lives. Tell students to follow the steps for paragraphs 1, 2, and 3 by answering the questions in the yellow boxes. They can refer back to Ponn Pet's story for more ideas.

4. Have them write their stories on regular paper, and then share them with a classmate. Papers can later be compiled into a class book.

5. As an alternate approach, provide each student with newsprint and markers. Have students write their stories and illustrate them. Post the stories in the classroom and allow students to read everyone's work and to write brief, signed comments to each other at the bottom of the paper (e.g., *I'm glad you are happy in the US.—Ali; I never saw snow before either.—Yadira; Nice work! —Marek*).

a. On your own. Tell about life in your native country and in the United States. List your ideas in a chart.

	In My Native Country	In the United States	Same or Different?
Climate			
People			
Food			
Language			
Customs			

b. Pairwork. Tell a partner about the ideas in your chart.

c. Write about the changes in your life. Use your chart for ideas.

Paragraph 1 Introduction	Where are you from? Why did you move here?
Paragraph 2	What was new or different for you here?
Paragraph 3 Conclusion	How do you feel about the changes in your life?

d. Share your writing with a classmate.

Inventions that changed the way we live

The way we live today is different from the way our grandparents and great-grandparents lived. In this section, you will read about some of the inventions that have made these changes possible.

1. Identify

a. Classwork. What do we use these things for? Share ideas with your classmates.

These inventions changed the way people live.

> ***Language Focus:***
>
> ***Identifying Purpose***
>
> Q: What do we use a sewing machine for?
> A: To make clothes.
>
> Q: What do we use a telephone for?
> A: To talk to people far away.

Air Conditioner (1911)

Personal Computer (1981)

Telephone (1876)

Sewing Machine (1846)

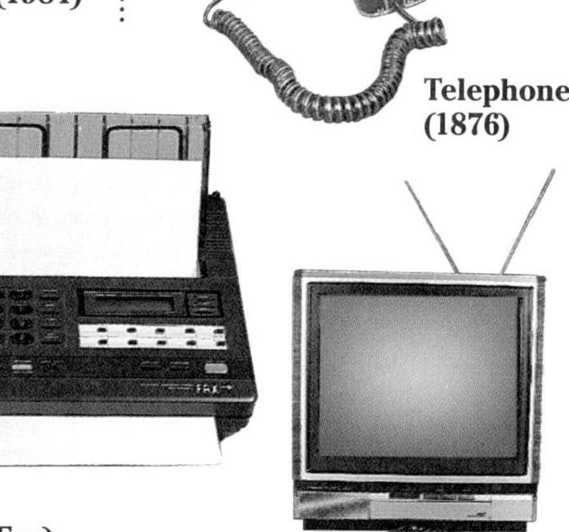

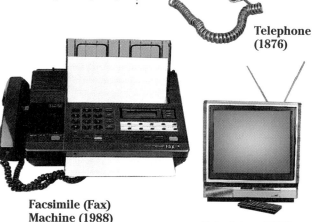

Facsimile (Fax) Machine (1988)

Television (1930)

Introduce the section by asking, *What is an invention?* Establish that an invention is something new (it didn't exist before) that someone has made. Write on the board, *invention = something new that someone has made.* Ask for examples of inventions and write them on the board as they are given. Ask, *Why do you think people invent things?* Elicit that people invent things to make life better and easier. Then read the title of the section and the three introductory lines aloud.

Activity 1: Identify

1. *Part a.* Have students look at the pictures on pages 113–114 as you name the inventions: air conditioner, personal computer, telephone, sewing machine, facsimile (fax) machine, television, vacuum cleaner, copy machine, electric washing machine, automobile, electric iron, tape recorder, pocket calculator. Then go back and ask, in random order, when each was invented. Point out that the original invention probably looked very different from the modern machine. Ask, *Did you ever see an antique (very old) automobile? An antique sewing machine or telephone?* Help students understand that an invention is not so much a thing as an idea or concept that is new. Once something has been invented, it is changed and improved as the years go by.

2. Using the model in the Language Focus box, ask the purpose of each invention. For example, ask, *What do we use the telephone for?*

3. *Part b.* Draw the chart on page 114 on the board or on a transparency. Call attention to the headings of the three columns: *Invention, What do you use it for?* and *What did people use before?* Use the sewing machine as an example. Write its name in the first column; then ask, *What do people use it for?* Elicit that they use it to make clothes, and write, *to make clothes* in the second column. Then ask, *What did people use before?* Elicit that they used their hands (and a needle and thread) before they had sewing machines. Write *their hands* in the third column.

(Continued on page 114.)

Activity 1: Identify *(continued)*

4. Have the students get in pairs. Distribute copies of AM 4/3 to each pair, or have them copy the chart on page 114. Have them work to complete the chart. They should list and answer questions about all 13 inventions pictured. Circulate and provide help or suggestions as needed.

(Suggested answers: Sewing machine—to make clothes; their hands. Telephone—to talk to people at a distance; telegraph or letter. Vacuum cleaner—to clean floor and rugs; brooms, dustpans, rug beaters. Automobile—to travel quickly; horse and buggy. Air conditioner—to make things cool; fans. Personal computer—to write letters, calculate, do homework; typewriter, pen and pencil. Facsimile machine—to send messages quickly; letters, telegrams. Television—to send news quickly; radio. Copy machine; to make copies; carbon paper. Washing machine—to wash clothes; their hands [and washboard in tub]. Electric iron—to press clothes; irons heated on stove. Tape recorder—to make or take notes; pencil and paper. Pocket calculator—to do math quickly; pencil and paper.)

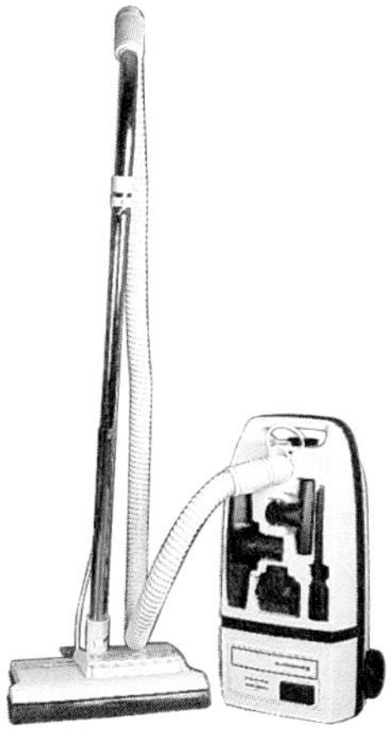

Vacuum Cleaner (1869)

Copy Machine (1959)

Electric Washing Machine (1911)

Automobile (1885)

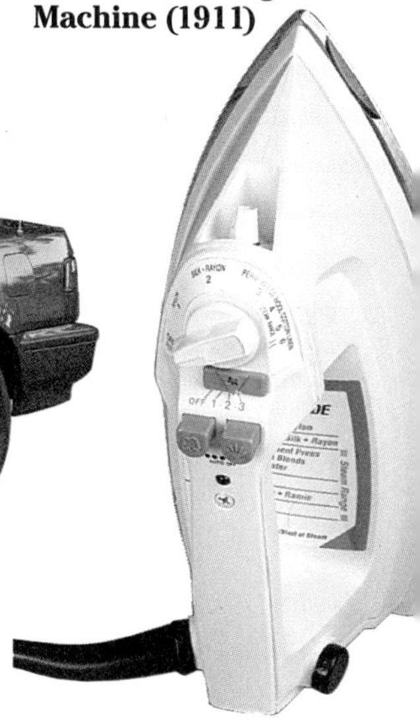

Electric Iron (19

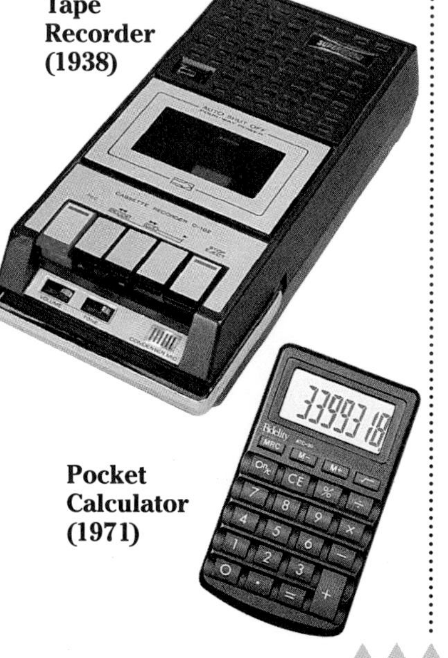

Tape Recorder (1938)

Pocket Calculator (1971)

b. Pairwork. Answer the questions in a chart. Then share answers with your classmates.

Invention	What do you use it for?	What did people use before?
sewing machine	*to make clothes*	*their hands*
telephone	*to talk to people at a distance*	
vacuum cleaner		
automobile		

Compare

Pairwork. Take turns telling about life in the past and today. Use your chart from Activity 1 for ideas.

Student A: People used to *make clothes by hand*.
Student B: Today they *use sewing machines*.

Student B: People used to *travel by horse*.
Student A: Today they *travel by car*.

Evaluate

a. Pairwork. Choose one invention. List the advantages and disadvantages of this invention.

Invention: *washing machine*

Advantages +	**Disadvantages** –
You can wash clothes quickly.	*It uses a lot of water.*
You can save a lot of time.	

b. Share your ideas with the class. Together, answer this question:

Do the advantages outweigh the disadvantages? (Are the advantages more important than the disadvantages?)

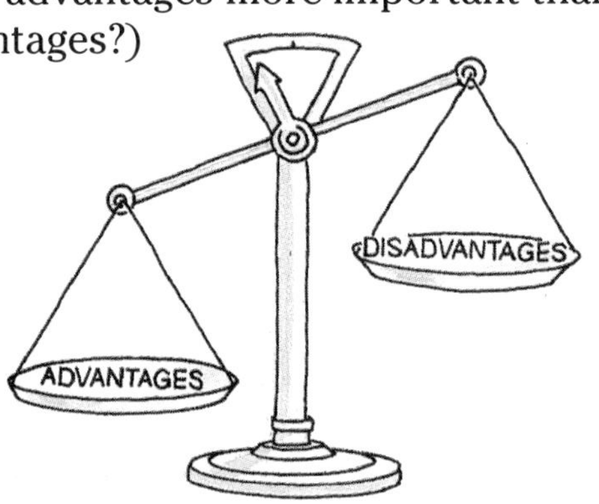

Thomas Edison invented 1,093 things. Among his inventions are the phonograph, the light bulb, and the motion picture projector.

Activity 2: Compare

Have students change partners. Tell them to take turns telling about life in the past and today. They can use their charts for ideas. Ask two students to demonstrate by reading the examples in the text. Student A: *People used to make clothing by hand.* Student B: *Today they use sewing machines.* Remind students to use *used to* and *today* in their answers.

Activity 3: Evaluate

1. *Part a.* Read the instruction line aloud. Ask students, *What are advantages?* (good things) *What are disadvantages?* (bad things or problems) Have students study the example of the washing machine. Ask, *What are the advantages of the washing machine?* (You can wash clothes quickly. You can save a lot of time.) Ask, *What are the disadvantages?* (It uses a lot of water.) Elicit other disadvantages for the washing machine. (It must use electricity. It is expensive to buy.)

2. Tell students to follow the example on page 115 and write about another invention. They should list both advantages and disadvantages for it.

3. *Part b.* Have pairs share ideas with the class. One partner can read the advantages and disadvantages; the other can pose the question to the class: *Do the advantages outweigh the disadvantages?* More proficient students may be able to comment further.

Activity 4: Match

1. Read the instruction line aloud. Ask students to read the dates aloud chorally. Read the question to the class, *What helps you to date the photographs?* Explain that as they do this activity, they will be making deductions. Ask them to look at the picture of the woman on the telephone. Ask, *What date is this picture?* Have two different pairs demonstrate the examples in the Language Focus box. (Student A: *It can't be 1850.* Student B: *Why?* . . .) Explain that the use of *must be* means probably.

2. Continue asking about each picture. Prompt students if necessary: *It can't be* ____.

(Answers will vary but possible answers are [clockwise from the large street scene]: 1. It can't be 1910 because the street has no automobiles. It must be 1850 because there are horses and buggies. 2. It can't be 1850 because there is a car. It must be 1950 because it's an old fashioned car. 3. It can't be 1950 because there is a computer. It must be 1990 because of the computer. 4. It can't be 1850 because there are cars. It must be 1910 because these are very early/old cars. 5. It can't be 1950 because of the modern cars. It must be 1990 because of the modern cars and bus. 6. It can't be 1990 because of the black dial telephone. It must be 1950 because of the clothes and the telephone.)

4. Match

Classwork. Match the photographs and the years.

1850 **1910** **1950** **1990**

What helps you to date the photographs?

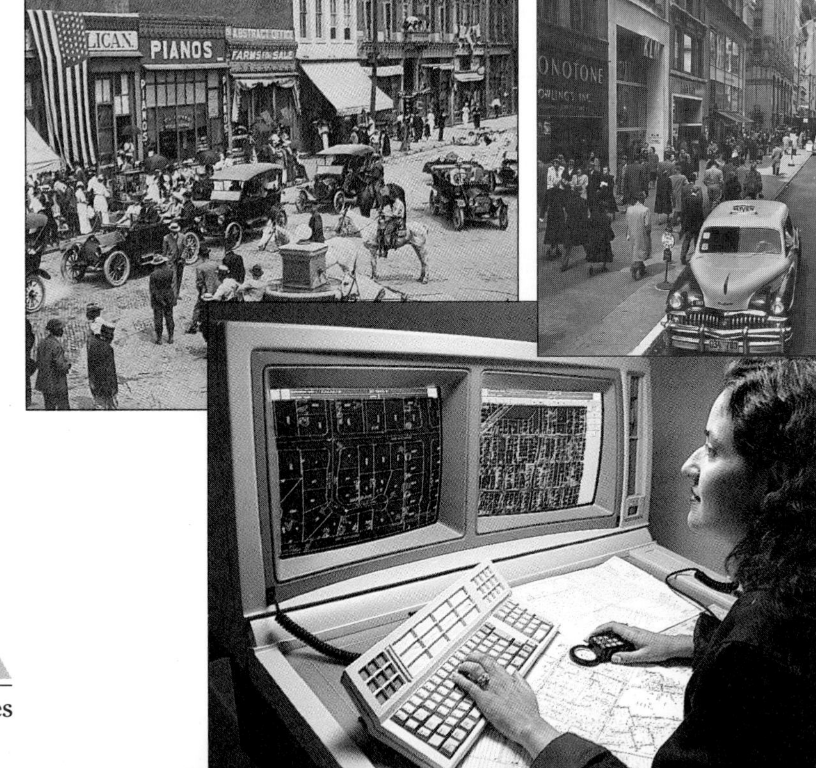

Language Focus:
Making Deductions

A: It can't be 1850.
B: Why?
A: Because she's talking on the telephone.

A: It must be 1950.
B: Why?
A: Because she's using an old-fashioned telephone.

5. Make a K-W-L Chart

a. Groupwork. Choose one of these inventions. Write your ideas about this invention in a K-W-L chart.

Plow

Paper

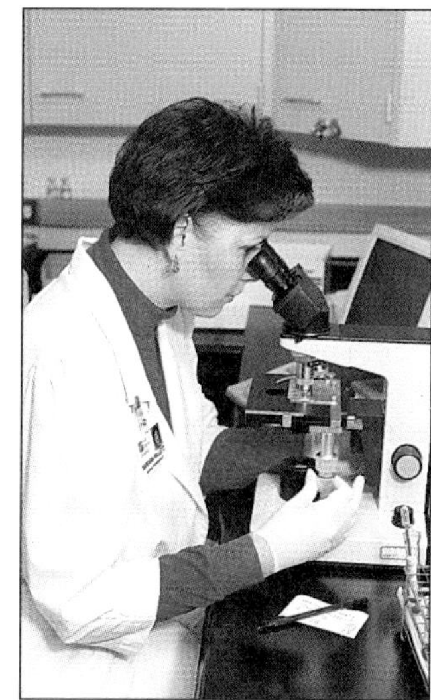

Microscope

Answer these questions before you read the passage.

Answer this question after you read the passage.

Invention: *Paper*

Know	Want to Know	Learned
What do you know about this invention?	**What do you want to find out?**	**What did you learn?**
Paper is made from trees.	*Who invented paper?*	

b. Share your chart with the class.

Study Strategy:

Making a K-W-L Chart

Making a K-W-L chart is a good way to get ready to read.

Activity 5: Make a K-W-L Chart

1. *Part a.* Have students work in small groups for this activity. Divide the class into 3 or 6 groups. Pass out 1 copy of AM 4/4 to each group, or have them copy the chart on page 117. Have groups decide which invention they want to read about: paper, the plow, or the microscope. If a group cannot decide, or if too many groups pick the same one, assign inventions to ensure balance within the class.

2. Have a volunteer read aloud the Study Strategy box: Making a K-W-L Chart. Ask students to look at the sample chart on page 117. Ask, *What do you know about this invention? What answer is in the example?* (Paper is made from trees.) Ask, *What do you want to find out?* Elicit: *Who invented paper?* Tell students that they will be adding more statements and questions to these two categories. Remind them that after they read, they will answer the question, *What did you learn?*

3. *Part b.* Before the reading, have each group share the statements from the *Know* column and the questions from the *Want to Know* column with the class.

Activity 6: Shared Reading

1. This activity will require careful strategy, since groups will be working independently on different readings. Ask each group to turn to their chosen reading, look at the pictures, and read the captions. This will preview the content and some of the unfamiliar vocabulary. Have groups do round robin reading (one paragraph or sentence read aloud by each member of the group).

2. Have the groups read the passage about their invention. If they encounter unfamiliar vocabulary, they can note these words and try to determine meanings together. You can explain any remaining words as you circulate among the groups.

3. After all groups have finished the reading, have them return to their K-W-L charts to answer: *What did you learn?* as they listen to the tape.

4. If your groups need more structure, you may want to write these steps on the board for them to follow:

For your story:

1. Look at pictures and read captions
2. Round robin reading (turn taking)
3. Define new vocabulary words
4. Listen to tape
5. Answer: What did you learn?

Circulate among the groups during this activity to help with vocabulary and ensure that students stay on task.

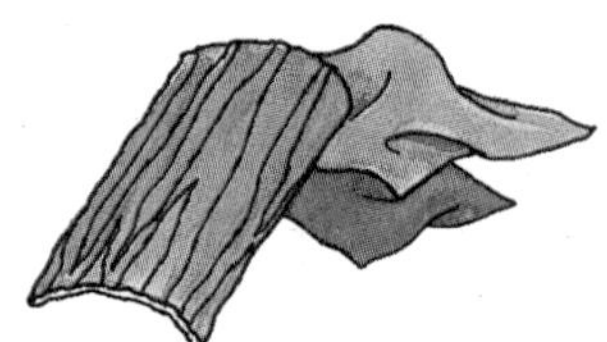

The first paper was made from the bark of trees and old rags.

Before paper was invented, people carved information on stone.

Thousands of years ago, people wrote on wet clay. Then they baked the clay tablets until hard.

6. Shared Reading

Read or listen to the section about your group's invention and complete your K-W-L chart.

Paper

Before paper was invented, people wrote on materials such as stone, clay tablets, and parchment. But none of these writing surfaces worked very well. Stone was difficult to carve. Clay tablets were heavy to carry around, and parchment was expensive to make. Around A.D. 105 a Chinese man by the name of Ts'ai Lun invented a much better writing surface—paper. It is believed that Ts'ai Lun used the bark of trees and old rags to make paper. His paper was light, easy to write on, and cheap to make. The Chinese kept the invention of paper a secret for several hundred years. But eventually, people in other parts of the world learned the art of paper making.

Paper was a very important invention because it provided a way to record information easily and cheaply. With paper, people could more easily make copies of written information. This made it possible to communicate ideas and information to a larger number of people.

Today, there are more than 7,000 different kinds of paper. Much of this paper is used for written communication, but we also use it to make paper products like cardboard boxes and paper plates.

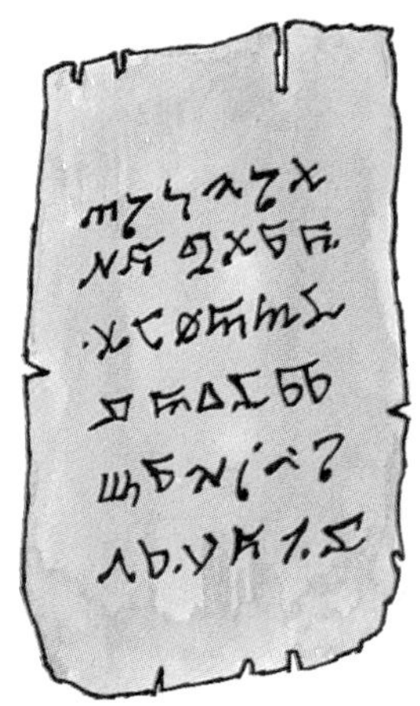

Parchment was made from the skin of animals.

The Plow

Thousands of years ago people discovered that plants grow better in soil that has been loosened. For a long time, farmers used sharp sticks, rocks, and other objects to loosen the soil. Then about 8,000 years ago, someone in the Middle East came up with the idea for a plow. These early plows were simple forked sticks pulled by a person. About a thousand years later, people began using oxen to pull simple plows. Today, many farmers use tractors to pull huge plows.

The plow was a very important invention because it allowed people to farm more land and grow more food. Because farmers could grow more food, fewer people died of starvation.

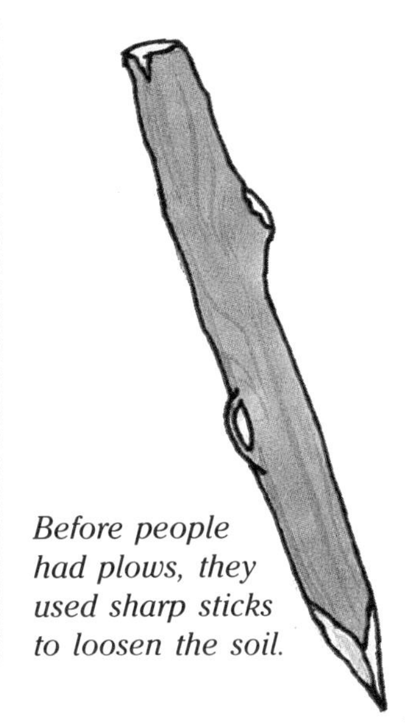

Before people had plows, they used sharp sticks to loosen the soil.

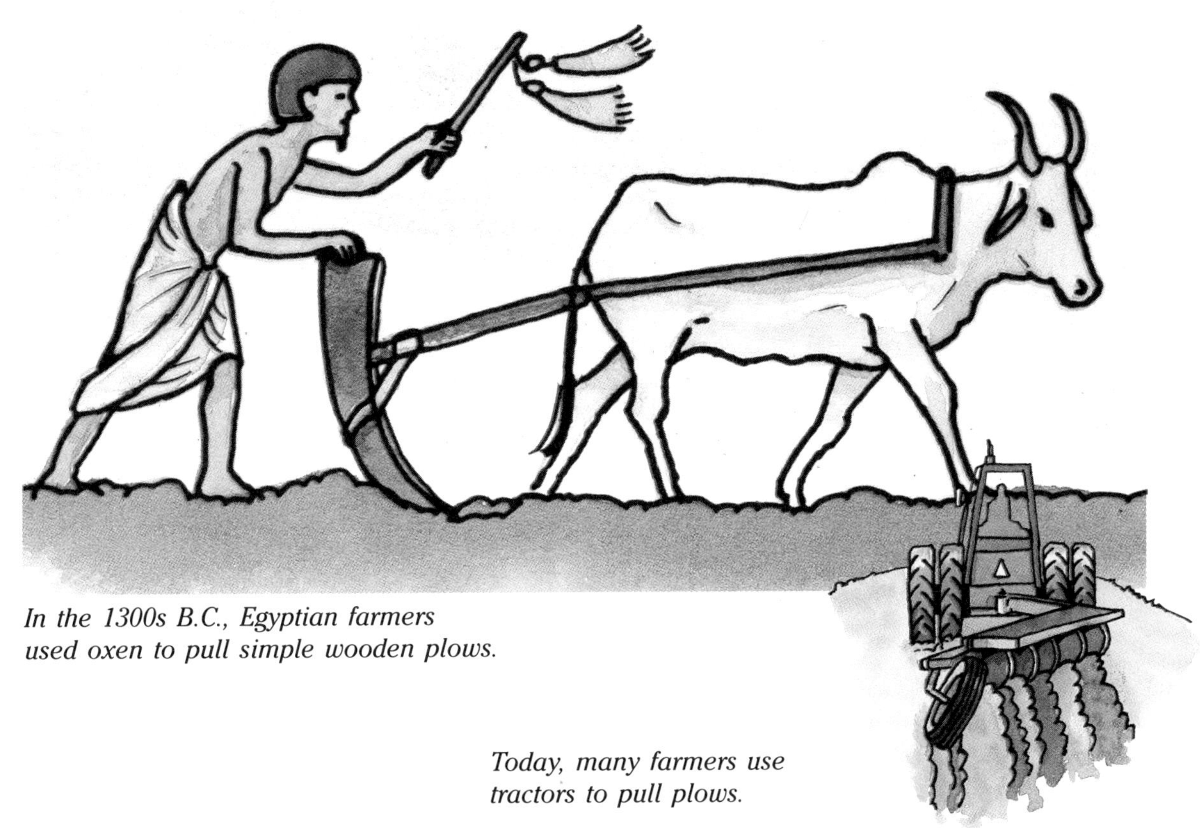

In the 1300s B.C., Egyptian farmers used oxen to pull simple wooden plows.

Today, many farmers use tractors to pull plows.

Activity 7: Test Your Knowledge

1. Have students remain in their groups. Ask them to look at the Language Focus box on Asking "Wh" Questions. They will each take a turn asking one of these questions about their invention and having the other group members answer it. They will follow the example, *What is a plow used for? To loosen the soil, etc.* Encourage students to remember the answers because they are "experts" about their invention.

Activity 8: Interview

1. Have students get into new groups. Be sure that new groups are balanced with "experts" on paper, the plow, and the microscope.

2. Pass out a copy of AM 4/5 to each student or have them copy the chart on page 121. For less proficient students, go over each category on the chart and ask them to give you the full question (e.g., Used for? = What is ____ used for? etc.).

3. Have students first complete the charts for their own inventions.

4. Then have students ask each other the full questions about the other inventions. Students will write the answers for each invention on the chart.

5. Check charts together as a class, and have students keep them for use in the next two activities.

Activity 9: Ask Questions

1. Give students time to study their charts and the "Wh" questions. You may scramble the groups again or keep them the same.

2. Read the instructions aloud.

3. Demonstrate how to play the game by having one student give an answer from the chart. His or her teammates must give the correct question. For example, Student A: *Ts'ai Lun.* Student B: *Who invented paper?*

(Continued on page 121.)

The Microscope

A microscope magnifies things, or makes them look larger. The simplest kind of microscope is a magnifying glass, which has one convex lens.

More than a thousand years ago, people used water-filled glass globes and rock crystals as magnifying glasses. Then in the 1300s, people learned how to make more powerful lenses. They used these lenses to make eyeglasses. In the 1600s, Anton van Leeuwenhoek, a Dutch merchant, found a way to make an even better lens. His lens could magnify things more than 200 times their natural size. In 1674, Leeuwenhoek, using a single lens microscope, was the first person to observe bacteria (very small organisms).

The invention of the microscope made it possible for scientists to learn how certain bacteria cause disease and infection. With this knowledge, scientists were able to look for ways to stop the spread of disease. Millions and millions of lives were saved because of the microscope.

A magnifying glass makes objects look larger.

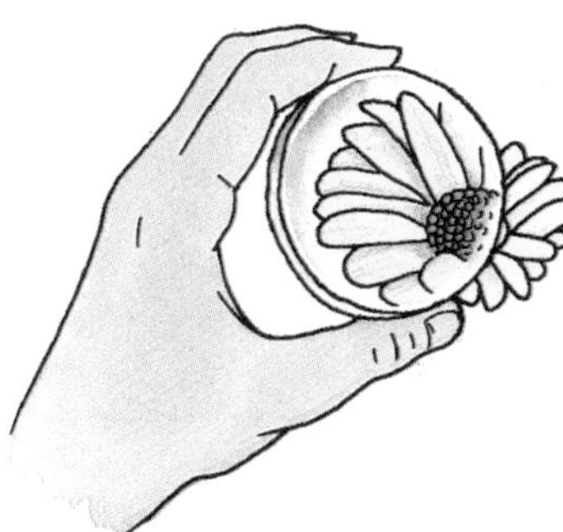

A convex lens is thicker in the middle than at the edges. It can make objects look larger.

You can observe bacteria with a microscope.

More than a thousand years ago, people used water-filled globes and rock crystals to magnify objects.

7. Test Your Knowledge

Groupwork. Take turns asking and answering questions about your group's invention.

Example: **Q:** *What is a plow used for?*
A: *To loosen the soil.*

8. Interview

Groupwork. Get together in new groups. Ask questions about the other inventions. Write your classmates' answers in a chart.

Language Focus:

Asking "Wh" Questions

- What is _____ used for?
- What did people use before _____ was invented?
- Who invented _____________?
- When was _____ invented?
- Why was the invention of the _____ important?

Invention	Used For?	Use Before?	Who?	When?	Why important?
Paper Plow Microscope					

9. Ask Questions

Groupwork. Follow these instructions to play a game:

- One person reads an answer from the chart in Activity 8.
- Without looking at the chart, your teammates match the answer with a question.

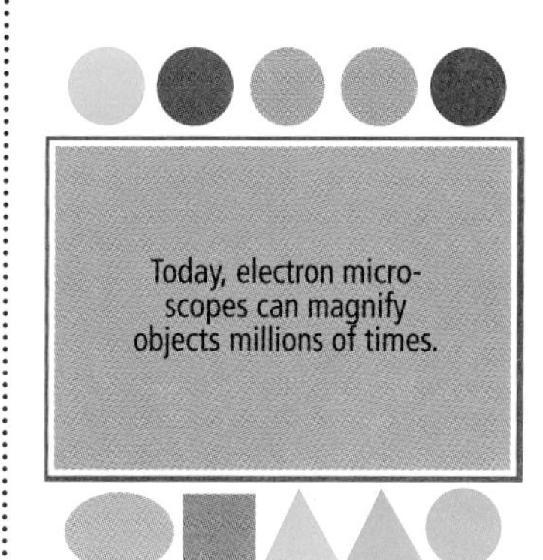

Today, electron microscopes can magnify objects millions of times.

Example:

Answer	*Question*
Ts'ai Lun	*Who invented paper?*
at least 6,000 years ago	*When was the plow invented?*

4. You may play the game in different ways. One option is to divide the whole class into two teams and have each team take a turn. A score-keeper can tally a point for each correct question for each team. A time-keeper (or you) can keep a 10 second time limit for a teammate to give the question. If the team cannot answer, the other team may answer and win a point. Another option is to have students play the game in small groups. Have the student giving the answer award a point to the first person who correctly gives the question. (No interrupting!) A score sheet should list each teammate's name and 1 point should be awarded for each correct question. At the end of 5–10 minutes, the individual with the most points wins.

Activity 10: Analyze

1. Review or introduce *cause* and *effect.* Say, *The effect is what happened; the cause is what made it happen.* Explain that each invention is a cause. Students will use their charts from Activity 8 to find effects.

2. Have students look at their charts. Ask, *Which category on the top of the chart gives effects?* (Why important?). Tell students to use this information as they give the effects of the three inventions.

3. Have volunteers make complete sentences giving effects for each invention (e.g., *The invention of paper made it possible to record information easily.*). Students can write these sentences on the board for additional practice.

Activity 11: Evaluate

1. *Part a.* Have students work in small groups. Tell them to look back at the inventions on pages 113–114. Working together, they should choose the five most important inventions.

2. *Part b.* Pass out a copy of AM 4/6 to each group or have them copy the chart at the bottom of page 122, allowing space for five inventions. Have groups list their five inventions on the *cause* lines. Then have them determine an effect for each one.

3. Have groups study the example as a volunteer reads it aloud (e.g., *The invention of the television made it possible to get news quickly.*).

4. *Part c.* Groups should reach consensus on the most important invention on their list. A person from each group can read this invention to the class. Have someone tally the most important inventions to see if groups thought alike or differently.

Language Focus:

Identifying Cause and Effect

- The invention of paper made it possible to record information easily.
- The invention of the plow made it possible to grow more food.

10. Analyze

Classwork. What did these inventions make it possible for people to do? Share ideas with your classmates.

CAUSE	EFFECT
The invention of paper	*made it possible to record information easily*
The invention of the plow	
The invention of the microscope	

11. Evaluate

a. Groupwork. What were the five most important inventions of all time? List your ideas.

b. Groupwork. Why were these inventions important? List your ideas.

CAUSE	EFFECT
The invention of the *television*	*made it possible to get news quickly*
The invention of ______	
The invention of ______	

c. Groupwork. Together, choose the most important invention on your list. Tell why you think it was the most important invention. Report your ideas to the class.

A changing population

The population of the earth is changing rapidly. You will find out why in this section.

1. Solve a Word Problem

a. Pairwork. Read this word problem and answer the questions.

Each day, about 400,000 babies are born around the world. On the same day, about 140,000 people die.

- How many more people are there in the world today than there were yesterday?
- How many more people will there be in a week? In 10 years?
- How is the world's population changing? Is it increasing, decreasing, or staying the same?

b. Get together with another pair. Tell how you solved the word problem.

Student text page 123

Introduce the section by having students count 5 seconds (one one thousand, two one thousand, etc.) or watch it on the clock. Tell them that before the 5 seconds were up, a baby was born somewhere in the world. About every 5 seconds, a baby is born. What do they think about this fact? Read the title and the introduction aloud.

Activity 1: Solve a Word Problem

1. *Part a.* Have students work in pairs. Read the word problem aloud. Send a volunteer to the board and ask him or her to write the number for 400,000. Then send another volunteer to write the number for 140,000.

2. Tell students to read each question and figure out the answer. Circulate to assist less proficient students with this task. Students should keep their math calculations for each question.

(Answers: 1. There are 260,000 more people in the world today. (400,000 – 140,000 = 260,000) 2. There will be 1,820,000 more people in a week. (26,000 × 7 = 1,820,000) 3. In 10 years, there will be 946,400,000 more people. [1,820,000 × 52 = 94,640,000 in a year; 94,640,000 × 10 = 946,400,000]. The population is increasing.)

3. *Part b.* Have pairs share their answers and math strategies. For less proficient students, have volunteers do the calculations on the board so everyone can see how they arrived at the answers.

Activity 2: Read a Graph

1. Tell students they are going to study about the world population and how it has changed. Say, *A line graph can help you to see the changes over time.* Have volunteers read the instruction line and the italicized caption. Ask questions to help students interpret the graph: *How many people were there in AD500?* (200 million); *In what year did the population reach 500 million?* (1650); *What will the population be in 2000?* (6 billion); *By how much did the population grow between 1940 and 1990?* (by 2.5 million; the population doubled). Then ask the key question, *Why do you think the earth's population began to increase rapidly in the mid-1800s?*

2. Have students work in small groups. Pass out one copy of AM 4/7 to each group or have them copy the Guesses/Text Information chart from the bottom of the page. Tell them to write their guesses on the lines under *Guesses.* If students have trouble thinking of possibilities, remind them that they should remember some things about the mid-1800s from earlier activities in this unit.

2. Read a Graph

Groupwork. Study the graph and answer the question below.

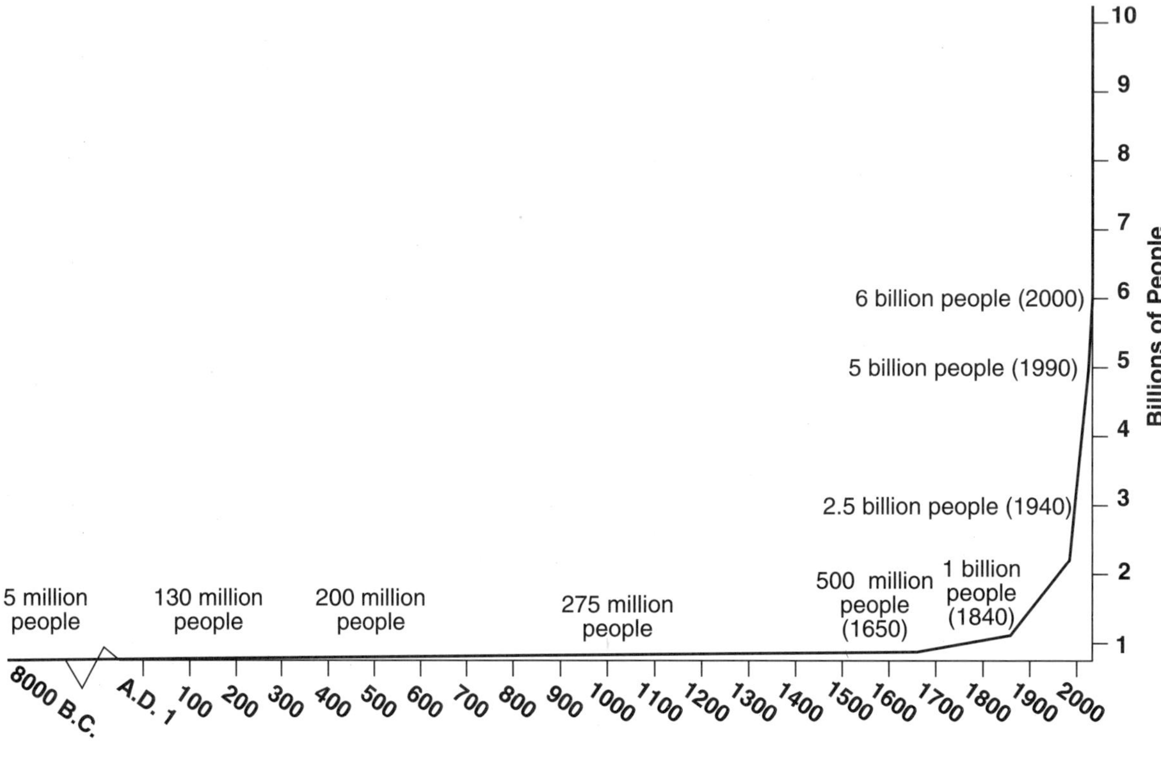

This line graph shows how the earth's population has changed. For thousands of years, the population increased very slowly. Since the mid-1800s, however, the earth's population has increased rapidly.

Study Strategy:

Reading a Line Graph

A line graph shows how something changes over time.

Why do you think the earth's population began to increase rapidly in the mid-1800s?

Guesses	Text Information

Shared Reading

a. Read to check your guesses from Activity 2.

My, How We've Grown

Why has the world's population grown so fast in the last 150 years? Beginning in the 1800s, many aspects of human life changed. Farms grew in size and number. New farming methods and better seeds increased annual harvests. People had more food to eat, and countries began buying and selling goods throughout the world. With the invention of new machines, people moved these goods—and themselves—quickly, first in steamships, then in trains, cars, and airplanes.

After farming methods and transportation improved, cheap food became available to more people. Before these discoveries, famines—severe shortages of food—regularly caused widespread starvation. Famine is now a rare event in most parts of the world.

In addition to inventing ways to grow more food, scientists also discovered what caused some deadly diseases and infections. These scientists found out that certain bacteria (very tiny organisms) make us sick when they enter and grow in our bodies. After the invention of the microscope, scientists could see these tiny life forms and could learn how they caused sickness.

This important breakthrough helped to stop the spread of illnesses that pass rapidly from person to person through a population. These widespread diseases, known as epidemics, included malaria, influenza, and yellow fever.

An epidemic can strike people of all ages and can cause sudden declines in population. The last worldwide epidemic—in this case, of influenza—occurred between 1918 and 1919. In those years, the flu killed roughly 20 million people around the world.

b. Complete the chart in Activity 2. Then share your group's chart with the class.

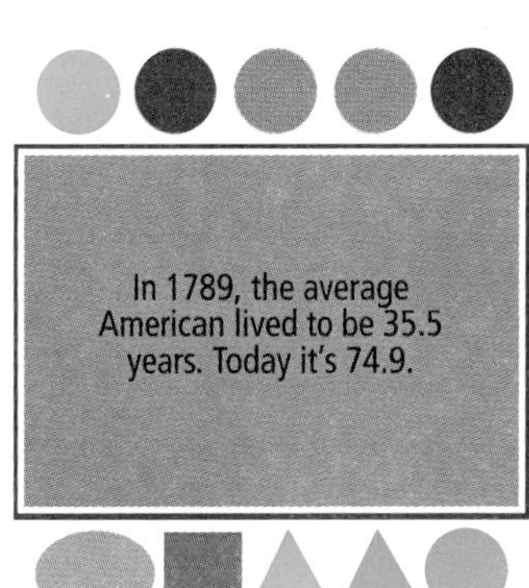

In 1789, the average American lived to be 35.5 years. Today it's 74.9.

Activity 3: Shared Reading

1. *Part a.* Have students read the selection "My, How We've Grown." Tell them that they will be working on new vocabulary later, so they should read only for reasons why the population increased rapidly in the mid-1800s. Have students read a second time or play the tape and have them read as they listen for extra practice.

2. *Part b.* While they read the second time or listen to the tape, students will complete their charts from Activity 2, filling in the Text Information column.

3. Have each group report its guesses and actual text information from their chart.

4. Have students read the information for the average life span in the pink box. Ask, *How much longer does the average American live now than in 1789?* (39.4 years longer). Ask, *How did you get that answer?* (subtract 35.5 from 74.9).

Activity 4: Make a Word Map

1. Introduce the activity by having a student read the Study Strategy box. Have students study the model in the text while you ask, *How many words are explained in this word map?* (3); *What are they?* (famine, bacteria, and epidemic); *What 3 pieces of information are given for each word?* (definition, characteristics, and examples).

2. Give a copy of AM 4/8 to each student or have them copy the word maps on page 126. Tell students to use information from the reading on page 125 to complete the word map. They can also add their own ideas.

(Suggested answers: Famine. definition: a shortage of food; characteristics: causes widespread starvation; rare in most places today; example: famine in Somalia in 1992. Bacteria. definition: very tiny organisms; characteristics: enter and grow in our bodies; cause deadly diseases and infections; examples: pneumococci, streptococci. Epidemic. definition: widespread diseases; characteristics: can strike people of all ages; can cause sudden declines in population; examples: malaria, influenza, yellow fever, polio.)

Activity 5: Classify

1. Have students work in pairs. Tell them that using context is an important way to learn new vocabulary. Ask a student to read the Study Strategy box on page 127. Put this example on the board: *New farming methods and better seeds increased annual harvests.* Ask, *What do you think "harvest" means?* (gathering in and bringing home the crops from the fields). Ask, *What words helped you to define "harvest"?* (farming, seeds, annual). Then underline these words in the example to emphasize use of context.

2. Have pairs use the context to find the meaning of each word. (Possible answers: bacteria—very tiny organisms; epidemic—widespread disease; famine—shortage of food; harvest—gathering crops from the fields; illness—sickness; infection—a disease caused by bacteria; starvation—death or suffering because of hunger)

(Continued on page 127.)

4. Make a Word Map

Classwork. Use information from page 125 to complete these word maps. Add your own ideas, too.

Study Strategy:

Making a Word Map

Making a word map is a good way to collect information about a new word.

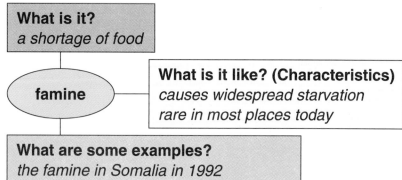

Example:

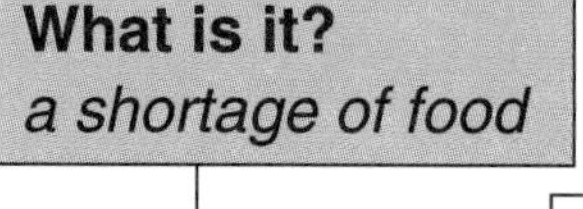
What is it?
a shortage of food

famine

What is it like? (Characteristics)
causes widespread starvation
rare in most places today

What are some examples?
the famine in Somalia in 1992

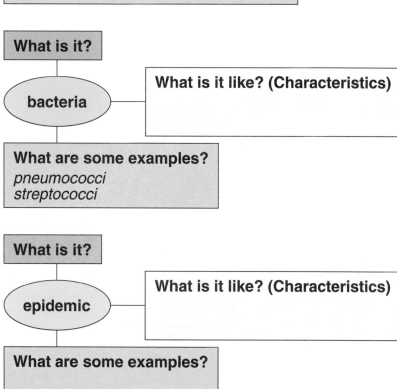

What is it?

bacteria

What is it like? (Characteristics)

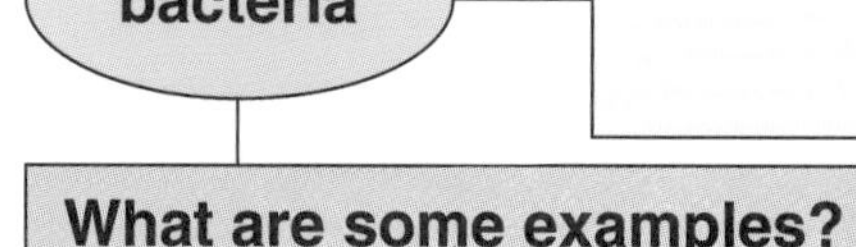
What are some examples?
pneumococci
streptococci

What is it?

epidemic

What is it like? (Characteristics)

What are some examples?

5. Classify

Pairwork. Find these words in the reading on page 125. Use context to guess the meaning of each word. Then put the words into two groups.

bacteria	*harvest*	*sick*
epidemic	*illness*	*starvation*
famine	*infection*	*seeds*

Words related to food	**Words related to disease**
______	______
______	______
______	______

Study Strategy:
Using Context

Use the words and ideas around a new word to guess its meaning.

6. Identify

a. Pairwork. For each pair of sentences, identify the cause and the effect.

1. a. Farmers used new farming methods and better seeds. *cause*
   b. Farmers were able to grow more food. *effect*
2. a. The harvests were larger each year. ______
   b. Food became cheaper. ______
3. a. People could send food to different parts of the world. ______
   b. New means of transportation were available. ______
4. a. People could send food to areas without food. ______
   b. Fewer people died of starvation. ______
5. a. Fewer people died. ______
   b. Scientists discovered the cause of some diseases. ______

Activity 5: Classify *(continued)*

3. Then distribute AM 4/9 or have students copy the two-column chart at the top of page 127. Have pairs classify the words according to *Words related to food* or *Words related to disease*. They can write the vocabulary words on the chart in the appropriate categories. (Caution them not to write in the book.)

Answers:

Words related to food: famine; harvest; seeds; starvation. **Words related to disease:** bacteria; epidemic; illness; infection; sick.

Activity 6: Identify

1. *Part a.* Begin by reviewing cause and effect. (See Teacher Notes for Activity 10 on page 122.) Read the instruction line aloud. Ask a volunteer to read the example. (a. Farmers used new farming methods and better seeds = cause. b. Farmers were able to grow more food = effect.)

2. Distribute a copy of AM 4/10 to each student or have them number their papers 1 to 5, with an a. and a b. space under each number. Have partners work together to complete the activity.

(Answers: 1. a. cause b. effect; 2. a. cause b. effect; 3. a. effect b. cause; 4. a. cause, b. effect; 5. a. effect, b. cause.)

3. *Part b.* (page 128) Before students continue work with the sentence completion, have them read the example in the Language Focus box at the top of page 128: *Farmers were able to grow more food because they used new farming methods.* Write this sentence on the board. Underline the two clauses: (1) *Farmers were able to grow more food* (2) *because they used new farming methods.* Ask, *Which part of the sentence states the cause?* (2); *Which part states the effect?* (1).

4. Have pairs complete the rest of the exercise.

(Suggested answers: 2. Food became cheaper because the harvests were larger each year. 3. People could send food to different parts of the world because new means of transportation were available. 4. Fewer people died of starvation because people could send food to areas without food. 5. Fewer people died because scientists discovered the causes of some diseases.)

Activity 7: Write

Have students work in groups of three. Give each group a copy of AM 4/11 and one pencil or have students copy the question and the three incomplete sentences on a piece of paper. Groups can first discuss what the three reasons are, and which one is the most important. If they have trouble giving reasons, suggest that they look back at the reading on page 125 for ideas. After students reach consensus, they can take turns passing the paper and pencil, and each can write a reason.

(Possible answers: The most important reason is that scientists discovered what caused some deadly diseases and infections. Another reason is that farming methods improved so more food was produced. Another reason is that transportation improved so food was transported to countries around the world.)

Activity 8: Share Ideas

1. *Part a.* Have students look again at the graph on page 124. Ask, *What do you think the world population is right now?* (Between 5 and 6 billion people.) Say, *Some people believe that the rapidly increasing population will cause many problems in the future. What problems might this increase in population cause?* Have students discuss this question in small groups. Prompt groups, if necessary, to think about people and their needs (food, air, water) and diminishing natural resources. Students can brainstorm ideas and write them on a list.

2. *Part b.* Have groups choose one problem from part a and discuss it further. Ask, *What can people do to solve this problem?* Circulate among the groups during discussions to assist less proficient students.

3. Have groups report their problem and their solution to the class.

b. Complete these sentences.

1. Farmers were able to grow more food because ______________________.
2. Food became cheaper because ______________________.
3. People could send food to different parts of the world because ______________________.
4. Fewer people died of starvation because ______________________.
5. Fewer people died because ______________________.

Language Focus:
Identifying Cause and Effect

Farmers were able to grow more food because they used new farming methods.

Language Focus:
Giving Reasons

- One reason is that ______ .
- Another reason is that ______ .
- The most important reason is that ______ .

7. Write

Groupwork. Take turns writing answers to this question:

Why has the earth's population grown rapidly in the past 150 years?

First student: The most important reason is that ______________________.

Second student: Another reason is that ______________________.

Third student: Another reason is that ______________________.

8. Share Ideas

Groupwork. Discuss these questions. Then report the results of your discussion to the class.

a. What problems might the increase in population cause?

b. Choose one of the problems from part a. Tell what people can do to solve this problem.

9. Make a Line Graph

a. Groupwork. Use the statistics below to make a line graph.

U.S Population, 1900–1990

Year	Total Population
1900	76,212,168
1910	92,228,496
1920	106,021,537
1930	123,202,624
1940	132,164,569
1950	151,325,798
1960	179,323,175
1970	203,302,031
1980	226,542,203
1990	248,709,873

b. Share your graph with the class.

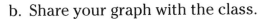

China has the highest population in the world with over 1.1 billion inhabitants (21% of the world's population)

10. Analyze

Groupwork. Use your line graph to answer these questions:

1. In which ten-year period did the population of the United States increase the least? Choose one answer.

   Between 1910 and 1920

   Between 1930 and 1940

   Between 1950 and 1960

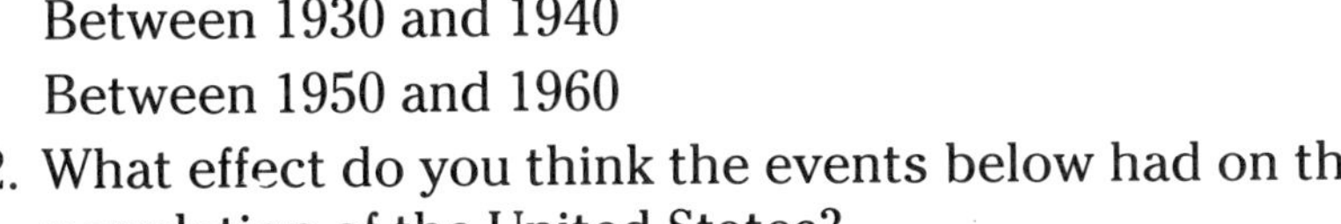

2. What effect do you think the events below had on the population of the United States?

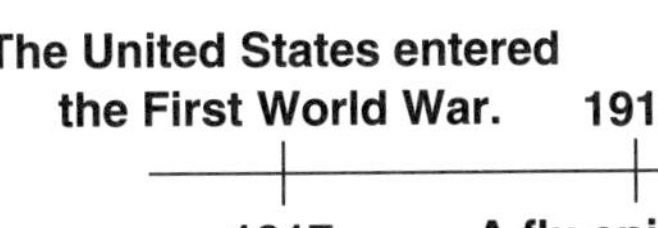

The United States entered the First World War.
1917
1918
A flu epidemic killed hundreds of thousands of people in the United States.
The United States entered the Second World War.
1941
1959
Alaska and Hawaii became part of the United States.

Activity 9: Make a Line Graph

1. *Part a.* Have students look again at the line graph on page 124. Point out (or review) the horizontal axis. Ask, *What information is given on the horizontal axis?* (years from 8000 B.C. to A.D. 2000) Ask, *What information is given on the vertical axis?* (billions of people, from 1 to 10 billion) Ask, *What does this graph show?* (change in the population of the earth) Then say, *You're going to make a similar graph to show change in the population of the United States from 1900 to 1990.*

2. Have students look at the statistics on page 129. Say, *These are the facts you will use to make your graph.* Put the students in groups and give each group a piece of graph paper or a copy of AM 4/12. Be sure students can correctly read the numbers: ask them to read several aloud. Ask, *What numbers will you put on your vertical axis?* Elicit that they will use millions from 75 to 250. Suggest they put a mark for every 10 million starting with 70 at the bottom. On the horizontal axis they will put the numbers 1900 to 1990, one mark for each ten years from left to right. Point out that the statistics are not in even ten millions. Ask, *Where will you graph 76,212,168?* Elicit that they will graph it between 70 and 80 million, but closer to 80 than to 70. Have groups work independently on their graphs. Circulate to help as needed.

3. *Part b.* Have groups post their graphs in the classroom and check to see if they are alike.

Activity 10: Analyze

Put students in their groups again. Have them read the instructions and work together to answer the questions.

(Answers: 1. 1930–1940. 2. 1917, decrease in population; 1918, decrease; 1941, decrease; 1959, increase.)

Begin with a demonstration. Place the desks or chairs of three students as far as possible from you and from the rest of the class. Be sure that it is clear that they are not part of the group. Ignore students' questions, and start the lesson. Read the title and the introduction aloud. Then ask students, *Is there something wrong here? What is different?* Students will answer that three students have been separated from the rest of the class. Ask, *Can I do that? Why not?* Elicit that all students have the right to learn and must be included. Invite the three back to the group and ask how they felt about being excluded. Write *segregation = separation* on the board. Explain to students that segregation of the three students was against their rights. They were treated differently from the other students, when everyone should have been treated equally. Now explore the meaning of *rights*. Can they give some examples of rights? (e.g., rights to life, freedom, happiness, equal education, employment, housing, etc.) Then ask, *What is the job of the government regarding people's rights?* (to protect them; to see that all people have these rights)

Activity 1: Think-Pair-Share

1. *Part a.* Read the instructions and the questions to students. If possible, share one of your own experiences of being treated unfairly. If they have difficulty thinking of an experience, prompt them by saying that this experience could have happened at home, at school, at work, on a sports team, etc.

2. *Part b.* Have students get into pairs and share their story with their partner. They should listen carefully because they will re-tell their partner's story.

3. *Part c.* Combine two pairs. Each student will tell his partner's story to another student.

Activity 2: Preview

1. *Part a.* Have students work in small groups for this activity. Explain that the pictures in a reading are important and help to explain meaning. Write the "Wh" question words on the board: *who,*

(Continued on page 131.)

Working for social and political change: Rosa Parks

All citizens in the United States have certain basic rights. If a law unfairly restricts these rights, people can challenge the law, or work to change it. Throughout the history of the United States, people have worked to gain and protect their rights. In this section, you will look at the way one group of people worked to change a law.

1. Think-Pair-Share

a. On your own. Think about a time when someone treated you unfairly.

- What did they do?
- How did you feel?
- What did you do?

b. Tell your story to a partner. Listen carefully to your partner's story.

c. Get together with another pair. Tell your partner's story.

2. Preview

a. Groupwork. Choose one of the photographs on pages 131–133. Write five questions about the photograph.

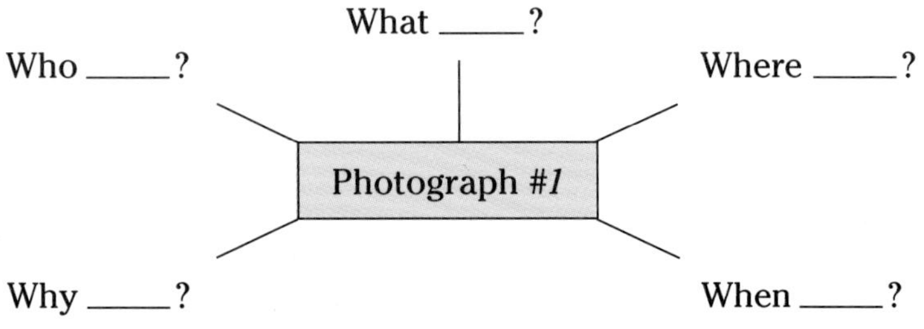

b. Share your questions with the class. Together, think of possible answers.

c. The passage on pages 131–133. is about a group of people who wanted to change a law. What law do you think they wanted to change? Use the pictures to make a prediction.

3. Shared Reading

Read or listen to find answers to your questions.

Taking Action for Change

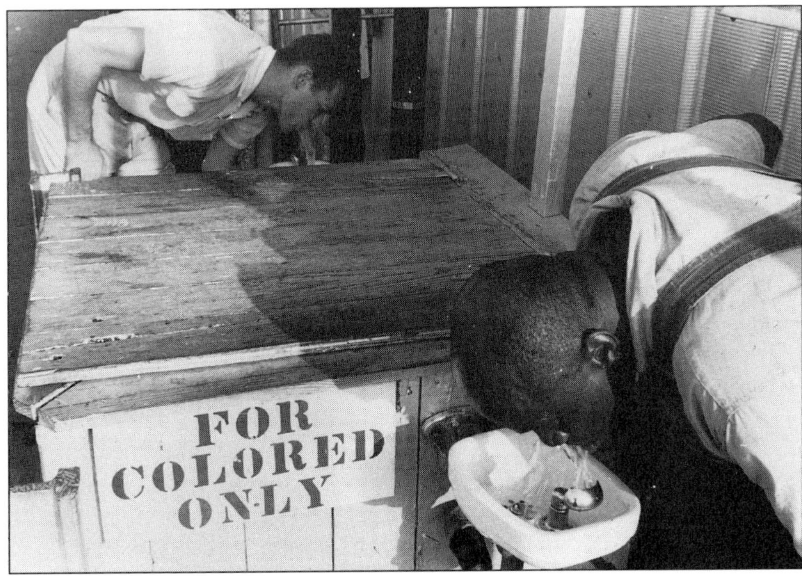

Before 1964, many places in the United States had laws that segregated, or separated, black and white Americans. These laws forced black Americans to use separate schools, restrooms, restaurants, and other public facilities. Usually, the facilities for black people were not as good as the facilities for white people.

Activity 2: Preview *(continued)*

what, when, where, why. Ask a volunteer to make a question about picture 1, using one of the question words. Write the question on the board as an example.

2. Groups will look at the three pictures and choose one. Ask them to write five questions about their photograph in a diagram like the one on page 131. Try to ensure that each of the three photographs is chosen by a group.

3. *Part b.* Have each group put their diagram and questions on the board or on a transparency. Have members of the group direct their questions to the class to elicit possible answers.

4. *Part c.* Read the instructions aloud. Ask students to look again at the pictures and answer the question in part c.

Activity 3: Shared Reading

1. Before having students read or listen to the tape, go through the selection to find vocabulary you think may be unfamiliar to your students. Write the words in context-rich sentences. Go over them together and have students determine the meaning from the context (e.g., The woman *refused* to stand up, and stayed in her seat.). (Exclude *segregated, challenged,* and *boycotted*—see Activity 6 on page 134.)

2. Have students read the selection silently. Then have them listen to the tape and write answers for their preview questions.

In some cities, black people had to sit in the back of public buses. When the white section in the front of the bus was full, black people had to give their seats to white people.

In 1955, Rosa Parks challenged the unfair bus law in Montgomery, Alabama. When a bus driver asked Rosa Parks to give her seat to a white person, she refused. The police arrested Rosa Parks and took her to jail. In her autobiography, Rosa Parks describes this event:

> One evening in early December 1955 I was sitting in the front seat of the colored section of a bus in Montgomery, Alabama. The white people were sitting in the white section. More white people got on, and they filled up all the seats in the white section. When that happened, we black people were supposed to give up our seats to the whites. But I didn't move. The white driver said, "Let me have those front seats." I didn't get up. I was tired of giving in to white people.
>
> "I'm going to have you arrested," the driver said.
>
> "You may do that," I answered.
>
> Two white policemen came. I asked one of them, "Why do you all push us around?"
>
> He answered, "I don't know, but the law is the law and you're under arrest."

In response to Rosa Parks's arrest, the black citizens of Montgomery, Alabama, decided to boycott the buses. For 381 days, they refused to ride the buses. Instead, they organized car pools or walked to work. By boycotting the buses, they hoped to force the city to change its unfair segregation laws. But the city refused to listen even though the bus company was losing a lot of money.

Thirteen months after the boycott began, the U.S. Supreme Court ruled that segregation in public transportation was unconstitutional. Black people could no longer be forced to sit in the back of buses or give their seats to white people. The day after the segregation laws were changed, Rosa Parks got on a bus and took a seat in the front. It had taken more than a year, but the black people of Montgomery had won a great victory.

Many people were inspired by Rosa Parks's courageous action. They decided to challenge the unfair segregation laws in restaurants, schools, and other public places. In case after case, the Supreme Court ruled that segregation was illegal. Then in 1964, Congress passed a law that forbade segregation in most public facilities. Passage of this law was an important step in protecting the rights of all U.S. citizens.

133

Activity 4: Share Ideas

Work with the class to answer the discussion/comprehension questions. Encourage everyone to participate by telling students to give their answer and then turn to another student and ask: *"What do you think?"* The other student should respond, *"I agree"* or *"I disagree."* More proficient students can give reasons for agreeing or disagreeing.

(Possible answers: a. Rosa felt angry and upset. b. Her actions got her arrested. c. The people in Montgomery decided to boycott the buses to show support for Rosa and agreement with her. Their goal was to force the city to change its unfair segregation laws. d. The bus boycott caused transportation problems for the citizens of Montgomery. It caused the bus company to lose a lot of money. e. Rosa Parks was a heroine because she can be admired for her bravery and strength. She was not afraid to stand up for her beliefs.)

Activity 5: Retell

Have students get into pairs. Each partner will retell Rosa Park's actions on December 1, 1955. Encourage pairs to give as much detail about the story as they can.

Activity 6: Define

1. *Part a.* Have students choose an answer from the italicized words above each statement. Ask them to write their answers on a piece of paper. Caution them not to write in the book. Students should do this part of the activity from memory.

2. *Part b.* Have students work with a partner and compare answers. They can write or underline the words in the context that helped them to choose their words.

3. Pairs can find these sentences in the reading selection and note the words the author used to express these ideas.

(Answers: 1. kept apart—segregated, 2. disagreed with—challenged, 3. stop using—boycott.)

(Continued on page 135.)

4. Share Ideas

Classwork. Share ideas about Rosa Parks. Here are some questions to think about:

a. How do you think Rosa Parks felt when the bus driver asked her to move?

b. What effect did Rosa Parks's action have?

c. Why do you think people in Montgomery decided to boycott the buses? What was their goal?

d. What problems do you think the bus boycott caused for the citizens of Montgomery? For the bus company?

e. A heroine is a woman who is admired for her bravery, strength, or goodness. Do you think Rosa Parks is a heroine? Why or why not?

5. Retell

Pairwork. In your own words, tell what Rosa Parks did on December 1, 1955.

6. Define

a. On your own. Choose a word or words to complete each sentence.

brought together/kept apart

1. Many places in the United States had laws that ________________, or separated, black and white Americans. These laws forced black Americans to use separate schools, restrooms, and other public facilities.

agreed with/disagreed with

2. Rosa Parks ______________ the unfair bus segregation laws. When a bus driver asked her to give her seat to a white person, she refused.

use/stop using

3. The black citizens of Montgomery decided to ___________ the public buses. For 381 days, they refused to ride the buses.

b. Pairwork. Compare sentences. Then answer these questions:

1. What words and ideas in the sentences helped you to choose a word?
2. Find the sentences above in the text on pages 131–133. What words did the writer use? Use context to guess the meaning of these words.

7. Analyze

Classwork. What effect did the actions below have? List your ideas.

CAUSE	EFFECT
Rosa Parks refused to give up her seat.	______________ ______________
The police arrested Rosa Parks.	______________ ______________
The Supreme Court declared that segregation on public buses was unconstitutional.	______________ ______________ ______________

Activity 7: Analyze

Ask students, *Which tells what happened, cause or effect?* (effect) *What does cause mean?* (to make something happen) Explain that events in the story of Rosa Parks had many different effects or results. Have a volunteer read the first cause: Rosa Parks refused to give up her seat. Ask, *What effects did this have on the driver, on the other passengers?* Have volunteers read the other two causes and elicit possible effects from the class.

(Possible answers: 1. The driver called the police; the other black passengers were probably surprised; the other white passengers were probably angry. 2. Black citizens wanted their rights; they boycotted the buses. 3. Black people no longer had to give their seats to white people; black people could sit anywhere they wanted on the buses; black people challenged other segregation laws.)

Activity 8: Shared Reading

Play the tape of the play and have students read as they listen. Then discuss the following questions: *What is the title of the play? What is a heroine? What does "unexpected" mean? Why do you think Rosa Parks was an unexpected heroine? Which story of Rosa Parks do you like better—the story or the play? Why?*

Classwork. Here's Rosa Parks's story in the form of a play. Listen and read along.

CAST

Narrator
Rosa Parks
First woman
Another bystander
Bus Driver
Passengers on bus (3)
First policeman
Second policeman
Mr. E. D. Nixon

The Unexpected Heroine

SCENE 1

NARRATOR: Some historical turning points start out uneventfully. Such is the story of Mrs. Rosa Parks.

FIRST WOMAN: (*approaching bus stop*) Hello, Rosa. How are you?

ROSA PARKS: All right. How are you?

FIRST WOMAN: Fine—just tired after a hard day's work.

ANOTHER BYSTANDER: I hope we can get a seat. It's a shame—the few seats they have for colored people on the bus.

ROSA PARKS: It sure is. Here comes the bus.

NARRATOR: The bus pulls up and the three women get on and pay their fares.

FIRST WOMAN: Just like I thought. There are not many seats left for us. Rosa, you take this one. I'll get one farther back.

ROSA PARKS: Thank you.

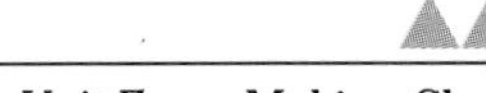

NARRATOR: Rosa Parks had just started to relax when the bus stopped again and several white passengers got on. Most of the new passengers found seats, but one man was left standing. The bus driver noticed that man and called to Rosa Parks and three other black people sitting beside her and across the aisle from her.

BUS DRIVER: Let me have those seats.

NARRATOR: At first, no one stood up. Then the bus driver spoke again.

BUS DRIVER: You all better make it light on yourselves and give me those seats.

NARRATOR: The other three people stand up, but Rosa Parks remains seated.

BUS DRIVER: (*to Rosa Parks*) Are you going to stand?

ROSA PARKS: No, sir, I'm not.

BUS DRIVER: If you don't stand up, I'll call the police and have you arrested.

ROSA PARKS: I understand.

NARRATOR: With that, the bus driver gets off the bus. Passengers begin whispering to each other.

FIRST PASSENGER: I wonder what's going to happen.

SECOND PASSENGER: I don't know.

FIRST PASSENGER: I'm not going to stay around to find out. I'm getting off this bus.

THIRD PASSENGER: Look, here comes the bus driver with two policemen.

FIRST PASSENGER: (*to Rosa Parks*) Did the driver ask you to stand?

137

ROSA PARKS: Yes, he did.

FIRST PASSENGER: Well, why didn't you stand?

ROSA PARKS: I don't think I should have to stand up. Why do you all push us around?

FIRST PASSENGER: I don't know, but the law's the law, and you're under arrest.

NARRATOR: Rosa Parks stands up when the policeman tells her that she is under arrest. They get off the bus and the two policemen walk her to the police car. One carries her purse; the other, her shopping bag.

SCENE 2

NARRATOR: At the police station, Rosa Parks calls Mr. E. D. Nixon, who is former president of the state and local NAACP.*

ROSA PARKS: Hello, Mr. Nixon. This is Rosa Parks. I'm calling to let you know that I've been arrested for refusing to give up my bus seat.

MR. E. D. NIXON: You are one brave woman, Mrs. Parks. I'll be right there to post bail. Then we'll see what we can do.

NARRATOR: Mrs. Parks was released from jail. Mr. Nixon called Rev. Ralph Abernathy and Rev. Martin Luther King, Jr., and the three started planning the famous bus boycott in Montgomery, Alabama. It was the beginning of the civil rights movement. Eventually, the buses in Montgomery were successfully desegrated.

*NAACP—The NAACP, or National Association for the Advancement of Colored People, was organized in 1910. This organization plays an important role in the modern civil rights movement. Using legal means, it works to gain equal rights for all Americans.

138

9. Reader's Theater

Work in groups. Act out *The Unexpected Heroine.*

10. Write

On your own. Follow these instructions to write about someone you admire:

a. List the names of people you admire. (These can be relatives, friends, or famous people.)

b. Choose one person on your list to write about. Think of words and phrases to describe this person.

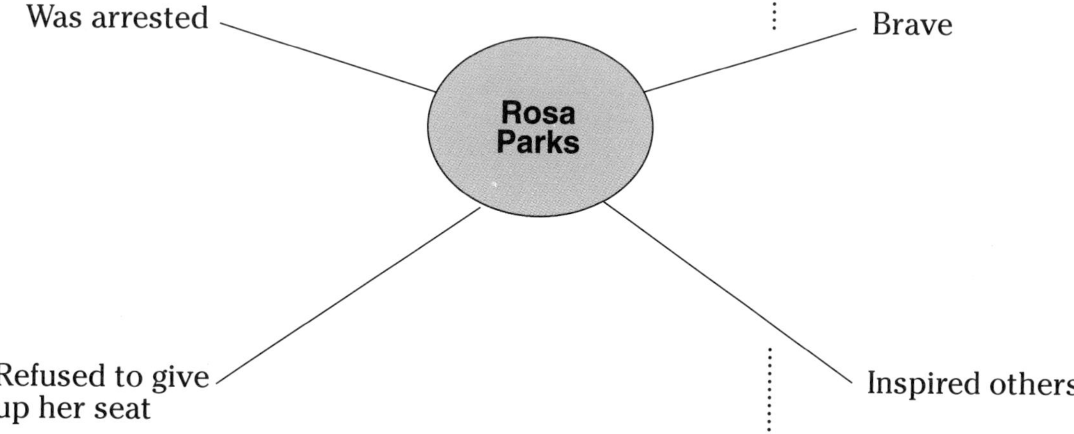

c. Use your ideas to write a "two-word" poem. Each line in your poem should have only two words. You can write many lines or just a few.

Example: *Rosa Parks*
brave woman
said, "No"
inspired many
to work
for change

d. Share your poem with the class.

Activity 9: Reader's Theater

Have students work in groups to dramatize the play. Tell them to use gestures and read with expression. Encourage them to use props (purse, shopping bag, telephone) and set the "stage" appropriately with chairs as bus seats, etc.

Activity 10: Write

1. *Part a.* Have students list the names of people they admire (friends, relatives, or famous people). Remind them that *admire* means to think highly of someone. As an example, think out loud and write your own list of people you admire on the board. As you list their names, mention qualities and achievements about them that you admire. Try to include some names that students recognize.

2. *Part b.* Tell students to choose one person on the list to write about. Have them study the cluster diagram of Rosa Parks in the text, and then do a cluster diagram for their person.

3. *Part c.* Read the instruction line and the two-word poem about Rosa Parks aloud. Have students write at least three lines; more proficient students can write longer poems.

4. *Part d.* Have students read their poems aloud to the class. Written poems with a photo or drawn picture of the subject can be displayed in the classroom.

Activity Menu

Read and explain the activities to the class. Then have students individually or in small groups select a project for a class or homework assignment. Projects can later be displayed in the classroom as they are shared with the class.

Activity Menu

Choose one of the following activities to do.

1. Guess the Year
Find photographs taken at different times in the past. Show your classmates the photographs and ask them to guess the year.

2. What's Changing?
Choose one place to observe at different times during the day (e.g., the school cafeteria, the street on which you live, the view from a window). Record your observations on a chart. In writing, tell how this place changed during the day. Share your writing with the class.

Time of Day	Observations

3. Take a Poll
What invention would you have a hard time living without? Ask ten to twenty students. Record their answers on a bar graph.

4. Who's the Inventor?
Choose an invention that interests you. Look for information to answer the questions in the chart on page 121. Present the results of your research to the class.

5. Illustrate
Choose a device—something that you use every day. Find out how this device works. Then illustrate this device to show your classmates how it works.

6. Compare Life in the Past with Today

List everything that you use in one day. This might include things like a radio, pencil, and toothbrush. Tell what you used each thing for. The next day, read over your list. Put an X next to the items that were NOT available 100 years ago. For each of these items, tell what you think people used 100 years ago.

7. What's in the Kitchen?

Draw a kitchen as it might look in 1800, 1920, 1992, or 2500. Show the latest inventions of the day.

8. How Fast Does It Grow?

Plant a morning glory seed (or some other fast-growing plant). Take a weekly measurement of its height, and record the data on a line graph. In writing, describe how the plant changed over time.

9. Research

Many people have worked for social and political change in the United States. The list below names just a few of these people. Look in the library for information about one of these people. What did this person try to change? Share your information with the class.

Frederick Douglass	Sojourner Truth
Harriet Tubman	William Lloyd Garrison
Lucretia Mott	Cesar Chavez

10. Learn about the Modern Civil Rights Movement

Collect information about other important events in the modern Civil Rights Movement. Use the information to make a timeline.

11. Is the Population of Your School Changing?

How many students are there in your school this year? How many were there each year for the past ten years? See if your school office has this information. Then make a line graph showing how the population of your school has changed over time. Suggest possible reasons for any changes in population. Then interview someone in your school office for an explanation.

141

Read on . . .

The Microscope

1. Read the poem aloud for the students. Then discuss the following questions: *What change did Anton Leeuwenhoek make in his life? What interesting things did he study under the microscope? What did the Dutch people think of him? Why?*

2. After the discussion, read the poem again for students to appreciate its meaning. Then have them read it aloud. Individual students or pairs can read lines or stanzas. Have students practice until their reading is fluent. Tape record their rendition and use it as a review on another day.

Read on . . .

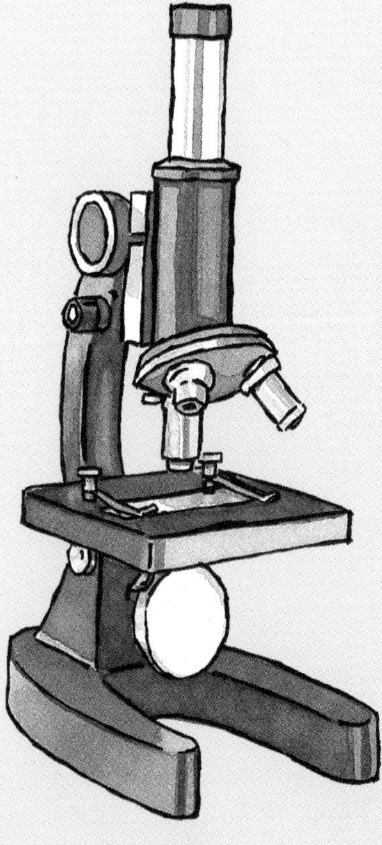

The Microscope

Anton Leeuwenhoek was Dutch.
He sold pincushions, cloth, and such.
The waiting townsfolk fumed and fussed
As Anton's dry goods gathered dust.

He worked, instead of tending store,
At grinding special lenses for
A microscope. Some of the things
He looked at were:
mosquitoes' wings
the hairs of sheep, the legs of lice,
the skin of people, dogs, and mice;
ox eyes, spiders' spinning gear,
fishes' scales, a little smear
of his own blood,
and best of all,
the unknown, busy, very small
bugs that swim and bump and hop
inside a simple water drop.

Impossible! Most Dutchmen said.
This Anton's crazy in the head.
We ought to ship him off to Spain.
He says he's seen a housefly's brain.
He says the water that we drink
Is full of bugs. He's mad, we think!

They called him *dumkopf*, which means dope.
That's how we got the microscope.

—*Maxine Kumin*

Change

The summer
still hangs
heavy and sweet
with sunlight
as it did last year.

The autumn
still comes
showering
gold and crimson
as it did last year.

The winter
still stings
clean and
cold and white
as it did last year.

The spring
still comes
like a whisper
in the dark night.

It is only I
who have changed.

—*Charlotte Zolotow*

Student text page 143

Change

1. Have students identify seasons by picture without looking at the text. Then read the poem to the class. Have students paraphrase each stanza and find important words that characterize each season. Ask, *Why does the poet say only she has changed?*

2. Have students in groups of 5 read the entire poem, 1 student per stanza. Have each group recite before the class.

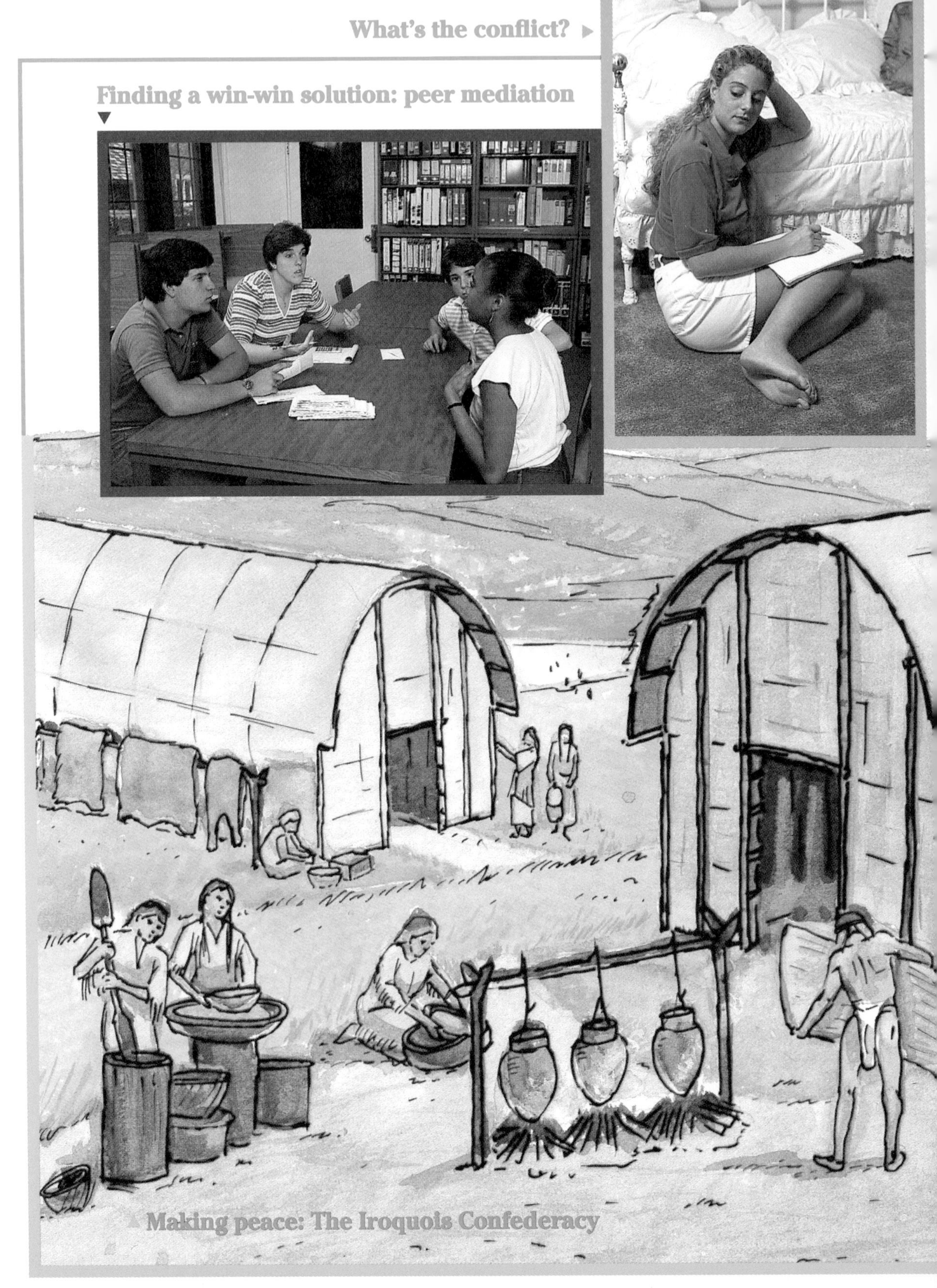
What's the conflict?
Finding a win-win solution: peer mediation
Making peace: The Iroquois Confederacy

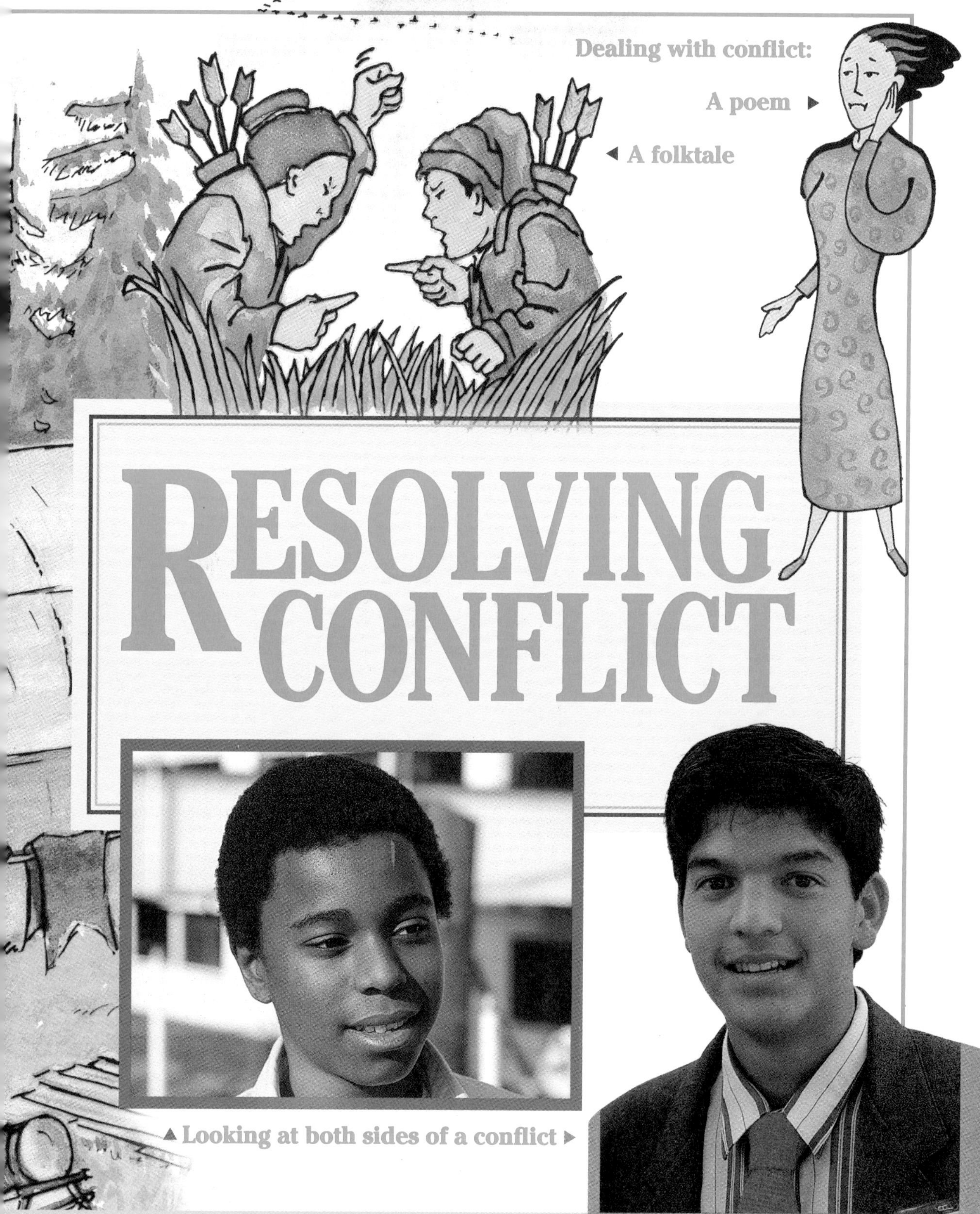
Dealing with conflict:
A poem
A folktale
RESOLVING CONFLICT
Looking at both sides of a conflict

A: I think it was a good movie.

B: I didn't like it at all. ▶

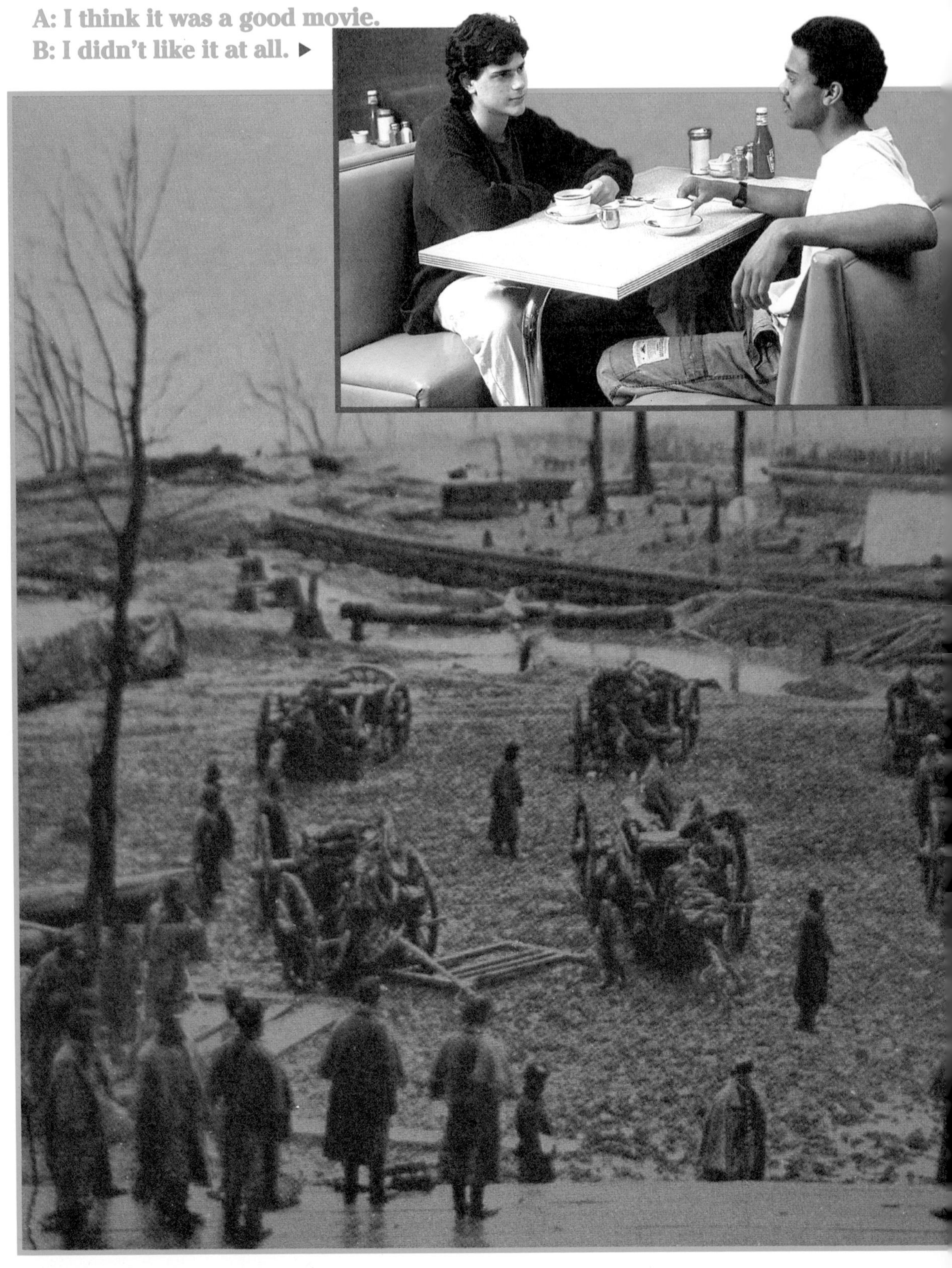

▲ The American Civil War lasted for four years. During this conflict, more than 600,000 people died.

What's the Conflict?

Write a Definition

a. Classwork. What is conflict? Study the pictures and captions and write a definition.

b. Look up the word *conflict* in a dictionary. Write the dictionary definition.

c. How is your definition similar to the dictionary? Different?

The soccer game is at three o'clock today and so is my music lesson. ▼

◂ A: I want you to babysit your brother this afternoon.

B: But I want ▸ to go out with my friends.

Activity 1: Write a Definition

1. *Part a.* Write the question *What is conflict?* on the board. Tell students to look at the pictures and captions on pages 146–147 as well as the unit opening pages as you brainstorm ideas. Write their ideas on the board. Then write two columns, *Class definition* and *Dictionary definition*. Write *Conflict is . . .* under each column.

2. Ask students to choose ideas from the list on the board to complete the statement *Conflict is. . . .* Then have a volunteer write the class definition in the appropriate column.

3. *Part b.* Have a volunteer look up *conflict* in the dictionary. Ask this student to write the definition under the *Dictionary definition* on the board.

4. *Part c.* Ask students how the two definitions are similar and different. Have a volunteer underline the similarities in the two definitions.

Activity 2: Listen

1. *Part a.* Pass out a copy of AM 5/1 to each student or have them copy the chart at the top of page 148. Tell students that they will listen to three conversations. In each one there is a conflict. As they listen, they will write both sides of the conflict. Play the tape or read the conversations in the tapescript.

(Answers: 1. One person wants to go outside. The other person doesn't. 2. One person thought the movie was great. The other person thought it was awful [bad]. 3. One person says it's his book. The other person says it's her book.)

2. *Part b.* Students should perceive the angry tone and the name-calling in the third conversation. In the first two dialogues, there were honest disagreements. Write the word *liar* on the board. Explain that this is an example of name-calling. Ask, *What does* liar *mean?* Elicit that it means someone who doesn't tell the truth. Ask, *Do you see any differences between the conflicts in the first two conversations and the conflict in the third conversation?* Elicit that the first two conversations are good, acceptable, appropriate forms of disagreement, while the third one is not.

Activity 3: Quickwrite

1. *Part a.* Ask students to read the Study Strategy box. If your students have not done quickwriting before, you may want to demonstrate the strategy for them. (See Teacher Notes, page 44.) Read the instructions and the four questions aloud. Give students time to think about an incident and then time them as they write for five minutes. Quickwrite along with them to stimulate their writing.

2. *Part b.* Have students share their ideas with a partner. If students do not write the quickwrite in a notebook that they always have for this class, collect their writing. It will be used for a comparison with a later quickwrite in this unit on page 165.

2. Listen

a. Classwork. Listen to the three dialogues and answer the question below.

Dialogue	What is the conflict?
1	One person wants to go outside. The other person ________.
2	One person ________. The other person ________.
3	One person ________. The other person ________.

b. Classwork. Listen to the dialogues again. How is the third dialogue different? Share ideas with your classmates.

Study Strategy:

Quickwriting

Quickwriting is a good way to explore ideas. When you quickwrite, try to write without stopping.

3. Quickwrite

a. On your own. Think about a time when you disagreed with someone. Quickwrite about this disagreement for five minutes. Here are some questions you might think about:

- Who did you disagree with?
- What was the disagreement about?
- What happened in the end?
- How did you feel in the end?

b. Share ideas from your quickwriting with a classmate.

Dealing with conflict: A folktale

People deal with conflict in different ways. In the folktale on page 153, two people have a disagreement. When you read the story, you will find out how they deal with conflict.

1. Analyze

Classwork. Study the cartoon and answer these questions:

a. What do the two donkeys want to do?
b. What problem do they have?
c. How do they solve the problem?

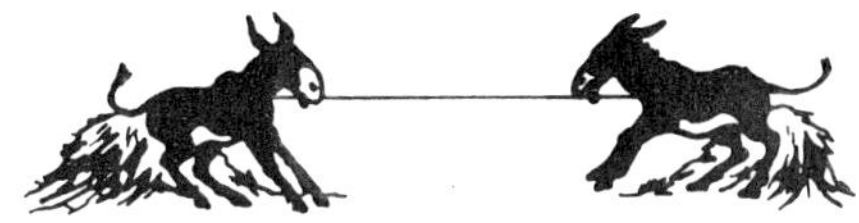

Activity 1: Analyze

Explain that the cartoon tells a story about two donkeys. Ask, *What do the two donkeys want to do?* (eat the straw or hay) *What problem do they have?* (They are tied together, but the rope doesn't let them eat from their own piles.) *What are things that they try?* (They pull away facing each other and pull apart with backs to each other—nothing works.) *How do they solve the problem?* (They work together; first they eat from one donkey's pile of hay and then from the other's.) Ask further, *How did the donkeys feel when they were fighting each other?* (angry) *When they were working together?* (happy).

Activity 2: Match

1. *Part a.* Ask, *What is the donkeys' conflict?* (They each want to eat from their own pile of hay.)

2. *Part b.* Tell students to recall the conversations from page 148, Activity 2. Say, *There are different ways to deal with conflict. Look at the diagram on page 150, and decide how the donkeys dealt with their conflict.* To help students understand the terms, ask about each in turn, *What does* postpone *mean?* get help? etc. To answer the question, students look at the pictures and read the captions. Ask, *What did the donkeys do?* (compromised).

3. *Part c.* Have students work in groups of four. Tell them they will first listen to four conversations. Then they will read them on page 151. Have them close their books and listen to the conversation.

4. Give a copy of AM 5/2 to each group, or have them copy the chart at the bottom of page 151. Have groups open their books to page 151, read the conversation, and follow the steps on page 150 (identify the conflict, etc.). Each person should take a turn being group discussion leader for one of the dialogues. He/she will then write the way in which the people dealt with the conflict on the chart on the activity master after the group has reached consensus.

5. Have each member of the group report the answers for the steps to the class.

2. Match

a. Classwork. Look again at the cartoon. What is the conflict?

b. How did the donkeys in the cartoon deal with the conflict? Choose one of the ways shown in the diagram below.

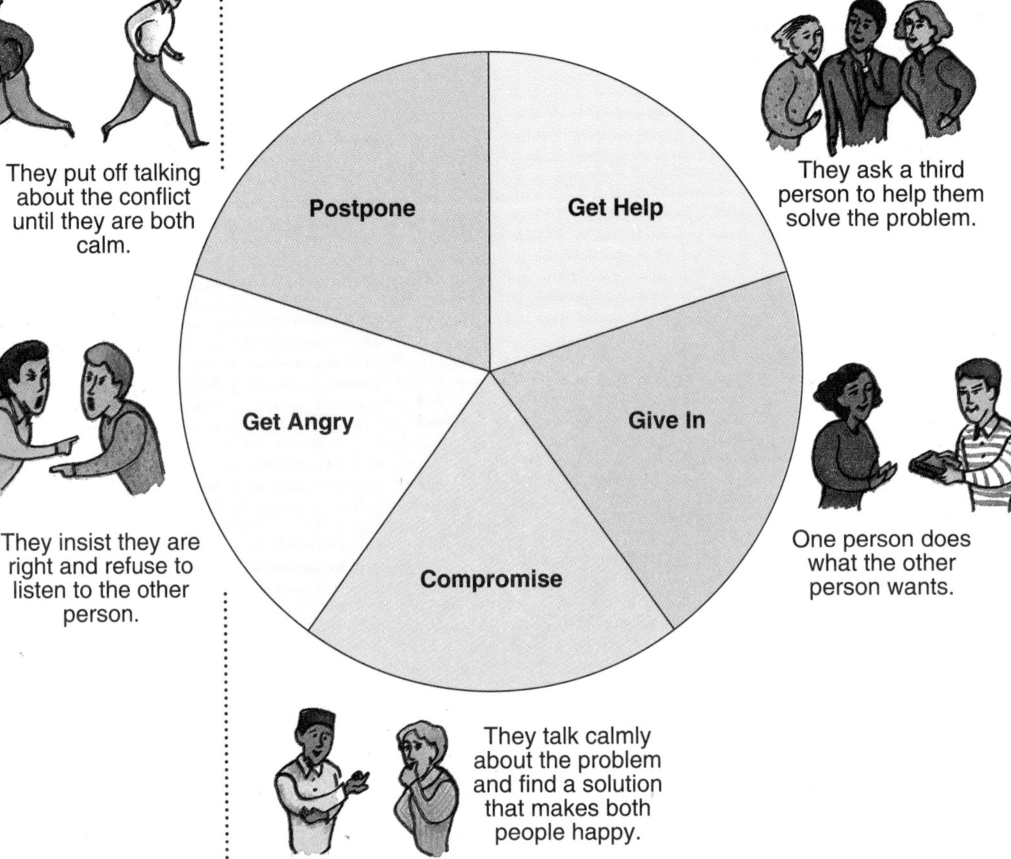

Postpone
They put off talking about the conflict until they are both calm.
Get Help
They ask a third person to help them solve the problem.
Give In
One person does what the other person wants.
Compromise
They talk calmly about the problem and find a solution that makes both people happy.
Get Angry
They insist they are right and refuse to listen to the other person.

c. Groupwork. Listen to the four dialogues on page 151. Then read them and follow these steps.

1. Identify the conflict.
2. Tell how the people deal with the conflict. (Use the diagram above for ideas.)
3. Share your ideas with the class.

Dialogue

1. A: Let's go somewhere.
   B: No, I don't want to.
   A: Why? Are you tired?
   B: Yeah.
   A: OK. Then let's stay here.

2. A: Can I read the story aloud?
   B: Well, I really wanted to.
   A: Then you read the first half and I'll read the second half.
   B: OK.

3. A: Why didn't you call me?
   B: I did call, but you weren't home.
   A: I don't believe you.
   B: It's true.
   A: OK. OK. I'm going to go for a walk. Let's talk about it later.

4. A: I think we should invite everyone to the party.
   B: We can't do that. That's too many people.
   A: So what?
   B: But we won't have enough food.
   A: Are you sure? Let's see what Julia thinks.

Dialogue	How do they deal with the conflict?
1	__________
2	__________
3	__________
4	__________

Activity 3: Predict

1. Read the instruction line aloud. Before students guess what the disagreement is about, have them study the pictures of food. Ask, *What does* stewed *mean?* (cooked in liquid like juice or sauce) *What does* roasted *mean?* (baked in an oven in dry heat).

2. Ask one student his or her prediction. Repeat and rephrase his or her answer to model making guesses from the Language Focus box (e.g., *Maybe they disagree about. . . .*).

Activity 4: Preview

1. Ask students, *What are information "Wh" question words?* As they name them, write them on the board: *who, what, where, when, why.* Have students get into small groups. Distribute a copy of AM 5/3 to each group or have them copy the chart at the bottom of page 152. Ask the class to look at the top picture on page 153 and the diagram on page 152. Have a volunteer read the sample question: *What is he pointing at?*

2. Tell groups to choose one of the three pictures and write five information questions about that picture. Assist less proficient students with this task.

3. *Part b.* Starting with groups that chose picture 1, have each group ask the class their questions. Classmates will study the pictures and guess possible answers.

3. Predict

Classwork. In the story *Stewed, Roasted, and Live?,* two people have a disagreement. Think about the title of the story. What do you think the disagreement is about?

***Stewed* and *roasted* are ways to cook food.**

Language Focus:
Making Guesses

- The disagreement might be about ________.
- Maybe they disagree about ________.

Stewed tomatoes *Roast chicken*

4. Preview

a. Groupwork. Choose one of the pictures on page 153. Write five questions about the picture.

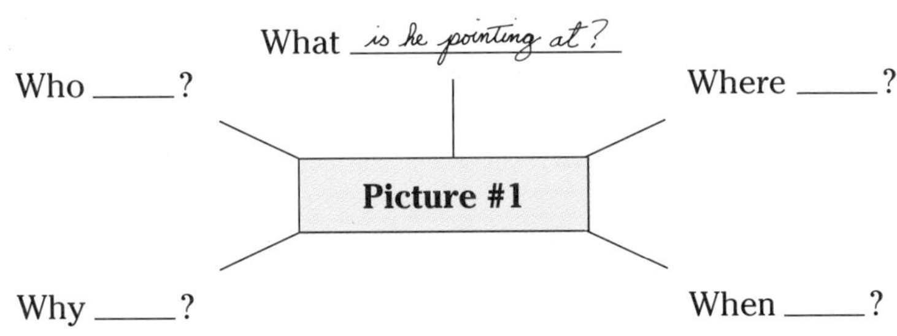

b. Share your group's questions with the class. Together, think of possible answers.

Study Strategy:
Using Pictures

Before you read, look at the pictures. Ask yourself questions about the pictures. This helps you get ready to read.

5. Shared Reading

Stewed, Roasted, or Live?
(A Chinese Folktale)

Two hunters were in the field all day. They were about to go home when they suddenly saw a flock of wild geese. Quick as a wink, they took out their bows and arrows and waited for the geese to fly overhead.

"They are very fat geese," said one hunter, licking his lips. "Think of it . . . stewed goose."

"Or roasted," said the other hunter. "I really like roasted goose."

"Stewed goose is better!"

"Oh, no. Roasted goose is better!" The first hunter looked angrily at his friend. His voice got louder. "Stewed!"

The second hunter looked angrily back at his friend. "ROASTED!" They glared at each other.

"Stewed!"

"Roasted!"

The two hunters stared angrily at each other for a long minute. Then they turned away and raised their bows to the sky once more.

But the geese were already far away.

Activity 5: Shared Reading

Have students use the pictures to understand important new vocabulary. Ask them to read the story silently. Play the tape and have them read a second time for extra practice.

Activity 6: Share Ideas

As a class, discuss the comprehension/discussion questions.

(Possible answers: a. Answers will vary. b. The hunters disagreed about how to cook the goose. c. They got angry. This was a bad way to deal with the conflict, because meanwhile the geese flew away. d. Anger never solves anything.)

Activity 7: Make a Story Map

1. *Part a.* Have students work in pairs. Ask a volunteer to read the Study Strategy box: Making a Story Map. On the board write the elements of the story: *title, characters, setting, problem, plot.* Before students look at the text or the activity master, ask, *What word tells what happened in the story?* (plot) *What does setting mean?* (where the story happened) *What are main characters?* (important people in the story) *What is a title?* (the name of the story) *What is another word for problem?* (conflict) Now pass out a copy of AM 5/4 to each pair or have them copy the story map at the bottom of page 154.

2. Tell pairs to complete the story map.

3. *Part b.* Have two pairs work together to compare their story maps and resolve any differences.

6. Share Ideas

Classwork. What's your reaction to the story? Discuss ideas with your classmates. Here are some other questions to think about:

a. Did you like this story? Why or why not?
b. What did the two hunters disagree about?
c. How did the two hunters deal with the conflict? Do you think this was a good way?
d. Folktales often try to teach something. What do you think this folktale is supposed to teach?

> ***Study Strategy:***
>
> ***Making a Story Map***
>
> Making a story map helps you understand a story.

7. Make a Story Map

a. Pairwork. Use information from the story to make a story map.

Stewed, Roasted, or Live?

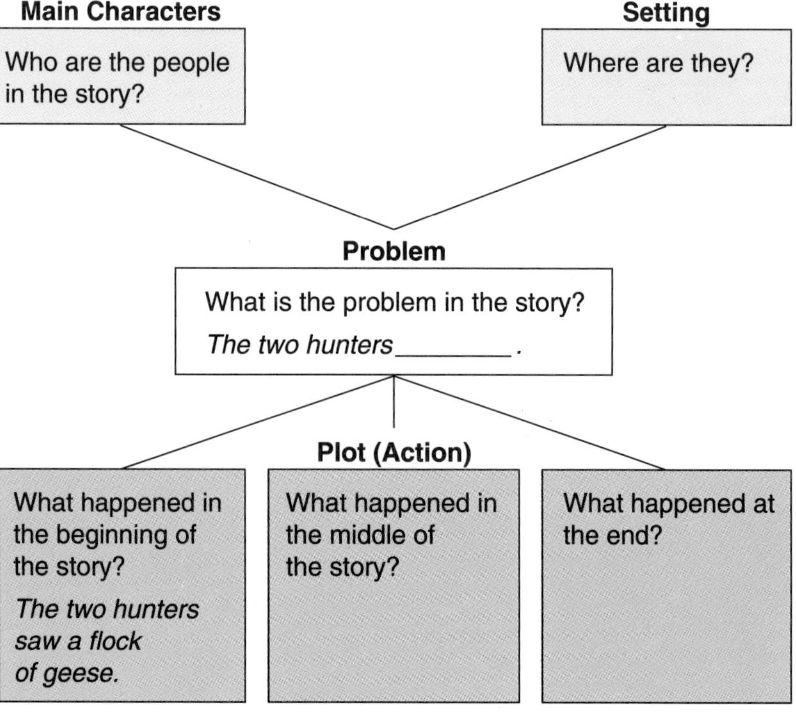

Main Characters
Who are the people in the story?
Setting
Where are they?
Problem
What is the problem in the story?
The two hunters ________.
Plot (Action)
What happened in the beginning of the story?
The two hunters saw a flock of geese.
What happened in the middle of the story?
What happened at the end?

b. Compare story maps with classmates.

8. Roleplay

Groupwork. Work in groups of three. Act out the story *Stewed, Roasted, or Live?*. Two people are the hunters in the story. One person is the narrator. Practice first. Then perform for the class.

9. Write

a. On your own. Choose one of these activities:

1. Imagine that you are one of the hunters. Write about what happened today. Tell how you feel about it.
2. Add to the story *Stewed, Roasted,* or *Live?*. Tell what the hunters did next.

  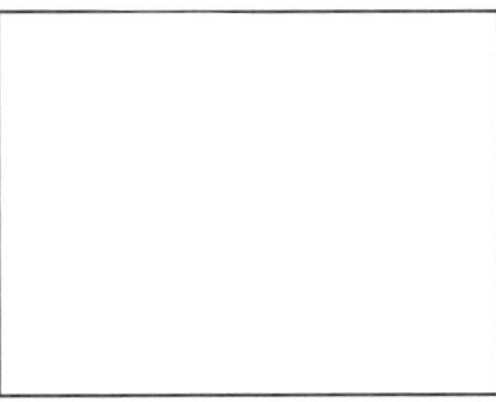

b. Share your writing with the class.

10. Write

a. Pairwork. Choose one of these ways of dealing with conflict:

compromise give in postpone

Write a new dialogue for the story. Show how the two hunters deal with the conflict in a different way.

New Dialogue

A: They are very fat geese.
Think of it . . . stewed goose.

B: ______________________________

A: ______________________________

b. Share your dialogue with the class.

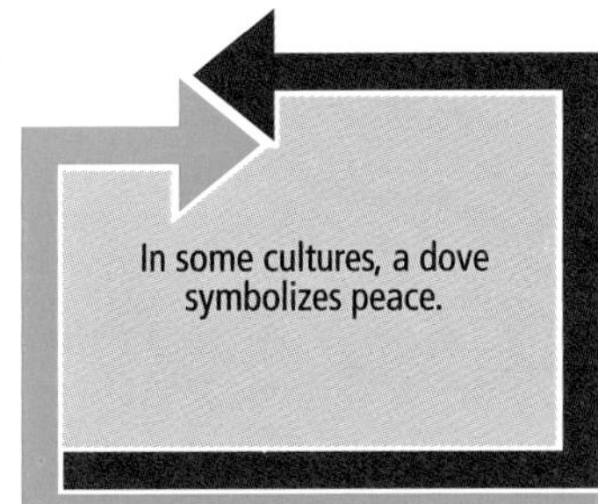

In some cultures, a dove symbolizes peace.

Activity 8: Roleplay

Have students work in groups of three for role-playing. Students will choose their own parts. Ask them to practice reading their parts with expressions and gestures. Have each group perform for the class.

Activity 9: Write

1. *Parts a and b.* Read the writing choices aloud. Tell students to do only one of the assignments. Encourage students to make a cluster diagram or list of words and ideas as a pre-writing activity. Draw the design of the cluster diagram on the board so students recall the format (see page 33). Allow them enough time to think of their story and to develop it adequately. Circulate during this activity to prompt less proficient students.

2. Have students read their stories to the class.

3. As an alternate activity, provide students with newsprint and color markers. Have them write and illustrate their story. Post their writing in the classroom and allow time for them to read classmates' writing.

Activity 10: Write

1. *Part a.* Review terms with students. Ask, *What does* compromise *mean?* give in? postpone? Put students in pairs. For this activity you may want to pair a less proficient with a more proficient student.

2. Have students note the format for a dialogue. They should begin with the line: *"They are very fat geese. Think of it . . . stewed goose."* Tell students to write, on a piece of paper, several exchanges (lines) between the two hunters. Their dialogue will show a new solution—compromising, giving in, or postponing.

3. *Part b.* Have pairs roleplay their dialogues for the class. After each pair performance, the class must guess the means of conflict resolution—compromising, giving in, or postponing.

4. Read the culture note about the dove. Ask a volunteer to draw a dove on the board. Ask students: *Does the dove mean peace in your first culture?*

Activity 1: Identify

1. Draw the cluster diagram on page 156 on the board. Read the instructions aloud. Ask, *What does "miserable" mean?* (very unhappy) Ask, *What might a friend do to make you feel miserable?* Write students' responses on the board. Ask, *If a friend called you a name, how would you feel?* (Be sure students understand that "call someone a name" means to call that person a bad name.) Elicit that it would make students unhappy or miserable. Write *call me a name* on the cluster diagram on the board in the same place it is on the cluster diagram in the book. Say, *If someone called me a name I would feel unhappy.* Give another example, such as, *If a friend said "I hate you," I would feel miserable.*

2. Elicit other examples of words and actions that make students unhappy. Encourage them to use the structure in the Language Focus box. As students share these ideas, add them to the cluster diagram on the board.

Activity 2: Shared Reading

1. Tell students that they are going to read a poem about feeling miserable. Point out that the word *misery* means *a miserable feeling.* Model the poem for the class. Then have students read it, first silently, then aloud in various ways, e.g., all together; boys first stanza, girls second; one stanza loud, the other soft.

Dealing with conflict: A poem

Language Focus:

Relating Cause and Effect

- If a friend called me a name, I would feel unhappy.
- If a friend ______, I would feel miserable.

When people get angry, they sometimes say things that hurt other people. That's what the poem in this section is about.

1. Identify

Classwork. Read the title of the poem below. What might a friend do or say that would make you feel miserable, or very unhappy? Share ideas with your classmates.

a friend's action — things that would make me feel miserable — a friend's words

calls me a name

2. Shared Reading

Read this poem aloud several times.

Misery

Misery is when your
very best friend
calls you a name she really
didn't mean to call you at all.

Misery is when you call
your very best friend a name
you didn't mean to call her, either.

—*Langston Hughes*

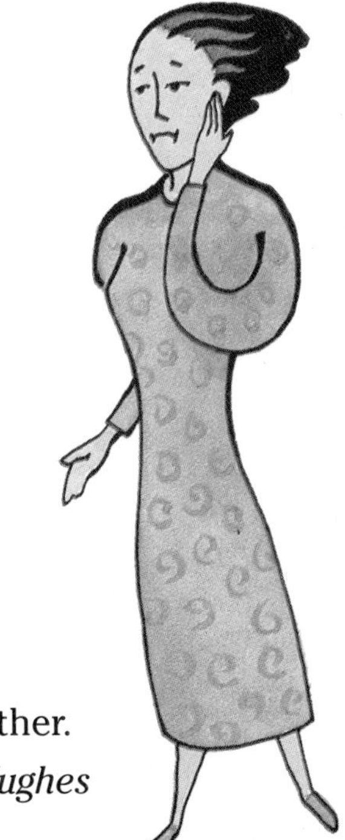

3. Share Ideas

Classwork. Share ideas about the poem with your classmates. Here are some questions that you might think about.

a. What is "misery" to the poet? Do you agree or disagree?

b. Why do you think a friend might call you a name?

c. How would you feel if someone called you a name? What would you do?

d. Do you think name-calling is a good way to deal with conflict? Why or why not?

4. Write

a. Groupwork. Choose an idea from your cluster diagram in Activity 1. Use this idea to write a poem.

Misery is when ________________________
____
____
____
________________________________.

Misery is when you ______________________
____
____
____
________________________________.

b. Read your poem to the class.

Activity 3: Share Ideas

1. Discuss the poem with the class. They talked earlier about how they would feel if someone called them a bad name. Point out that the poem goes further than this. Ask, *What new elements does it add?* (It's your best friend who calls you a name; your best friend didn't mean it; you feel equally bad when you call your best friend a name and don't mean it.)

2. Discuss the questions about the poem as a class. Opinions will vary. To encourage participation by the entire class, have everyone stand up. After a student voices an opinion about one of the questions, he or she may sit down. Add other questions, for example, *Why do people say things they don't really mean? What can they do about it? Why do they feel just as bad when they hurt someone as they do when someone hurts them?* Ask if anyone in the class has ever been in this situation. How did it feel? What did they do?

Activity 4: Write

1. *Part a.* Put students in small groups. Have them look again at the poem on page 156 and note how Hughes focuses on one idea. Groups can parallel "Misery" by using one idea from the cluster diagram on the board. Distribute paper to each group (caution them not write in the book) and have group members work cooperatively to choose an idea and write their poem.

2. *Part b.* Have the groups share their poems with the class.

Ask students: *What do you think the title means? What is a win-win solution?* Elicit student opinions and then read the introduction aloud.

Activity 1: Identify

1. *Part a.* Tell students: *You will listen to two conflicts between students. Just as you are going to work together now, Shawn and Leila and Marta and Yan are supposed to work together. Read the questions on page 159 before you listen to the tape.*

2. Play the tape or read the stories to the students.

3. Have students work together in groups of three. Pass out one pencil and one copy of AM 5/5 to each group or have students copy the chart on page 160. Suggest that each student in the group ask one of the questions and record the group's answers for Shawn and Leila and Marta and Yan. That student then passes the paper and pencil to the next member, and so on. Students can read the stories again as they look for answers.

4. Have each group report one or two answers to the class. If other groups disagree, ask them to challenge the other group's information.

(Suggested answers: *Shawn and Leila.* Conflict: Shawn wants to write about Rosa Parks, but Leila doesn't. How to deal? They compromise. Solution: They choose another person they both admire. *Marta and Yan.* Conflict: Yan wants them to do interviews together, but Marta can't. How to deal? Yan gets angry, won't listen to Marta's explanation. Solution: They don't work together at all.)

5. *Part b.* Ask, *Which of these solutions is a win-win solution?* (Shawn and Leila's) *Why?* (It's a compromise—both are satisfied).

Finding a win-win solution

The best way to resolve a conflict is to find a solution that makes everyone happy. That's a win-win solution. In this section, you will read about some strategies for finding a win-win solution.

1. Identify

a. Groupwork. Read or listen to these stories and answer the questions in the chart.

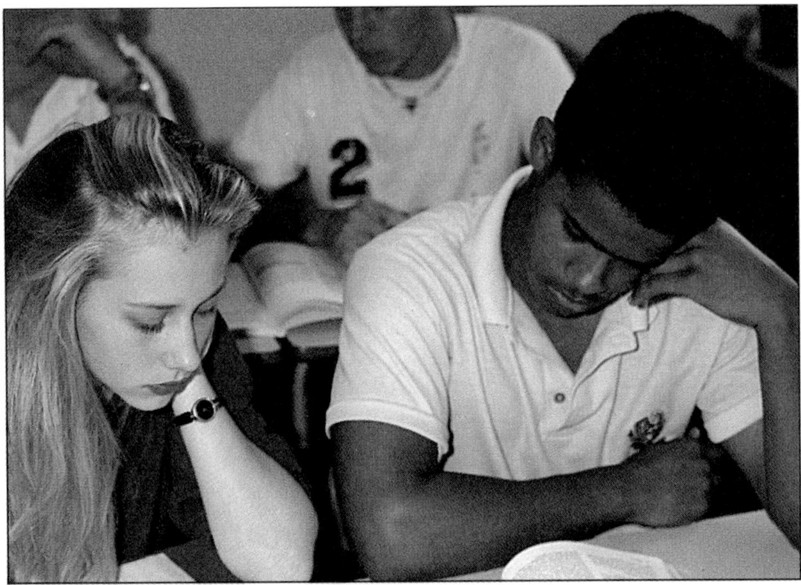

1. Shawn and Leila are working together on a class project. They have to write a report about a famous person in history. Shawn wants to write about Rosa Parks because he's interested in the Civil Rights Movement. Leila has already read a lot about Rosa Parks, and she wants to write about someone different. After talking about it, they decide to write about Martin Luther King, Jr., a leader in the Civil Rights Movement.

2. Marta and Yan have to interview people outside school and then make a report to the class. Yan suggests that they do the interviews together after school, but Marta says she can't. Yan gets angry because he doesn't want to do all the work. He tells Marta that she is lazy. Marta tries to tell Yan that she can't do the interviews because she has to babysit after school. But Yan refuses to listen. He says he'll do the work himself, and then he walks away.

	Shawn and Leila	Marta and Yan
What is the conflict?		
How do they deal with the conflict?		
What solution do they reach?		

b. Classwork. A win-win solution allows both people to feel good. Which of the solutions above is a win-win solution? Why?

2. Analyze

Classwork. Read the title of the article on page 160 and study the picture. What do you think the students in the picture are discussing? Share ideas with your classmates.

Activity 2: Analyze

Read the instructions aloud. Ask students to look at the people, their expressions and gestures. Ask, *What are these students doing?* (resolving a conflict).

Activity 3: Shared Reading

1. Introduce unfamiliar vocabulary *(fistfight, disputants, peer mediators, training, maintain, put someone down).* You may want to list these terms on the board with simple definitions.

2. Play the tape or read the selection to the class.

3. Read the information about conflict resolution in the right margin of page 161. Have students find out and report back if there is a conflict resolution or peer mediation committee in their school. If not, should there be? Discuss.

Finding a Win-Win Solution

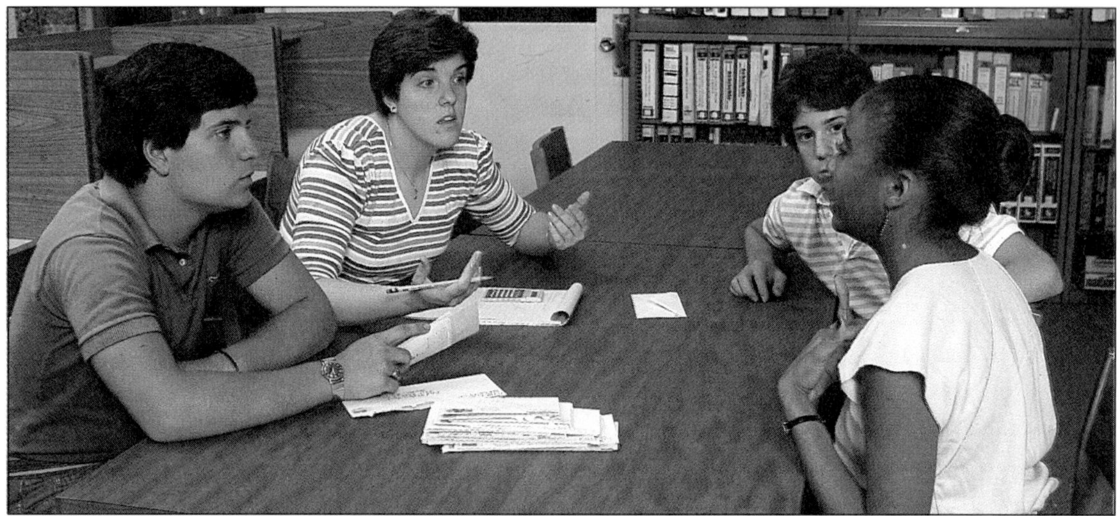

Two students started arguing at school. One student called the other one a name, and a fistfight began.

What can be done to prevent fights like this at school? In some schools, the disputants (the two students with a disagreement) sit down with peer mediators. Peer mediators are students with special training in conflict resolution.

Peer mediators help the disputants to communicate peacefully. Here are some of the communication strategies they use:

1. State your own feelings clearly but don't be accusatory. Begin with "I feel . . ." instead of "You always . . ."
2. Don't interrupt or finish another person's sentences.
3. Listen carefully to what the other person is saying. Try to see the other person's side of the disagreement.
4. Maintain eye contact with the other person.
5. Ask questions to make sure that you understand the other person.

6. Repeat the other person's ideas as you understand them.
7. Never put anyone down. Saying things like "You're stupid" makes communication difficult.
8. Try to find a solution that makes both people happy.

Peer mediators never judge the disputants. They don't decide who is right and who is wrong. Instead, they help the two students to find their own "win-win" solution. A "win-win" solution allows everyone to feel good.

Peer mediation often succeeds simply because it gets people to talk to each other. And getting people to communicate is the first step in finding a win-win solution.

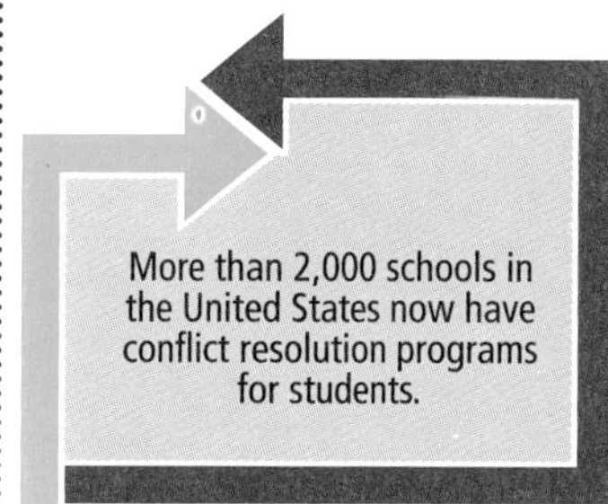

More than 2,000 schools in the United States now have conflict resolution programs for students.

4. Identify

a. On your own. Decide if these sentences are true or false.

	True	False
1. Peer mediators are usually teachers.	____	____
2. Disputants are people with a disagreement.	____	____
3. "I feel angry" is an example of an accusation.	____	____
3. "You're lazy" is an example of a put-down.	____	____
3. Peer mediators find a"win-win" solution for the disputants.	____	____
4. The disputants decide who is right and who is wrong.	____	____
5. Peer mediators help other people to communicate clearly.	____	____

b. Compare ideas with a partner. Show where you found the information in the reading.

c. Report your *True* answers to the class. Rewrite the false statements to make them true.

Language Focus:

Agreeing

- It's true that disputants are people with a disagreement.
- It's true that ________________.

Activity 4: Identify

1. *Part a.* Have students do the true-false sentences individually on AM 5/6, or have them number their paper 1 to 7 and write *true* or *false* next to each number. If they don't remember an answer, they can look back at the reading.

2. *Part b.* Have pairs compare their answers. Let them take turns pointing out where the answers can be found in the reading. Ask them to follow the example in the Language Focus box for agreeing: *It's true that. . . .*

3. *Part c.* Ask volunteers to read the true statements. After students rewrite the false statements on AM 5/6 or on their paper to make them true, have volunteers read them to the class.

(Answers for corrected false statements: Peer mediators are students. "I feel angry" is an example of stating feelings.)

Activity 5: Share Ideas

1. Discuss the comprehension/discussion questions as a class. Encourage students to voice an opinion. (Answers will vary.)

Activity 6: Evaluate

1. *Part a.* Play the tape or read the dialogue to the students. Ask volunteers to read the parts for Leila and Shawn. A third student can act as narrator.

2. *Part b.* Students should recall that the communication strategies listed on the chart for this activity were first presented in Activity 3—Shared Reading. Now they will evaluate a situation to determine if these strategies were used. Have students get into pairs. Pass out a copy of AM 5/7 to each pair or have them copy the chart on page 163.

3. Have pairs read each strategy and put a check in the appropriate column if it is used by Shawn and/or Leila.

4. Ask each pair to join another pair to check their charts and find the strategies in the dialogue.

5. Share Ideas

Classwork. Share ideas about the reading with your classmates. Here are some questions you might think about:

a. Do you think peer mediation is a good way to resolve conflict at school? Why or why not?
b. Would it be easier to discuss your feelings with a peer or with a teacher? Why?
c. Do you think it is difficult to be a peer mediator? Why or why not?
d. Why is it important to understand the other person's side of the conflict?
e. Why is it a good idea to find a win-win solution to a conflict?

6. Evaluate

a. Pairwork. Listen to this dialogue. Then read it aloud.

Shawn and Leila have to write a report about a famous person in history. Here's what happens when they try to choose a person to write about:

Shawn: Why don't we write about Rosa Parks?
Leila: Can't we write about someone else?
Shawn: Why?
Leila: I've already read a lot about Rosa Parks. I'd like to learn about someone different.
Shawn: But I'm really interested in the Civil Rights Movement.
Leila: So you want to write about the Civil Rights Movement?
Shawn: Yeah.
Leila: Well, could we write about someone else in the Civil Rights Movement?

Shawn: I suppose so. Like who?

Leila: What about Martin Luther King, Jr., or Ralph Abernathy?

Shawn: OK. Sounds good to me.

b. Pairwork. Tell which communication strategies Shawn and Leila use.

Communication Strategies	Shawn	Leila
States his or her feelings.		
Doesn't interrupt.		
Listens carefully.		
Tries to see the other person's side.		
Asks questions.		
Repeats the other person's ideas.		
Doesn't put the other person down.		
Tries to find a win-win solution.		

7. Apply

a. Pairwork. Listen to this dialogue. Then read it aloud and answer the questions on page 164.

Yan and Marta have to do a school project together. For this project, they have to interview people outside school. Here's what happens when they discuss the project:

Yan: Let's do the interviews today.

Marta: I can't, Yan.

Yan: Come on. We have to get the information.

Marta: I know but I . . .

Yan: You know, Marta, you never want to help. You're lazy.

Marta: That's not true. You don't understand. I . . .

Yan: I do understand. I understand that I have to do all the work.

Activity 7: Apply

1. *Part a.* Play the tape or read the dialogue. Then have volunteers read the parts of Yan, Marta, and the narrator.

2. Ask pairs to read the questions at the top of page 164 so that they better understand the conflict. Then they can write short answers on their own paper.

(Continued on page 164.)

Activity 7: Apply *(continued)*

3. *Part b.* Ask groups to rewrite the dialogue to have Marta and Yan follow the strategies listed on page 163. As they write, circulate among the pairs to check their answers for part a and assist less proficient students with the task.

(Answers for part a: 1. Yan, 2. Yan, 3. Yan—He said that Marta was lazy.)

4. *Part c.* Have each pair roleplay their dialogue for the class. As an extra challenge, classmates can evaluate each pair's dialogue to see if it includes the communication strategies listed on page 163.

Activity 8: Self-evaluate

1. Pass out copies of the evaluation chart on AM 5/8 or have students copy the chart on page 164. Say, *You have read about a number of strategies to use when you disagree with someone. Think about yourself. Which strategies do you use? Put a check mark in the appropriate column for each strategy on the chart. Think carefully before you fill out your chart. Do you really use a particular strategy "always" or "never"? Be honest with yourself—this chart is for you to keep, not for others to look at.*

2. You may want to have students tape their completed charts in their notebook for this course. It could serve as a reminder to work toward better communication and conflict resolution. Suggest that they look at it from time to time to remind themselves of these important strategies and to reevaluate themselves in terms of them.

3. As an extension activity, if your school has a peer mediation program, invite a member to speak to the class. Ask the mediator to share information about his/her training and experience. Encourage the class to ask questions about the program.

1. Who was accusatory? ______________
2. Who interrupted the other person? ______________
3. Who put down the other person? ______________
   How? ______________________________

b. Pairwork. Rewrite the dialogue. Make sure Yan and Marta follow the communication strategies on page 163.

c. Read your dialogue to the class.

8. Self-evaluate

On your own. What strategies do you use when you disagree with someone? Complete an evaluation chart.

	Always	Usually	Sometimes	Never
I state my feelings clearly.				
I avoid accusing the other person.				
I avoid interrupting the other person.				
I look at the other person.				
I ask questions to make sure I understand the other person.				
I repeat the other person's ideas.				
I avoid putting down the other person.				
I try to find a win-win solution.				

Looking at both sides of a conflict

It's impossible to find a win-win solution to a conflict if you don't know what the other person is thinking and feeling. In this section, you will find out how two people think and feel about a conflict.

1. Quickwrite

a. On your own. Look back at your quickwriting from page 148. Write about the disagreement again, but this time write from the other person's point of view.
b. What was easy or difficult about this assignment? Share ideas with your classmates.

2. Shared Reading

Pairwork. Choose one of the conflict situations from pages 165–166. Read or listen to both sides of the story.

Two Sides of a Conflict

Laurie's side of the story:
There's a guy in my class who can't pronounce my last name. No one else has trouble saying it, but he gets it wrong every time. I think he says it wrong on purpose. I try to laugh about it, but it really makes me angry.

Mario's side of the story:
There's a new student at school. She has a real long last name, and I can't pronounce it correctly. I feel stupid because every time I say her name, I get it wrong. She laughs when I say it wrong, so I guess it doesn't matter.

Activity 1: Quickwrite

1. *Part a.* Have students read their quickwrite from page 148. They should recall the incident in which they disagreed with someone. Give students five minutes to write the other person's side of the argument.

2. *Part b.* Some students may have found this quickwrite easy, while others may have found it difficult. Ask students what was easy and what was difficult about this activity.

Activity 2: Shared Reading

1. Have students work in pairs for this activity. First have them choose one situation, either Laurie and Mario's or Rigoberto and Don's. Divide the class according to the situation chosen. On one side of the room have students listen to Mario and Laurie's taped dialogue. On the other side of the room, pairs listen to Rigoberto and Don's taped dialogue.

2. Then have pairs read their situation in the text. Encourage them to read carefully so they will remember the details of each person's point of view.

Activity 3: Report

1. *Part a.* Have each partner take one person's side. Partners will take turns telling each other their character's point of view, one part at a time.

2. *Part b.* Have one pair for Mario and Laurie's situation get together with a pair for Rigoberto and Don's situation. Each pair will report both sides of their story to the new pair.

Activity 4: Write

1. *Part a.* Have pairs write dialogues for their disputants. Each partner will write the lines for the disputant he/she knows best. Encourage them to look at the list of strategies on page 166 to see if they are including the steps for successful conflict resolution.

2. *Part b.* Pass out a copy of AM 5/9 to each pair or have them copy the chart at the bottom of page 166. Have each pair get together with the same pair from Activity 3. As partners read their dialogues, the other pair will listen and put a check by the communication strategies that the disputants follow.

Rigoberto's side of the story:
I don't understand my friends Don and Mark. I've been eating lunch with them at school for two years. Now my friend Carl wants to eat with us, but Don and Mark don't want him to. Carl is not like everybody else—he has learning problems. But he's on the soccer team with me, and he's my friend. Why can't Don and Mark accept him, too? Now I'm afraid Carl and I won't have anyone to eat with.

Don's side of the story:
What is Rigoberto trying to do? We have this nice group of guys who always eat together. Why does Rigoberto have to invite Carl to eat with us? Carl makes us feel uncomfortable, and some kids are always making fun of him. They'll probably make fun of us now.

3. Report

a. Pairwork. Retell each person's side of the story. Take turns reporting an idea.
b. Get together with another pair. Tell them both sides of the story. Listen to their story.

Language Focus:
Reporting Someone's Ideas

- Laurie says that a guy in her class can't pronounce her name.
- She says that he gets it wrong every time.

4. Write

a. Pairwork. Write a dialogue in which the two people try to find a win-win solution to the conflict.
b. Get together with another pair. Listen to their dialogue. Identify their communication strategies.

	Laurie	*Mario*
States his or her feelings.		
Doesn't interrupt.		
Listens carefully.		
Tries to see the other person's side.		
Asks questions.		
Repeats the other person's ideas.		
Doesn't put the other person down.		
Tries to find a win-win solution.		

A plan for peace

For many years, the Iroquois people fought among themselves. But in the 1400s, a remarkable plan for peace ended the fighting. In this section, you will read about the Iroquois plan for peace.

1. Define

Groupwork. Complete the sentences below:

Examples: *Peace is a lion and a lamb living together!*
Peace is the world without war.

Peace is ______________________________.

Peace is ______________________________.

Peace is ______________________________.

2. Make a K-W-L Chart

Classwork. Use the pictures and captions on pages 168–169 to make a K-W-L chart.

Answers these questions before you read the story.

Answer this question after you read the story.

Know	Want to Know	Learned
What do you know about the Iroquois people from the pictures?	What do you want to find out?	What did you learn?

Study Strategy:

Making a K-W-L Chart

Making a K-W-L chart is a good way to get ready to read.

Student text page 167

Tell the class that conflict and conflict resolution occur among all people and in all cultures and societies. They are going to learn about the Iroquois, a very old culture in America, and the Iroquois plan for peace. Read the title and the introduction aloud.

Activity 1: Define

1. Have students work in groups of three. Ask a volunteer to read the examples of definitions of peace: *Peace is a lion and a lamb living together! Peace is a world without war.* Encourage students to be creative as each person in the group comes up with a different definition of *peace.*

2. Have groups share their definitions with the class.

Activity 2: Make a K-W-L Chart

1. Begin by giving the rationale for the activity and read the Study Strategy box aloud: *Making a K-W-L Chart is a good way to get ready to read.* Tell students to study the pictures and read the captions on pages 168–169 to see what they already know about the Iroquois. Put the K-W-L Chart on the board or on a transparency. Elicit some information for the K column (e.g., *the Iroquois lived in New York*). Continue writing or have a volunteer write students' ideas under the K column.

2. Then ask students: *What do you want to find out about the Iroquois?* Elicit questions and write or have volunteers write them on the chart (e.g., *How many Iroquois are there today?*). Remind students that they will complete the L (Learned) column after the reading.

Activity 3: A Plan for Peace

1. Read the selection and circle new vocabulary for your class. Then contextualize these words in context-rich sentences. For example, wise—*The wise leader made intelligent decisions for her people.* Write these sentences on the board or on a transparency and have students determine meaning from context as a class. (Do not include *Iroquois Confederacy, sachems,* or *Great Council*—see Activity 7 on page 171.)

2. Have students read the selection silently. Then play the tape or read the selection to the class and have them read as they listen for additional practice. After students have listened to the tape, return to the K-W-L chart on the board and elicit what they have learned. Write this information to complete the chart.

3. If students have unanswered questions about the Iroquois, help them find additional reading material such as articles from encyclopedias, history books, or simple library books on the subject. As a follow-up activity, students can find out more information and then share it with the class in short oral reports.

3. A Plan for Peace

A Plan for Peace

Six hundred years ago, five tribes of the Iroquois people lived in the area south of Lake Ontario. The people in these five tribes were similar in a number of ways. They spoke closely related languages. They had similar religious beliefs. They lived in villages and farmed the land. Despite these similarities, conflict among the tribes was common. Sometimes these conflicts erupted into warfare.

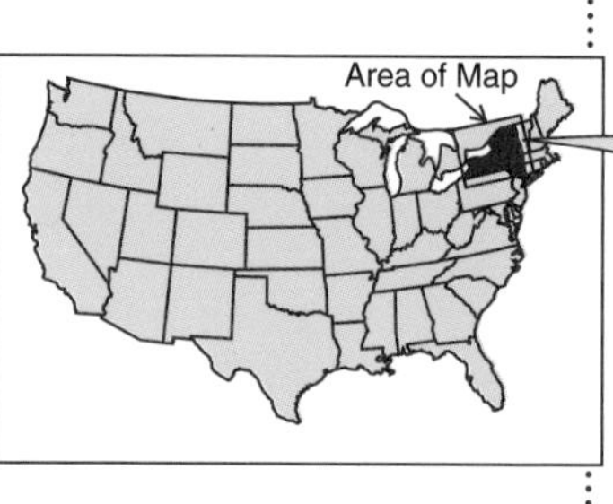

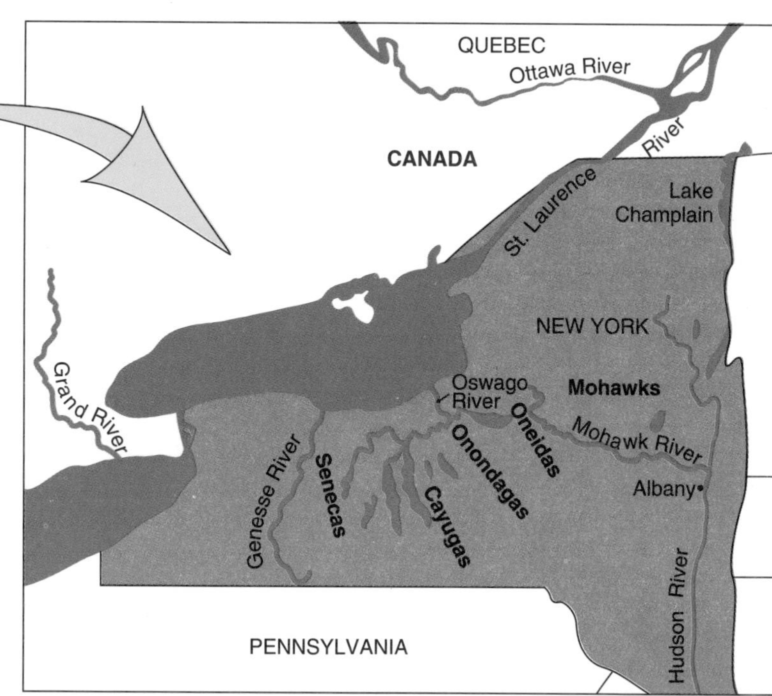

Six hundred years ago, five tribes of Iroquois people lived south of Lake Ontario. Today, this area is part of the state of New York.

One reason for the fighting was a custom known as blood revenge. If someone in one tribe killed a person in another tribe, that person's family had to seek revenge—they had to kill someone in the other person's family. As long as the blood revenge custom existed, there could never be peace among the tribes.

Iroquois people lived in villages and farmed the land. Each village was made up of a number of longhouses. Many families lived together in a longhouse.

According to legend, a wise person known as the Great Peacemaker found a way to bring peace to the tribes. He convinced the tribes to join together in a confederacy, or family of tribes. The confederacy was a permanent form of government designed to help the tribes live together in peace.

The Iroquois Confederacy had a constitution, or set of laws. According to the constitution, each tribe continued to govern itself. To settle disputes between tribes, however, the constitution set up a Great Council. The Council was made up of representatives from each tribe. These representatives were called sachems, or peace chiefs. All of the sachems were men, but they were chosen and advised by women in each tribe.

The Great Council met at least once a year to resolve conflicts and to make new laws. Each sachem could express his opinion to the Council. If there was disagreement, the sachems tried to reach a compromise. No decision could be made until everyone agreed.

There are 20,200 Iroquois people in the U.S. and Canada.

Activity 4: Take Notes in a Chart

1. Have students work in pairs. Read the Study Strategy box aloud. Tell students to study the chart as you go over it. Ask, *What is the topic of paragraph 1?* (description of the Iroquois tribes) *What details and examples are given?* (They lived south of Lake Ontario, etc.)

2. Pass out a copy of AM 5/10 to each pair or have them copy the chart on page 170. Have pairs re-read the selection and complete the chart.

Activity 5: Test Your Knowledge

1. Tell students they will make questions about their chart to review information with another pair. As they do this, they will be asking for and giving information about the past. Write the two questions from the Language Focus box on the board. *Where did the Iroquois people live? Were the tribes similar?* Ask students, *Which words in the question tell you that these questions are about the past?* (did and were). Underline these words in the questions on the board.

2. Have two students demonstrate by asking and answering the questions in the Language Focus box. Then have them ask their partners questions about the information on their charts. Remind students to use *did* and *was/were* in past questions. Circulate among pairs as they do this activity to listen for correct questions.

The Iroquois Confederacy was the first form of democracy in North America. Many people believe it was a model for the government of the United States. In the U.S. government, for example, each state sends representatives to the U.S. Congress. This is similar to the government of the Iroquois Confederacy.

The Great Council of the Iroquois Confederacy continues to meet each year. As in the past, it works to solve problems and resolve conflicts peacefully.

Study Strategy:

Taking Notes

When you take notes, write only the most important ideas.

4. Take Notes in a Chart

Pairwork. Look back at the reading and take notes in a chart.

Paragraph	Topic (What's the paragraph about?)	Details and Examples
1	description of the Iroquois tribes	▪ lived south of Lake Ontario ▪ were similar in many ways ▪ there was conflict between tribes
2	reason for fighting	
3	plan for peace	
4		
5		

Language Focus:

Asking For and Giving Information About the Past

Q: Where did the Iroquois people live?
A: South of Lake Ontario.

Q: Were the tribes similar?
A: Yes, they were.

5. Test Your Knowledge

Pairwork. Get together with another pair. Take turns asking and answering questions about the information in your chart.

Example: Q: *Where did the Iroquois people live?*

A: *South of Lake Ontario.*

6. Write

Groupwork. Follow these steps:

a. Write three true sentences about the Iroquois Confederacy.
b. Write three false sentences about the Iroquois Confederacy.
c. Mix up your sentences.
d. Read your sentences to the class. Ask your classmates to identify the true sentences.

7. Make a Word Map

Pairwork. Use information from pages 168–170 to complete these word maps. Add your own ideas, too.

Iroquois Confederacy

Definition *(What was it?)*	Purpose *(What was it for?)*	Characteristics *(What was it like?)*
a family of tribes *a form of government*		

sachems

Definition *(What were they?)*	Purpose *(What were they for?)*	Characteristics *(How would you describe them?)*

Great Council

Definition *(What was it?)*	Purpose *(What was it for?)*	Characteristics *(What was it like?)*

Study Strategy:

Making a Word Map

Making a word map is a good way to collect information about a new word.

Activity 6: Write

1. Have students work in groups of three. As a class, first read the steps of the activity aloud. For less proficient students, write an example on the board (e.g., *Iroquois tribes lived south of Lake Ontario.*). Ask, *Is this sentence true or false?* (true).

2. Have each student in the group make up one true and one false statement. Students in the group can check each other's sentences or improve upon them as needed. Each sentence should be different from the others.

3. Have students mix up their sentences.

4. Each member of the group will read two sentences to the class. Classmates will say *true* or *false* after each statement.

Activity 7: Make a Word Map

1. Have students work in pairs. Pass out AM 5/11 to each pair or have them copy the word maps on page 171. Review the word map format with students. Ask, *What three terms will you define?* (Iroquois Confederacy, sachems, and Great Council). Ask, *What three kinds of information will you find for each word?* (definition, purpose, and characteristics).

2. Have pairs read the instruction line and then complete their word maps.

(Suggested answers: Iroquois Confederacy Definition: family of tribes, form of government. Purpose: help tribes live together in peace. Characteristics: Constitution, Great Council. Sachems Definition: peace chiefs. Purpose: represent their tribes in Great Council. Characteristics: men chosen and advised by women. Great Council Definition: group of representatives called Sachems. Purpose: settle disputes between tribes. Characteristics: tried to reach compromises, met at least once a year, still meet yearly.)

3. Have pairs compare charts and resolve any differences.

Activity 8: Compare

1. *Part a.* Ask students, *What was the Iroquois Confederacy?* (a form of government). Tell them that in this activity they will compare the Iroquois government to the U.S. Government.

2. Have students work together in small groups. Tell them to look back at the reading when they need information about the Iroquois Confederacy. Groups will also discuss what they know about the U.S. Government.

3. Distribute copies of AM 5/11, or have students copy the chart on page 172. Have groups work together to reach consensus for each point in the chart.

(Answers: All points in the chart should be checked.)

4. *Part b.* Ask students to look at the Language Focus box. Have a volunteer read the two examples: *Both governments have a constitution. The Iroquois government has a constitution and so does the U.S. government.* Ask, *Which sentence would be a better beginning for a paragraph comparing the Iroquois Confederacy and the U.S. government?* (The second one, since it names both governments.)

5. Ask groups to discuss appropriate ways to compare the other ideas in the chart. Each member of the group should then write down the sentences that the group agrees on.

6. Have a member of each group read the group's paragraph to the class.

7. As a follow-up exercise, see what information students know about the U.S. government. Ask, *In a democracy, how do people have a voice in government?* (They vote for their leaders and lawmakers.) *What two kinds of lawmakers do people elect in the United States?* (senators and representatives) *What are the groups that are found under a central government in the United States?* (the 50 states).

8. Compare

a. Groupwork. Tell about the Iroquois Confederacy and the U.S. government. Complete a chart like this one.

	Iroquois Confederacy	U.S. Government
has a constitution		✔
is a democracy (people have a voice in government)		
is a representative democracy (people elect representatives)		
is a federal system (groups join under central government)		

Language Focus:

Making Comparisons

- Both governments have a constitution.
- The Iroquois government has a constitution and so does the U.S. government.

b. Compare the Iroquois Confederacy and the U.S. Government. Write several sentences.

9. Apply

Groupwork. In the Great Council of the Iroquois Confederacy, everyone had to agree on a decision. Try this activity to see if you can agree on a decision.

1. Your group can have the four items in the picture below. Think of different ways to share these items among the people in your group.

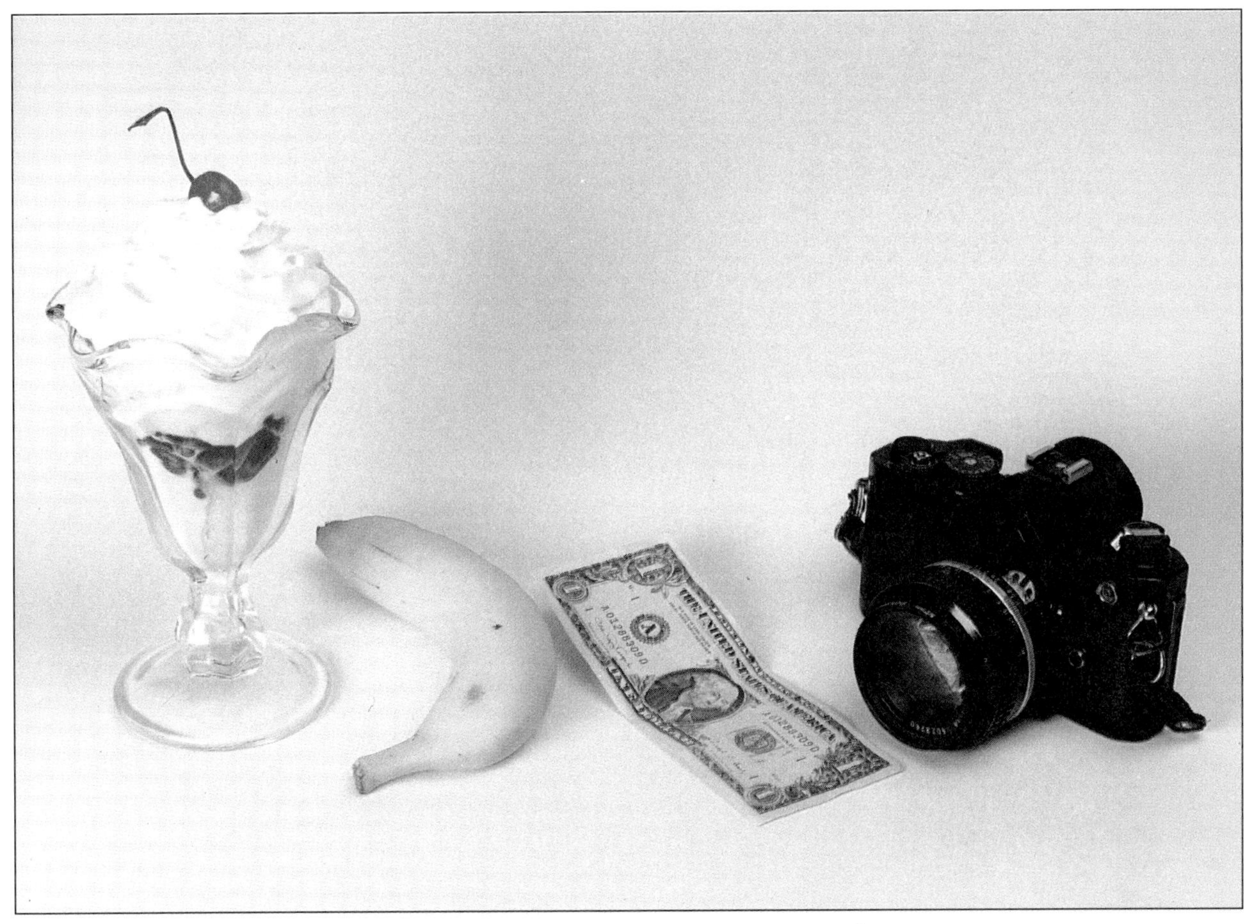

2. Choose one way to share the items. Make sure everyone in your group is happy with the final decision.
3. Report your decision to the class.

Activity 9: Apply

1. Have students work in groups of four for this activity. Read the introduction and the steps for the activity aloud. Have groups write down possible ways to share the items among their members. Although the items obviously have different value, students can think of several equitable ways to share them. Don't prompt them—see how creative they can be.

2. Have each group decide on one way to share the items. Everyone in the group must agree with the decision.

3. Have the groups report their decision to the class. Have the class vote on whose decision is the best.

Activity Menu

Read and explain the activities to the class. Then have students individually or in small groups select a project for a class or homework assignment. Projects can later be displayed in the classroom as they are shared with the class.

Activity Menu

Choose one of the following activities to do.

1. Make a Collage
How does a peaceful world look? Collect magazine pictures that suggest a peaceful world to you. Use them to make a collage.

2. Choose a Peacemaker
There are many monuments to wars and war heroes. Now, the National Foundation for Peace in Washington, D.C. wants to build monuments to peace and peace heroes. Can you suggest an individual, group, or event that represents peace? Write a description of your representative of peace and tell how the monument might look.

3. Design a Game
Many games and sports are competitive—there is a winner and a loser. A more cooperative type of game allows everyone to win. Design a game in which everyone wins, and teach it to your classmates. You might think of a new type of game or rewrite the rules of an old game.

4. Read a Children's Book
A popular children's book by Katherine Scholes is called *Peace Begins With You.* For ten minutes, think about the title of the book. What ideas would you include in a book with this title? List your ideas. Then read the book to compare ideas with the author.

5. Analyze a TV Program
Watch for an example of conflict in a TV program. Take notes on the cause of conflict and how it is resolved. Then suggest other ways the conflict might be resolved.

6. Design a Peace Symbol

The dove is one symbol of peace. What are some other symbols of peace? Draw pictures of them, then design a new symbol for peace.

7. Write about a Conflict

Describe a conflict between two people. Tell each person's side of the conflict. Let your classmates read your story and suggest a win-win solution.

8. Read a Folktale

Choose another folktale and read it to your classmates. Together, make a story map telling about the folktale.

175

Read on . . .

Sharing a Culture

Ask students what they remember about the Iroquois culture. Besides the system of government, what else can they add?

In this brief reading, they will find out a little more about one of the oldest cultures in America. Read the selection or have students read it silently. Discuss these questions: *Why did the Iroquois plant white pine trees on their land? What else did we learn about this culture?*

Law of the Great Peace

Have students read only the title of this selection. Ask, *What do you think the Law of the Great Peace said? How do you think the Iroquois achieved this peace?*

Have students read the selection. Rephrase the pre-reading question: *What does the Law of the Great Peace say? When there is no more hostility or fighting, what is the result for the people? What does this reading tell us about resolving conflict?*

Read on . . .

Sharing a Culture

Cindy knows that understanding between cultures is at the root of peace. So she started studying under her grandmother to learn all about her own culture—the Oneida Indian Nation, part of the Iroquois Nation. Now she visits schools in New York state, sharing Iroquois songs and stories. One of her favorite stories is about the white pine, planted by the Great Peacemaker who directed the people to bury their weapons at its roots. To honor this message and to bring peace to the environment, Cindy and other Oneida children planted 1,200 white pines on the Oneida Nation Territory. "Planting trees brings us oxygen, holds more soil, and gives animals more homes," she explains.

Law of the Great Peace

I now uproot the tallest tree, and into the hole thereby made, we cast all weapons of war. Into the depths of the earth, down into the deep underneath currents of water flowing to unknown regions, we cast all the weapons of strife. We bury them from sight and we plant again the tree. Thus shall the Great Peace be established, and hostilities shall no longer be known between the Five Nations, but peace to the united people.

A Kingdom Lost for a Drop of Honey
(A Burmese Folktale)

One day the King and his chief minister were standing by the palace window, eating roasted rice and honey. They laughed so much that they spilled some honey on the windowsill.

"We have spilled some honey, Your Majesty," said the chief minister. "Let me wipe it off."

"My dear chief minister," laughed the king, "you are an important person. It is beneath your dignity to do it. And if we call a servant to wipe it away, he will disturb our pleasant conversation. So leave the spilt honey alone."

They went on eating and laughing while a drop of honey dripped down the windowsill onto the street below.

"Chief Minister, said the king, leaning forward, "a drop of the honey has fallen on the street and a fly is now eating it."

The chief minister looked and saw a spider attacking the fly. The king looked down again and saw a lizard eating the spider. The king and minister continued to eat and laugh and soon they saw a cat eating the lizard.

When a dog attacked the cat, they did not stop laughing and eating. They did not stop laughing even when they saw the owner of the cat and the owner of the dog arguing and fighting.

Soon friends of both sides joined in the fight. Still the king and his minister continued to laugh and eat. Before long the fighting spread to other streets. Only then did the king order the palace guards to stop the fighting. However, by that time, the palace guards had also joined the fight, as some of them supported the owner of the dog while others supported the owner of the cat.

In the next few hours, civil war broke out and the palace was destroyed together with the king and the chief minister.

A group of judges went to the Princess Learned-in-the-Law and asked for her advice. She listened to their story and then she said: "My Lord Justices, remember that there is no such thing as a minor disagreement. You must never wait and do nothing. You must deal with each conflict right away, no matter how unimportant it may be. Remember always, my Lords, the story of the kingdom which was lost because of one drop of honey."

Burmese Folktale

Student text page 177

A Kingdom for a Drop of Honey

Read the selection aloud to the students. Have students make a drawing of interlinking circles (like a chain) on the board as a graphic organizer to show the sequencing of the folktale. Write *honey* in the first circle. Then in each successive circle have volunteers write the next animal or person(s) who enter the conflict. Assist students in phrasing the later entries into the conflict.

The chain should look like this:

honey—fly—spider—lizard—cat—dog—owner of cat—owner of dog—friends of owner of cat—friends of owner of dog—palace guards—opposing palace guards—people—people.

Ask, *What happened at the end of the folktale? Why did this happen? What is the lesson that this folktale teaches?*

Choosing Foods

Merriam, Eve. *How to Eat a Poem* in *A Sky Full of Poems*. Dell Publishing, 1986.

Soto, Gary. *Ode to La Tortilla* and *Ode to Pomegranates* in *Neighborhood Odes*. Harcourt Brace Jovanovich.

Jones, Mary Ellen. *Seeds of Change, Readings on Cultural Exchange after 1492*. Addison-Wesley, 1993.

Perl, Lila. *Junk Food, Fast Food, Health Food.* Houghton Mifflin, 1980.

Tatchell, Judy, and Wells, Dilys. *You and Your Food*. Usborne Publishers, 1985.

Life Science Library. *Food and Nutrition.* Time Inc.

International Food Library. Rourke Publishing.

Ontario Science Center. *Foodworks*. Addison-Wesley.

Copp, Vicki. *Science Experiments You Can Eat*. Harper and Row, 1972.

Albynt, Carole Lisa, and Sihaiko Webb, Lois. *The Multicultural Cookbook for Students*. Oryx Press, 1993.

Sending Messages

Baylor, Byrd, comp. *Why Dogs Don't Talk Anymore* in *And It Is Still That Way, Legends told by Arizona Indian Children*. Trails West Publishing, 1976.

Selected and Adapted in Spanish by José Griego y Maestas. Retold in English by Rudolpho A. Anaya. *The Man Who Knew the Language of Animals* in *Cuentos, Tales from the Hispanic Southwest*. The Museum of New Mexico Press, 1980.

Hayes, Joe. *La Llorona* (The Crying Woman) in *The Day It Snowed Tortillas, Tales from Spanish New Mexico*. Mariposa Publishing, 1990.

Krashe, Robert. *The Twelve Million Dollar Note: Strange but True Tales of Messages Found in Seagoing Bottles*. Thomas Nelson Publishers, 1977.

Ardley, Neil. *Music*. Eyewitness Books, Alfred A. Knopf, 1989.

How Animals Behave. Books for World Explorers, National Geographic Society, 1984.

Mountfield, Anne. *Looking Back at Sending Messages*. Schoolhouse Press, Needham, 1988.

Musical Instruments of the World. Facts on File, 1976.

Setting Goals

Spier, Peter. *We the People, the Constitution, and the United States of America*. Doubleday and Company, 1987.

Faber, Doris and Harold. *We the People*. Charles Scribner, 1987.

179

Johnson, Neil. *All in a Day's Work*. Little, Brown, and Company, 1989.

Westridge Young Writers Workshop. *Kid's Explore America's Hispanic Heritage*. Jon Muir Publications, 1992.

Berry, Joy. *Every Kid's Guide to Laws That Relate to School and Work*. Children's Press, 1987.

Schleifer, Jay. *Citizenship*. Rosen Publishing Group, Inc., 1990.

Career Discovery Encyclopedia. Volumes 1–6. Ferguson Publishing Company, 1990.

Bolles, Richard Nelson. *What Color Is Your Parachute?* Ten Speed Press, 1993.

VGM Careers for You Series, VGM Career Horizons. NTC Publishing Group, 1991.

Making Changes

Parks, Rosa. *Rosa Parks: My Story*. Dial Books.

Greenfield, Eloise. *Rosa Parks*. Crowell, 1973.

Myers, Walter Dean. *Now Is Your Time! The African-American Struggle for Freedom*. HarperCollins, 1991.

America's Civil Rights Movement, Teaching Kit. One free kit available per school upon written request from school principal. Send request to The Southern Poverty Law Center, Teaching Tolerance Project, 400 Washington Avenue, Montgomery, Alabama, 36104.

Roché, Joyce M., and Rodriguez, Marie. *Kids Who Make a Difference*. Mastermedia Limited, 1993.

Haber, Louis. *Black Pioneers of Science and Invention*. An Odyssey Book, Harcourt Brace Jovanovich, 1970.

Inventors and Discoverers, Changing Our World. National Geographic Society, 1988.

Panati, Charles. *Extraordinary Origins of Everyday Things*. Harper and Row, 1987.

Buchman, Dian Dincin, and Groves, Seli. *What If? Fifty Discoveries That Changed the World*. Scholastic Inc., 1988.

Winckler, Suzanne, and Rodgers, Mary M. *Population Growth*. Lerner Publications Company, 1991.

Resolving Conflict

Courlander, Harold, and Herzog, George. *Guinea Fowl and Rabbit Get Justice* in *The Cow Tail Switch and Other West African Stories*. Henry Holt and Company, 1947.

Teaching Tolerance (educational journal for teachers). Free subscription available upon written request to The Southern Poverty Law Center, Teaching Tolerance Project, 400 Washington Avenue, Montgomery, Alabama, 36104.

George, Phil. *Battle Won Is Lost* in *The Whispering Wind, Poetry by Young American Indians*. Edited by Terry Allen. Doubleday.

Exley, Richard and Helen, eds. *My World Peace, Thoughts and Illustrations from the Children of All Nations*. Passport Books, National Textbook Company, 1985.

Harrison, Michael, and Stuart-Clark, Christopher, comp. *Peace and War, A Collection of Poems*. Oxford University Press.

181

Junne, I.K., ed. *Two Foolish Friends* in *Floating Clouds, Floating Dreams, Favorite Asian Folktales*. Doubleday.

Htin Aung, Maung, and Trager, Helen G. *Partnership* in *A Kingdom Lost for a Drop of Honey* and *Other Burmese Folktales*. Parents Magazine Press.

Durell, Ann, and Sachs, Marilyn, eds. *The Big Book for Peace*. Dutton Children's Books, 1990.

McCall, Barbara. *The Iroquois*. Rourke Publications, 1989.

Tapescript Book 2

Unit One: Choosing Foods

Activity 4. Listen to the chant. Then chant with the tape.

I'm Hungry!

Pizza, pretzels, popsicles, and peanuts.

I'm hungry. I'm hungry. I'm hungry. I'm hungry.

Apples, peaches, strawberries, and cantaloupe.

I'd like some. I'd like some. I'd like some. I'd like some.

Mustard, ketchup, hamburgers, and hot dogs.

Just a little. Just a little. Just a little. Just a little.

Cabbage, carrots, cucumbers, and onions.

That's enough. That's enough. That's enough.

That's enough.

Tacos, tofu, tangerines, and lemonade.

I'm full! I'm full! I'm full!

Activity 1. Listen and write each customer's order.

Dialogue Number 1

Are you ready to order?
Yes. I'd like a hamburger and an order of fries.

Cheese on the hamburger?
No thanks.

Something to drink?
A small cola.

Anything else?
No, that's all.

Dialogue Number 2

Are you ready to order?
Yes. I'd like a tuna fish sandwich, please.

Anything to drink?
What kind of juice do you have?

Apple and orange.
I'll have a glass of apple juice.

Will that be all?
Yes. Thanks.

Dialogue Number 3

Can I take your order?
Yes. I'm going to have a pizza with onions and green peppers.

What size?
Small. And I'd like a small salad, too.

Something to drink?
A large orange soda.

Will that be all?
Yes, thanks.

Activity 2. Listen to this dialogue.

A: I'd like a chicken sandwich and a small salad, please.
B: For here or to go?
A: For here.
B: Anything to drink?
A: A lemonade, please.
B: What size?
A: Small.
B: Anything else?
A: No, that's all.
B: That'll be $5.05.

Activity 4. Listen to the dialogues. What are the people going to eat? List the foods.

Dialogue Number 1

A: Let's have peanut butter sandwiches for lunch.
B: Good idea.
A: What do you want to drink?
B: What about milk?
A: OK.

Dialogue Number 2

A: Let's have eggs for breakfast.
B: No, I don't think so. What about cereal?
A: OK. Do you want some juice?
B: Sure.

Activity 1. Listen.

A healthy diet contains food from different groups in the Food Guide Pyramid. But why do you need to eat different kinds of foods? To answer this question, you need to know about nutrients. You can't see nutrients, but they are the substances in food that keep you healthy. Foods contain different types and amounts of nutrients. No one food has all the nutrients you need. That's why you need to eat different kinds of food.

Activity 2. Listen.

Getting the nutrients you need

Nutrients are substances in food that help your body grow and stay healthy. Important nutrients in food are proteins, vitamins, minerals, carbohydrates, and fats. No one food has all the nutrients you need. That's why you need to eat different kinds of food.

Proteins

Your body needs proteins to grow and repair itself. Most foods contain some protein. Meat, fish, nuts, and cheese contain a lot of protein. Cereals and vegetables contain smaller amounts of protein.

Vitamins and Minerals

Vitamins and minerals help your body work properly. For example, the mineral calcium helps to build bones and teeth. Vitamin A helps your eyes see at night. Most people get enough vitamins and minerals by eating different kinds of food.

Carbohydrates

Carbohydrates give you quick energy. Your body needs this energy to move, grow, and keep warm. Good sources of carbohydrates are bread, rice, corn, fruit, and some vegetables like beets and peas.

Fats

Fats give you energy, too. Your body can store fat and use it later for energy. Everyone needs some fat in his/her diet. However, too much fat is bad for you. Some foods high in fat are butter, ice cream, sausage, and potato chips.

Your favorite food probably contains more than one kind of nutrient. For example, potatoes contain carbohydrates, vitamins, and minerals. Vegetables contain a lot of vitamins and minerals and some protein. An apple contains carbohydrates and vitamins. By eating different kinds of food, you can get the nutrients you need.

Activity 2. Listen.

How did the potato get to North America?

Five hundred years ago, potatoes grew in the Andes region of South America. They were an important food for the people who lived in these high mountains. In other parts of the world, however, people didn't know about potatoes.

The Spanish invaded South America in the mid-1500s. They learned of potatoes and took some back to Spain.

By 1570, white potatoes were growing in parts of Spain. By 1580, people in Portugal and Italy were also growing potatoes.

From Spain, potatoes traveled to France. In France, however, people were afraid to eat this new vegetable. They thought it was poisonous. Louis XVI, the King of France, tried to convince French people to eat potatoes. He even served them at the palace. But for many years, the French still refused to eat potatoes.

Potatoes reached England in a different way. In 1586, the English explorer Sir Francis Drake stopped in Colombia. There he probably picked up some potatoes and took them back to England. At first, the English refused to eat potatoes, too. Instead, they fed them to their pigs and chickens.

From England, the potato traveled to Ireland. The potato grew well in the poor soil of Ireland, and soon it was an important source of nutrients for Irish people.

In the early 1700s, Irish settlers brought the potato to North America. By 1750, many people in New England were growing and eating potatoes.

Unit Two: Sending Messages

Activity 4. Listen to the conversation and check your answers.

A: I made the team!
B: That's wonderful! When's your first game?
A: Next month.
B: What day next month?
A: On the 15th.
B: Who are you going to play?
A: The team from Baylor High.
B: Do you know anyone on the team?
A: No, I don't.

Activity 1. Listen to this music. What does it make you think of? How does it make you feel? As you listen, write your ideas.

Activity 3. Listen and check your guesses.

Making Music

A guitar is called a stringed musical instrument because it is made with strings stretched over a sounding box. Both the strings and the sounding box vibrate when the strings are plucked. Musicians know just how tense and how long to make the different-sized strings in order to create the high notes and low notes, or the pitch of music. Other stringed instruments include the violin, piano, and ukulele.

Wind instruments make musical sounds in a different way. A wind instrument is basically a hollow tube with a mouthpiece. When a musician blows into the mouthpiece, the air inside the tube vibrates. The length of vibrating air inside the tube is called the air column. By changing the size of the air column, the musician can make high and low notes. For example, making the air column shorter produces higher notes. Pipe organs, flutes, bugles, and saxophones are different kinds of wind instruments. They all depend upon vibrating air columns for their sounds.

Drums of different sizes and shapes are still another kind of musical instrument. Hitting a thin surface of a drum causes the surface to vibrate and produce sound. Hitting a drum hard makes a loud sound. Hitting it lightly makes soft sounds.

Activity 6. Listen and check your answers.

1. When you play a stringed instrument, the strings and sounding box vibrate.
2. When you play a saxophone, the air column vibrates.
3. When you pluck the strings on a guitar, they vibrate.
4. When you hit the surface of a drum, it vibrates.
5. When you hit a drum lightly, it makes soft sounds.
6. When you play a piano, the strings and sounding box vibrate.

Activity 4. Listen to this information about devices that help the deaf.

Devices That Help the Deaf

How does a deaf person know when his doorbell is ringing or when someone is calling her on the phone? Can a deaf person watch television? Wake up with an alarm clock? A hearing person can do all of these, but deaf people need special devices to help them.

Most hearing children don't know about the little tricks deaf people use. Here's a description of some of them.

A TDD, or a Telecommunication Device for the Deaf, helps deaf people talk on the telephone. When the phone rings, a light flashes. The person picks up the phone, puts on the TDD, and types and reads the conversation. Doorbells that flash a light when someone pushes the bell are also popular.

A closed-caption decoder makes it possible for a deaf person to watch TV. Many shows are closed-captioned for the hearing impaired. Words appear at the bottom of the screen and the person reads what's being said.

Hate waking up to a blaring alarm? Deaf people use vibrating clocks. The alarm shakes the pillow. It feels like an earthquake, but it makes us jump out of bed!

All of these devices help deaf people. There are many others that deaf people use at home, school, and work.

—By students at the Horace Mann School for the Deaf

Activity 8. Listen to this editorial.

Teaching Sign Language in Schools

We think hearing people should learn sign language as a separate class in school. Why? So that some day soon, all people in our country will be able to talk with deaf people.

If hearing people learned sign language, it would be easier for deaf people to communicate. We could communicate better with waiters in restaurants, clerks in stores, doctors, even hearing kids on the playgrounds.

Hearing people would quickly see the benefits. The most important is that they could make friends with deaf people. Many hearing people who know sign language say they like to sign with deaf kids and adults.

We know many hearing people who are curious to learn sign language. In the future, if more hearing people know sign, maybe a hearing person could become an interpreter for the deaf world.

We recommend that all schools offer sign language as an option for their students. It would make a big difference for all people.

—By students at the Horace Mann School for the Deaf

Unit Three: Setting Goals

Activity 1. Listen and read the captions.

I plan to go to college after high school. I want to work as a computer programmer after college. Someday I'd like to travel around the world.

I want to get good grades in school this year. I would also like to become a good basketball player. I hope to become a doctor. Someday I'd like to get married and have a family.

I plan to get a job next year. I'd like to work as a carpenter. I also hope to go to college part time.

Activity 5. Listen.

My Life's List

When John Goddard was fifteen years old, he made a list of things that he wanted to do during his lifetime. By the time he finished, there were 127 goals on his list.

Some of Goddard's goals involved travel and exploration:

- Explore the Amazon.
- Visit every country in the world.

Other goals dealt with learning new things:

- Play the flute and violin.
- Fly a plane.
- Type 50 words a minute.
- Make a parachute jump.

Some of his goals were intellectually demanding:

- Write a book.
- Compose music.

Other goals were physically demanding:

- Broad jump fifteen feet.
- Climb the Matterhorn.
- Ride an elephant, a camel, an ostrich, and a bucking bronco.

John Goddard was serious about his list of goals. Over the next 50 years, he reached 108 of the goals on his list. And he is still working to reach the remaining 19 goals.

Activity 2. Listen to these people talk about their careers.

Person Number 1: A Transportation Planner

What is your job?
I work as a transportation planner.

What do you do in your job?
I do a lot of research. I study the transportation needs of people—where they need to go and how. I use this information to predict where a town or city will need new roads, bus lines, etc. I also go to a lot of meetings to collect information. And I write a lot of reports, using a computer.

What do you like and dislike about your job?
I like looking for ways to solve problems. I spend a lot of time writing and I like that. I also like working in an office and getting a good salary. Sometimes I have to work outdoors in cold weather (counting cars) and I don't like that.

What kind of skills and training do you need?
You should be able to think about all sides of a problem. You should also be able to write clearly. To get a job as a Transportation Planner, you should get a college degree.

What can students do to prepare for this career?
They should study mathematics, science, and English. And learning to write clearly is important.

Person Number 2: Computer Specialist

What is your job?
I'm a computer specialist.

What do you do in your job?
I spend a lot of time fixing computers and helping people. I teach them how to use their computers. Computers are always changing, so I have to read a lot of technical books and magazines.

What do you like and dislike about your job?
I'm always learning something new—I like that. I also enjoy working with people. But sometimes I have too much work and I don't like that.

What kinds of skills and training do you need?
It's helpful to have a degree in Computer Science. You should also be able to communicate well with people.

What can students do to prepare for this career?
Take computer classes in high school. Use computers whenever possible. Get a college education.

Person Number 3: Sports Reporter

What is your job?
I write about sports for a newspaper.

What do you do in your job?
I go to sports games and write about them. I interview athletes and coaches. I spend a lot of time on the telephone talking to people and getting information. I also do a lot of typing.

What do you like and dislike about your job?
I like playing with words. I have to do lots of different things. Every day is different. I like that. I don't like spending so much time on the phone. Sometimes I have to work on the weekends and I don't like that.

What kinds of skills and training do you need?
You need good communication skills. A knowledge of sports helps, too. But most of all, you should be curious and observant.

What can students do to prepare for this career?
Read as many books as you can. Learn to type. Keep a diary. Writing is a skill that you can learn.

Person Number 4: Jewelry Designer

What is your job?
I'm a jewelry designer.

What do you do in your job?
I spend a lot of time drawing my ideas for a piece of jewelry. Then I work with special tools and materials to make jewelry. I also have to sell my work and keep records of my sales and expenses.

What do you like and dislike about your job?
I like almost everything about my job. I love making beautiful things. I like working by myself—I'm my own boss. I don't like keeping records, but it's an important part of the job.

What kinds of skills and training do you need?
First of all, you need to be creative. You also need to study art and learn to use special tools and materials. And you have to be good with your hands.

What can students do to prepare for this career?
Take art, math, and science courses. Draw a lot. Learn to use a computer.

Activity 4. Listen.

What are the goals of the U.S. government?

The U.S. government spends more than 1,000,000,000,000 (one trillion) dollars every year. It employs more than 3,117,000 people. It represents more than two hundred million people.

Why does the government spend so much money and employ so many people? To answer this question, just think about what the government has to do—what its goals are.

The goals of the U.S. government are stated in the Preamble (introduction) to the U.S. Constitution. The Constitution is a set of laws that define what the government can do. It also tells how the government should do these things. These laws were written more than 200 years ago when the United States became an independent country. The Preamble states that the goals of the government are to:

1. make sure all people are treated equally
2. promote peace within the United States
3. defend the country against attack
4. provide for the well-being for all people
5. protect our freedoms and make certain that our children have the same freedoms

And what does the U.S, government do to reach these goals? Here are a few examples:

- The U.S. government maintains a military force to defend the country. There are 2.1 million men and women in the U.S. Army, Navy, Marine Corps, and Air Force.
- It builds superhighways.
- It enforces laws that forbid discrimination, or unequal treatment, in public places such as restaurants and hotels.
- It provides loans for students who want to go to college. About five million students receive these loans each year.
- It provides food stamps to about 26 million people. People can use food stamps to buy food.
- It protects the right of people to protest, or express their disagreement with a law. If people think a law is unfair, they can express their disagreement peacefully.
- It provides a system of courts to settle disputes fairly and peacefully.
- It supports research into the causes and cures of disease.
- It makes sure that food is safe to eat.

Unit Four: Making Changes

Activity 3. Listen.

An Immigrant in the United States

I am a Cambodian immigrant refugee living in the United States. My family and I left Cambodia because of the war in the country where I was born. I can't believe that we are free in this country.

I was eight years old when I first saw different colored people. How strange, scary, and frightening to see white and black colored people, red and brown and yellow hair, blue, green, and brown eyes. I thought they had costumes on. My eyes had only seen brown-skinned people with black hair. The only pictures in books I had ever seen in my country were of Cambodian people who are of the brown race.

Everything was different here. The climate was so cold, and when I saw something white on the ground, I thought somebody went up in an airplane and dropped lots and lots of tiny pieces of paper down on the ground. It was the first time I saw snow. When I went to school, I couldn't speak English and the teacher didn't speak Khmer. I couldn't understand what to do. It was very difficult. Eating in the cafeteria at the beginning was so different. I had never seen or tasted milk and never eaten cheese or butter. I had never used a fork or a knife. There were about five other Cambodian kids in my room who had been in America longer, so they showed me how to use a fork and a knife. At first, I didn't like the foods—cheese, salad, pizza, and milk—so I threw them away. The foods I hated are some of my favorite foods now, like pizza, cheese, and milk.

American kids showed me how to play American sports and we became friends. Today, I feel very happy to be in America, a free country. The color of people doesn't scare me anymore. I think how silly it was to be afraid. Everyone is the same inside with the same feelings.

—By Ponn Pet

Activity 6. Listen.

Paper

Before paper was invented, people wrote on materials such as stone, clay tablets, and parchment. But none of these writing surfaces worked very well. Stone was difficult to carve. Clay tablets were heavy to carry around, and parchment was expensive to make. Around A.D. 105 a Chinese man by the name of Ts'ai Lun invented a much better writing surface—paper. It is believed that Ts'ai Lun used the bark of trees and old rags to make paper. His paper was light, easy to write on, and cheap to make. The Chinese kept the invention of paper a secret for several hundred years. But eventually, people in other parts of the world learned the art of paper making.

Paper was a very important invention because it provided a way to record information easily and cheaply. With paper, people could more easily make copies of written information. This made it possible to communicate ideas and information to a larger number of people.

Today, there are more than 7,000 different kinds of paper. Much of this paper is used for written communication, but we also use it to make paper products like cardboard boxes and paper plates.

The Plow

Thousands of years ago people discovered that plants grow better in soil that has been loosened. For a long time, farmers used sharp sticks, rocks, and other objects to loosen the soil. Then about 8,000 years ago, someone in the Middle East came up with the idea for a plow. These early plows were simple forked sticks pulled by a person. About a thousand years later, people began using oxen to pull simple plows. Today, many farmers use tractors to pull huge plows.

The plow was a very important invention because it allowed people to farm more land and grow more food. Because farmers could grow more food, fewer people died of starvation.

The Microscope

A microscope magnifies things, or makes them look larger. The simplest kind of microscope is a magnifying glass, which has one convex lens.

More than a thousand years ago, people used water-filled glass globes and rock crystals as magnifying glasses. Then in the 1300s, people learned how to make more powerful lenses. They used these lenses to make eyeglasses. In the 1600s, Anton van Leeuwenhoek, a Dutch merchant, found a way to make an even better lens. His lens could magnify things more than 200 times their natural size. In 1674, Leeuwenhoek, using a single lens microscope, was the first person to observe bacteria (very small organisms).

The invention of the microscope made it possible for scientists to learn how certain bacteria cause disease and infection. With this knowledge, scientists were able to look for ways to stop the spread of disease. Millions and millions of lives were saved because of the microscope.

Activity 3. Listen.

My, How We've Grown

Why has the world's population grown so fast in the last 150 years? Beginning in the 1800s, many aspects of human life changed. Farms grew in size and number. New farming methods and better seeds increased annual harvests. People had more food to eat, and countries began buying and selling goods throughout the world. With the invention of new machines, people moved these goods—and themselves—quickly, first in steamships, then in trains, cars, and airplanes.

After farming methods and transportation improved, cheap food became available to more people. Before these discoveries, famines—severe shortages of food—regularly caused widespread starvation. Famine is now a rare event in most parts of the world.

In addition to inventing ways to grow more food, scientists also discovered what caused some deadly diseases and infections. These scientists found out that certain bacteria (very tiny organisms) make us sick when they enter and grow in our bodies. After the invention of the microscope, scientists could see these tiny life forms and could learn how they caused sickness.

This important breakthrough helped to stop the spread of illnesses that pass rapidly from person to person through a population. These widespread diseases, known as epidemics, included malaria, influenza, and yellow fever.

An epidemic can strike people of all ages and can cause sudden declines in population. The last worldwide epidemic—in this case, of influenza—occurred between 1918 and 1919. In those years, the flu killed roughly 20 million people around the world.

Activity 3. Listen.

Taking Action for Change

Before 1964, many places in the United States had laws that segregated, or separated, black and white Americans. These laws forced black Americans to use separate schools, restrooms, restaurants, and other public facilities. Usually, the facilities for black people were not as good as the facilities for white people.

In some cities, black people had to sit in the back of public buses. When the white section in the front of the bus was full, black people had to give their seats to white people.

In 1955, Rosa Parks challenged the unfair bus law in Montgomery, Alabama. When a bus driver asked Rosa Parks to give her seat to a white person, she refused. The police arrested Rosa Parks and took her to jail. In her autobiography, Rosa Parks describes this event:

> One evening in early December 1955 I was sitting in the front seat of the colored section of a bus in Montgomery, Alabama. The white people were sitting in the white section. More white people got on, and they filled up all the seats in the white section. When that happened, we black people were supposed to give up our seats to the whites. But I didn't move. The white driver said, "Let me have those front seats." I didn't get up. I was tired of giving in to white people.
>
> "I'm going to have you arrested," the driver said.
>
> "You may do that," I answered.
>
> Two white policemen came. I asked one of them, "Why do you all push us around?"
>
> He answered, "I don't know, but the law is the law and you're under arrest."

In response to Rosa Parks's arrest, the black citizens of Montgomery, Alabama, decided to boycott the buses. For 381 days, they refused to ride the buses. Instead, they organized car pools or walked to work. By boycotting the buses, they hoped to force the city to change its unfair segregation laws. But the city refused to listen even though the bus company was losing a lot of money.

Thirteen months after the boycott began, the U.S. Supreme Court ruled that segregation in public transportation was unconstitutional. Black people could no longer be forced to sit in the back of buses or give their seats to white people. The day after the segregation laws were changed, Rosa Parks got on a bus and took a seat in the front. It had taken more than a year, but the black people of Montgomery had won a great victory.

Many people were inspired by Rosa Parks's courageous action. They decided to challenge the unfair segregation laws in restaurants, schools, and other public places. In case after case, the Supreme Court ruled that segregation was illegal. Then in 1964, Congress passed a law that forbade segregation in most public facilities. Passage of this law was an important step in protecting the rights of all U.S. citizens.

Unit Five: Resolving Conflict

Activity 2. Listen to these dialogues.

Dialogue Number 1

Let's go outside.
Do you really want to?
Sure. Don't you?
No, not really.
Why not?
Because it's cold outside.

Dialogue Number 2

That was a great movie.
Do you really think so?
Yeah. Why? Didn't you like it?
No. I thought it was awful.

Dialogue Number 3

That's my book.
No, it's not. It's mine.
I don't believe you. You're a liar.
You can't call me a liar!
Oh yeah?

Activity 2. Listen to these dialogues.

1. A: Let's go somewhere.
   B: No, I don't want to.
   A: Why? Are you tired?
   B: Yeah.
   A: OK. Then let's stay here.
2. A: Can I read the story aloud?
   B: Well, I really wanted to.
   A: Then you read the first half and I'll read the second half.
   B: OK.
3. A: Why didn't you call me?
   B: I did call, but you weren't home.
   A: I don't believe you.
   B: It's true.
   A: OK. OK. I'm going to go for a walk. Let's talk about it later.
4. A: I think we should invite everyone to the party.
   B: We can't do that. That's too many people.
   A: So what?
   B: But we won't have enough food.
   A: Are you sure? Let's see what Julia thinks.

Activity 1. Listen to these stories and answer the questions in the chart.

1. Shawn and Leila are working together on a class project. They have to write a report about a famous person in history. Shawn wants to write about Rosa Parks because he's interested in the Civil Rights Movement. Leila has already read a lot about Rosa Parks, and she wants to write about someone different. After talking about it, they decide to write about Martin Luther King, Jr., a leader in the Civil Rights Movement.
2. Marta and Yan have to interview people outside school and then make a report to the class. Yan suggests that they do the interviews together after school, but Marta says she can't. Yan gets angry because he doesn't want to do all the work. He tells Marta that she is lazy. Marta tries to tell Yan that she can't do the interviews because she has to babysit after school. But Yan refuses to listen. He says he'll do the work himself, and then he walks away.

Activity 3. Listen.

Two students started arguing at school. One student called the other one a name, and a fistfight began.

What can be done to prevent fights like this at school? In some schools, the disputants (the two students with a disagreement) sit down with peer mediators. Peer mediators are students with special training in conflict resolution.

Peer mediators help the disputants to communicate peacefully. Here are some of the communication strategies they use:

1. State your own feelings clearly but don't be accusatory. Begin with "I feel. . ." instead of "You always. . . ."
2. Don't interrupt or finish another person's sentences.
3. Listen carefully to what the other person is saying. Try to see the other person's side of the disagreement.
4. Maintain eye contact with the other person.
5. Ask questions to make sure that you understand the other person.
6. Repeat the other person's ideas as you understand them.
7. Never put anyone down. Saying things like "You're stupid" makes communication difficult.
8. Try to find a solution that makes both people happy.

Peer mediators never judge the disputants. They don't decide who is right and who is wrong. Instead, they help the two students to find their own "win-win" solution. A "win-win" solution allows everyone to feel good.

Peer mediation often succeeds simply because it gets people to talk to each other. And getting people to communicate is the first step in finding a win-win solution.

Activity 6. Listen to this dialogue.

Shawn and Leila have to write a report about a famous person in history. Here's what happens when they try to choose a person to write about:

Shawn: Why don't we write about Rosa Parks?

Leila: Can't we write about someone else?

Shawn: Why?

Leila: I've already read a lot about Rosa Parks. I'd like to learn about someone different.

Shawn: But I'm really interested in the Civil Rights Movement.

Leila: So you want to write about the Civil Right Movement?

Shawn: Yeah.

Leila: Well, could we write about someone else in the Civil Rights Movement?

Shawn: I suppose so. Like who?

Leila: What about Martin Luther King, Jr., or Ralph Abernathy?

Shawn: OK. Sounds good to me.

Activity 7. Listen to this dialogue between Yan and Marta.

Yan: Let's do the interviews today.

Marta: I can't, Yan.

Yan: Come on. We have to get the information.

Marta: I know but I . . .

Yan: You know, Marta, you never want to help. You're lazy.

Marta: That's not true. You don't understand. I . . .

Yan: I do understand. I understand that I have to do all the work.

Activity 2. Listen to these stories.

Story Number 1

Here's Laurie's side of the story:

There's a guy in my class who can't pronounce my last name. No one else has trouble saying it, but he gets it wrong every time. I think he says it wrong on purpose. I try to laugh about it, but it really makes me angry.

Here's Mario's side of the story:

There's a new student at school. She has a real long last name, and I can't pronounce it correctly. I feel stupid because every time I say her name, I get it wrong. She laughs when I say it wrong, so I guess it doesn't matter.

Listen to Story Number 1 again.

Story Number 2

Here's Rigoberto's side of the story:

I don't understand my friends Don and Mark. I've been eating lunch with them at school for two years. Now my friend Carl want to eat with us, but Don and Mark don't want him to. Carl is not like everybody else—he has learning problems. But he's on the soccer team with me, and he's my friend. Why can't Don and Mark accept him, too? Now I'm afraid Carl and I won't have anyone to eat with.

Here's Don's side of the story:

What is Rigoberto trying to do? We have this nice group of guys who always eat together. Why does Rigoberto have to invite Carl to eat with us? Carl makes us feel uncomfortable, and some kids are always making fun of him. They'll probably make fun of us now.

Listen to Story Number 2 again.

Activity 3. Listen.

A Plan for Peace

Six hundred years ago, five tribes of the Iroquois people lived in the area south of Lake Ontario. The people in these five tribes were similar in a number of ways. They spoke closely related languages. They had similar religious beliefs. They lived in villages and farmed the land. Despite these similarities, conflict among the tribes was common. Sometimes these conflicts erupted into warfare.

One reason for the fighting was a custom known as blood revenge. If someone in one tribe killed a person in another tribe, that person's family had to seek revenge—they had to kill someone in the other person's family. As long as the blood revenge custom existed, there could never be peace among the tribes.

According to legend, a wise person known as the Great Peacemaker found a way to bring peace to the tribes. He convinced the tribes to join together in a confederacy, or family of tribes. The confederacy was a permanent form of government designed to help the tribes live together in peace.

The Iroquois Confederacy had a constitution, or set of laws. According to the constitution, each tribe continued to govern itself. To settle disputes between tribes, however, the constitution set up a Great Council. The Council was made up of representatives from each tribe. These representatives were called sachems, or peace chiefs. All of the sachems were men, but they were chosen and advised by women in each tribe.

The Great Council met at least once a year to resolve conflicts and to make new laws. Each sachem could express his opinion to the Council. If there was disagreement, the sachems tried to reach a compromise. No decision could be made until everyone agreed.

The Iroquois Confederacy was the first form of democracy in North America. Many people believe it was a model for the government of the United States. In the U.S. government, for example, each state sends representatives to the U.S. Congress. This is similar to the government of the Iroquois Confederacy.

The Great Council of the Iroquois Confederacy continues to meet each year. As in the past, it works to solve problems and resolve conflicts peacefully.

Text permissions

We wish to thank the authors, publishers, and holders of copyright for their permission to reprint the following:

Black Misery by Langston Hughes. Copyright © 1969 by Langston Hughes. Reprinted by permission of Harold Ober Associates, Inc.

Bouki's Glasses from *The Piece of Fire and Other Haitian Tales* by Harold Courlander. Copyright © 1964 by Harold Courlander. Reprinted by permission of the author.

Change by Charlotte Zolotow from *River Winding*. Copyright © 1970 by Charlotte Zolotow. Reprinted by permission of the author and Edite Kroll Literary Agency.

David Klein by Mel Glenn from *Class Dismissed II*. Text copyright © 1986 by Mel Glenn. Reprinted by permission of Clarion Books/Houghton Mifflin Company. All rights reserved.

Deaf Donald by Shel Silverstein from *A Light in the Attic*. Copyright © 1981 by Shel Silverstein. Reprinted by permission of HarperCollins Publishers and Edite Kroll Literary Agency.

Devices That Help the Deaf by the students of the Horace Mann School for the Deaf in Allston, MA, and Marie Franklin, editor of The Fun Pages. Copyright © 1992 by the *Boston Globe*. Reprinted by permission of the *Boston Globe*.

Homero E. Acevedo II from *Kids Explore America's Hispanic Heritage*. Copyright © 1992 by John Muir Publications. Reprinted by permission of John Muir Publications.

How Do You Eat a Hot Fudge Sundae by Jonathan Holden from *Design for a House: Poems*. Copyright © 1972 by Jonathan Holden. Reprinted by permission of the University of Missouri Press.

How to Eat a Poem by Eve Merriam from *A Sky Full of Poems*. Copyright © 1964, 1970, 1973 by Eve Merriam. Reprinted by permission of Marian Reiner.

An Immigrant in the U.S. by Ponn Pet, age 11, from *Stone Soup, the magazine by children*. Copyright © 1990 by the Children's Art Foundation, Santa Cruz, California.

A Kingdom Lost for a Drop of Honey adapted by Helen G. Trager and Maung Htlin from *A Kingdom Lost for a Drop of Honey and Other Burmese Folk-Tales*. Reprinted by permission of Scholastic, Inc.

Law of the Great Peace adapted by John Bierhorst from *The Iroquois Book of the Great Law*. Copyright © by John Bierhorst. Reprinted by permission of John Bierhorst.

The Microscope by Maxine Kumin. Copyright © 1963 by Maxine Kumin. First published in *The Atlantic Monthly*. Reprinted by permission of Curtis Brown, Ltd.

From *My Story* by Rosa Parks. Copyright © 1992 by Rosa Parks. Published by Dial Books.

From *Our Endangered Planet: Population Growth* by Suzanne Winckler and Mary M. Rogers. Copyright © 1991 by Lerner Publications Company, Minneapolis, MN. Used with permission. All rights reserved.

A Round by Eve Merriam from *A Sky Full of Poems*. Copyright © 1964, 1970, 1973 by Eve Merriam. Reprinted by permission of Marian Reiner.

Sharing a Culture from *Learning Magazine*, November/December 1992. Copyright © 1992 by *Learning Magazine*. Reprinted by permission of *Learning Magazine*.

The Unexpected Heroine from *Take a Walk in Their Shoes* by Glennette Tilley Turner. Copyright © 1989 by Glennette Tilley Turner. Used by permission of Cobblehill Books, an affiliate of Dutton Children's Books, a division of Penguin USA, Inc.

That's Nice by Stephanie Todorovich from Perspectives 2. Copyright © 1991 by the Etobichoke Board of Education, Canada. Reprinted by permission.

Watermelons by Charles Simic from *Selected Poems*. Copyright © 1985 by Charles Simic. Reprinted by permission of George Braziller, Inc.

Younde Goes to Town from *The Cow-Tail Switch and Other West African Stories* by Harold Courlander and George Herzog. Copyright 1947 by Harold Courlander. Copyright © 1975 by Harold Courlander. Reprinted by permission of Henry Holt and Company, Inc.

Can We Talk? from 3-2-1 Contact Magazine. Copyright © 1992 by The Children's Television Workshop. Reprinted by permission.

Photo credits

Unit 1

Part Opener

xxii Clockwise from top left: © FourByFive, FPG, Int'l., © Superstock, FPG, Int'l.
1 Clockwise from bottom left: FPG, Int'l., FPG, Int'l., Nino Mascardi/The Image Bank

Text

4 FPG, Int'l.
5 FPG, Int'l.
11 © FourByFive
12 Top to bottom: FPG, Int'l., Bill Gallery/Stock Boston
26 © Martin Rogers

Unit 2

Part Opener

30 Clockwise from top right: © D. Chawda/Photo Researchers, Inc., Bill Gallery/Stock Boston

Text

47 Clockwise from top left: © Comstock, © Comstock, © Stock Imagery, Bob Daemmrich/ Stock Boston, © Marlene Ferguson/Index Stock Photography, Inc.
53 © Craig Aurnes/West Light
55 Clockwise from top right: Bettmann, © John Eastcott/Yva Momtiuk/Woodfin Camp & Assoc., Inc., © Brian Seed/Tony Stone World Wide, Ltd., © D. Chawda/Photo Researchers, Inc., © R. & S. Michaud/Woodfin Camp & Assoc., Inc., © Robert Frerck/Tony Stone World Wide, Ltd.
56 Bill Gallery/Stock Boston
57 Ultratec, Inc., Madison, WI
66 Lawrence Migdale/Stock Boston

Unit 3

Part Opener

68 Clockwise from top left: © Comstock, © Comstock
69 Clockwise from bottom left: © Comstock, FPG Int'l., © Stock Imagery, © Comstock

Chapter Opener

70 Clockwise from bottom left: © Bob Kramer, Stock Boston, © Comstock
71 © Comstock

Text

72 Courtesy of John Goddard
73 Clockwise from top right: © Eric Kamp/Index Stock Int'l., Inc., © Comstock, © Comstock, © Stock Imagery, © Sullivan/Index Stock Int'l., Inc., © Comstock, © Comstock
82 Left to right: © Stewart Cohen/Index Stock Int'l., Inc., © Stewart Cohen, © Comstock
83 © Comstock
86 Clockwise from top left: FPG Int'l., © Charles Feil/Stock Boston, © Phil Cantor/Index Stock Photography, Inc., AP/World Wide Photos
95 Clockwise from top left: © Comstock, © Daemmrich/Stock Boston, © Comstock, © Billy E. Barnes/Tony Stone World Wide, Ltd.
97 © Kenneth Garrett/West Light
98 Clockwise from top left: © Philip Wallick/FPG, Int'l., © Comstock, © Brooks Kraft/Sygma
99 Clockwise from bottom left: © Comstock, © David Grossman/Photo Researchers, Inc., FPG, Int'l.
104 © Robert Frerch/Woodfin Camp & Assoc., Inc.

Unit 4

Part Opener

106 © Ullisteltzer
107 Clockwise from top left: Stock Imagery, © MacDonald Photography/Stock Boston, AP/World Wide Photos

Chapter Opener

108 Clockwise from top right: © Ullisteltzer, © Comstock
109 Clockwise from top left: MC Tressin-Renault/Gamma-Liaison, © Lester Sloan/Woodfin Camp & Assoc., Inc., © Wolfgang Kaehler

Text

110 © Kindra Clineff/The Picture Cube
116 Clockwise from top left: © Index Stock Int'l., Inc., UPI/Bettmann, UPI/Bettmann, © Frank Pedrick/The Image Works, Bob Hautes/Stock Imagery, © Comstock
117 Clockwise from top left: Stock Imagery, © MacDonald Photography/Stock Boston, © Susan Van Etten
123 © Comstock
131 The Bettmann Archive
132 UPI/Bettmann
133 AP/World Wide Photos
143 Clockwise from top left: © Comstock, © Comstock, © Comstock, © Comstock

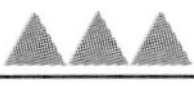

Unit 5

Part Opener

144 Left to right: © Antman/The Image Works, © Index Stock
145 Left to right: © John Lei/Stock Boston, © B. Daemmrich/The Image Works

Chapter Opener

146 Clockwise from bottom left: © Susan Van Etten, © R. Sidney/The Image Works
147 Clockwise from bottom left: © R. Sidney/The Image Works, © Alan Dorow/Actuality Inc., © Index Stock

Text

149 © David W. Johnson
158 © Steve Bourgeois/Unicorn Stock Photos
159 © Susan Van Etten
160 © Antman/The Image Works
165 Left to right: © Stewart Cohen/Index Stock Int'l., Inc., © Stewart Cohen/Index Stock Int'l., Inc.
166 Top to bottom: © B. Daemmrich/The Image Works, © John Lei/Stock Boston
174 © Susan Van Etten
176 Clockwise from top left: © Comstock, © Arnold Jacobs